Lazarus

Lessons Beyond the Tomb

Lazarus
Lessons Beyond the Tomb

Vinu V Das

Ti P

Tabor Press

ISBN 978-1-997541-21-9

Table of Contents

Chapter 1. "Lord, If You Had Been Here" — Learning to Trust God's Timing

When Mary and Martha sent word to Jesus that their brother lay gravely ill, they reached out not merely for physical healing but for the comforting presence of a Savior. Their plea—"Lord, if you had been here, my brother would not have died"— echoes the honest ache of every heart that yearns for God to arrive on our timetables. Yet in the very pause between the sisters' message and Jesus' arrival, we catch a glimpse of a deeper purpose at work. This moment of apparent absence serves as the backdrop for a lesson far richer than any immediate rescue: it is here, in the tension between need and delay, that faith is both tested and transformed.

As the narrative unfolds, we see that divine love does not always shortcut our seasons of waiting. Instead, God's delays invite us into a more profound dependence, compelling us to wrestle with questions of sovereignty, lament honestly over our pain, and cling to promises that feel distant. In these pages, you will be drawn into the geographical, cultural, and spiritual landscape of Bethany, where illness and hope collide. You will discover how the disciples' uncertainty, Martha's bold confession, and Jesus' measured response each illuminate a facet of trusting God's perfect timing—even when that timing defies our expectations.

1.1 Setting the Stage: Bethany, Sickness, and Sovereignty

1.1.1 Geographical & Social Context of Bethany

Bethany lay on the eastern slopes of the Mount of Olives, just two miles from Jerusalem, serving as a quiet village retreat for Jesus and His disciples (John 11:18). Its olive groves and guesthouses made it an ideal place for hospitality, where meals were shared and burdens lightened. In that agrarian setting, everyday life revolved around family ties and communal care—neighbors tended each other's fields and shared news at the well. Bethany was small enough that news of Lazarus's illness would spread immediately, yet close enough to Jerusalem's bustle that the social pressures of the city hovered nearby. The village's proximity to the Temple meant its residents were steeped in religious observance, observing Sabbath rules and purity laws (Luke 10:38). Mary and Martha, as hosts, bore responsibility for the family's honor and the household's welfare, so Lazarus's sickness threatened not only his life but their social standing. In today's lifestyle, we often lack that same neighborhood intimacy; we may live blocks away from friends yet feel isolated when crisis strikes. Yet learning from Bethany, we can rediscover "spiritual neighborhoods" by investing time in small groups, meal-sharing, and open-hearted presence. Understanding the physical and social contours of Bethany invites us to see that God often works through tight-knit communities rather than isolated individuals. May our modern "villages"—churches, small groups, neighborhoods—become places where sickness is met with prayer, presence, and practical care.

1.1.2 First-Century Jewish Customs Surrounding Illness and Burial

In Jesus' day, illness was often understood through both medical and spiritual lenses: physical suffering could be a symptom of sin or a call to deeper faith (John 9:2). When Lazarus fell sick, Mary and Martha would have observed strict protocols—consulting local healers, then rabbinic teachers if hope remained. If death approached, family members made preparations for burial within the same day, to avoid ceremonial uncleanness that persisted for seven days (Numbers 19:11-12). The mourners would tear their garments, throw dust on their heads, and wail in lament—a public ritual signaling profound grief (Matthew 11:17). Tombs were carved into rock, with narrow entrances sealed by heavy stones, a visual reminder that death's power was intended to be final. Yet Mary and Martha's plea to Jesus transcended custom, appealing to divine intervention that could override ritual law. In our modern lifestyle today, we segregate the sick— quarantine rooms, hospital wings—often out of fear rather than faith. The challenge for the twenty-first century believer is to practice presence over protocol, entering hospital rooms with compassion rather than retreating behind medical safety. We can honor both medical guidance and spiritual conviction, bringing prayer, laying on of hands, and heartfelt lament alongside modern treatment. By embracing the best of both worlds, we reflect the holistic care modeled in Bethany—body, soul, and community intertwined.

1.1.3 John's Narrative Purpose: Signs That Reveal Glory

From the opening chapter of his Gospel, John signals that Jesus' miracles are "signs" (σημεῖα) meant to point beyond the immediate to divine identity (John 2:11). Of the seven signs, raising Lazarus ranks as the climactic demonstration of authority over life and death (John 11:4). By framing each miracle with dialogues on belief, John invites his readers into a deeper trust—signs are not mere wonders but windows into the glory (δόξα) of God. In John 11, the delay and the tomb become integral to the sign, showing that true glory often emerges through suffering. The narrative arcs from conviction (Martha's confession) to compassion (Jesus weeps) to consummation (Lazarus called forth), each stage revealing facets of Christ's character. For modern readers, signs still abound: healed relationships, answered prayers, unexpected provision. Yet too often we consign these to coincidence rather than divine intervention. John's Gospel beckons us to reframe everyday blessings as "signs"—glimpses of a God who works out His purposes in our timelines. When our Wi-Fi goes out or a difficult conversation is softened, we can pause and ask, "Lord, what glory are You revealing?" This posture turns routine into revelation, cultivating a lifestyle today where every moment becomes an opportunity to attest to Jesus' power and love.

1.1.4 Key Characters Introduced: Lazarus, Mary, Martha, and the Disciples

Lazarus emerges not only as the beneficiary of a miracle but as a living testimony: his resurrection becomes proof that Jesus is "the resurrection and the life" (John 11:25). Mary, whose heart pours out tears at the tomb, teaches us that vulnerability before God is not a sign of weak faith but of authentic devotion (John 11:32). Martha, who moves swiftly to meet Jesus, reveals faith that acts even amid uncertainty: "I believe that You are the Christ" (John 11:27). The disciples, perplexed by Jesus' delay, demonstrate how proximity to Jesus does not guarantee perfect understanding (John 11:6-7). Collectively, these figures illustrate a spectrum of response: waiting, weeping, serving, and stumbling toward confession. In our contemporary lifestyle, we too fill similar roles—some are encouragers like Martha, some are contemplatives like Mary, and some are witnesses like Lazarus. Others among us wrestle with doubt, mirroring the disciples' questions. Healthy faith communities welcome all these responses, recognizing that each contributes to a fuller portrait of Christ's work. By identifying with these biblical personalities, we find both comfort and challenge: comfort in knowing our varied responses are normal, challenge in being invited into deeper trust. As you read this chapter, ask which character you most resemble today, and consider how God might be calling you to grow toward the fullness of faith modeled in Bethany.

1.2 Theological Paradox of Delay

1.2.1 "Jesus Stayed Two More Days": Love That Waits

The simple note that "Jesus stayed two more days in the place where He was" (John 11:6) can seem inexplicable until we recognize in it a posture of divine timing. This delay was not indecision but intentional—the Father and Son aligned their plan to magnify God's glory through resurrection rather than merely postpone death. Love that rushes is sometimes careless; love that waits is precise, honoring both the need and the purpose. In the modern rush of our lifestyles—instant messaging, one-click shopping, rapid streaming—patience can feel like a lost virtue. Yet God's pause reminds us that not every need is met on demand; some answers require incubation. Waiting becomes an avenue for grace, inviting us to trust in the unseen rather than the immediate. As we learn to wait, we practice dependence: acknowledging that our calendars are not God's calendar. In practice today, we can cultivate "holy pauses" by scheduling unplugged time, slowing our speech in prayer, and resisting the urge to fill every silence with activity. These disciplines echo Jesus' two-day wait, transforming our impatience into expectancy. Thus, divine delay reframes waiting not as absence but as appointment— an opportunity to align our hearts with heaven's clock.

1.2.2 Divine Providence vs. Human Urgency

Human urgency often masquerades as spiritual zeal: we mistake haste for holy passion and busyness for biblical devotion. Providence, by contrast, unfolds with sober care, weaving events together into a tapestry only God can see (Romans 8:28). In Bethany, Martha's hastened steps to meet Jesus reflect a good and godly concern, yet they also expose the tension between human timetables and divine agendas. Modern believers face similar tension when deadlines for work promotions collide with long-term calls to discipleship, or when family crises demand immediate attention that conflicts with scheduled devotionals. Recognizing the difference means asking, "Am I seeking God's timing, or my own?" and being willing to reorient plans when the Spirit redirects us. Daily practices—like holding our calendars lightly, praying over our "to-do" lists, and inviting accountability partners to question our hurried pace—help us submit urgency to providence. By doing so, we join a legacy of saints who paused in prayer before stepping into action. We then discover that God's solutions often arrive not with a bang but as a whisper, revealing His providence in ways our urgency would have missed. Thus, embracing divine providence over human urgency becomes a cornerstone of trusting God's timing.

1.2.3 Old-Testament Echoes of Waiting (Abraham, Joseph, David)

Scripture abounds with faithful figures who waited long before witnessing God's promise fulfilled. Abraham and Sarah received Isaac after decades of barrenness (Genesis 21:1-2), learning that God's promise does not expire but matures in His timing. Joseph endured years of prison and false accusation before rising to leadership in Egypt—and in that waiting, his character was forged for service (Genesis 41:14-16). David spent years in the wilderness, fleeing enemies and living as an outcast, yet those desert seasons shaped him into a shepherd-king after God's own heart (1 Samuel 16–30). Each story underscores that delays are not detours but developmental phases of divine training. In today's culture of instant gratification, we must resist the lie that immediate success equates to God's blessing. Instead, we can study these Old-Testament echoes to gain perspective: our current "wilderness" or "barren" seasons may be essential classrooms of trust. Practical steps include mentoring with mature believers, journaling God's faithfulness across past delays, and mapping personal timelines to see patterns of growth. By situating our waiting within this grand biblical narrative, we find solidarity and courage to persevere. These echoes then become living reminders that God's delays serve deep purposes beyond our immediate understanding.

1.2.4 Redemptive Delays in the New Testament (Jairus' Daughter, the Centurion)

Beyond Old-Testament prototypes, the Gospels record New-Testament instances where waiting became part of God's redemptive pattern. When Jairus begged Jesus to heal his daughter, a messenger interrupted: "Your daughter is dead"— yet Jesus still invited him to faith, turning apparent finality into fresh mercy (Mark 5:35-36). Similarly, the royal official's servant at Capernaum experienced healing only after Jesus declared, "Go; your son will live," underscoring that distance, delay, and declaration can converge in divine timetable (John 4:50). These narratives teach that God's interventions often transcend our definitions of "too late." In today's world, we may feel too old to start a new career, too wounded to rebuild relationships, or too drained to serve again. Yet the New-Testament pattern reminds us that redemptive delays are invitations to trust Jesus' word above circumstances. To embody this today, we can keep a "faith file" of past providences, practice prophetic proclamation over current challenges, and commit to steadfast intercession when hope seems extinguished. These actions mirror New-Testament faith, turning delays into declarations of divine sovereignty and grace.

1.3 Lament as Honest Faith

1.3.1 The Sisters' Message: "He Whom You Love Is Sick"

When Mary and Martha dispatched their urgent note—"Lord, he whom you love is sick" (John 11:3)—they appealed not only to Jesus' power but to His personal affection for Lazarus. This message reveals a theology of relationship: sickness is not merely a medical crisis but an opportunity to engage divine compassion. In first-century culture, a royal command or a teacher's decree held tremendous weight; here, the sisters leverage their personal bond to secure Jesus' attention. Their honest report sidestepped religious formalities, going straight to the heart of need. Today, we too can learn to speak plainly about our struggles—financial hardship, relational strain, mental health—trusting that Jesus cares more deeply than any counselor or physician. Honest confession becomes the soil for prayer, inviting God's presence into our most vulnerable moments. In practical terms, sharing burdens with trusted believers, writing frank journal entries to God, and naming our pain aloud in prayer groups embody this posture. By doing so, we follow Mary and Martha's lead: believing that our Savior's love is more powerful than any symptom. Their message reminds us that lament begins with naming our need before the One who loves us most.

1.3.2 "Lord, If You Had Been Here": Grief-Stricken Confession

Martha's words—"Lord, if you had been here, my brother would not have died" (John 11:21)—are raw, vulnerable, and utterly human. This confession blends grief with unspoken accusation, revealing that faith can coexist with disappointment. Remarkably, Jesus does not rebuke Martha for her lament; instead, He meets her at the intersection of sorrow and faith. Her statement models for us that honest questioning of God does not disqualify us from His presence. In contemporary life, we often feel pressure to mask doubt and disappointment behind polished spiritual platitudes. Yet Martha's grief-stricken confession grants us permission to bring our broken hopes openly before God. Practices such as writing unsent letters to God, creating art that expresses grief, or leading "lament liturgies" in worship provide healthy outlets for this honesty. Embracing our Martha moments shifts lament from mere complaint into the crucible of deeper trust. As we speak our sorrow, we find that Jesus stands not at a safe distance but draws near to bear our pain. Her confession teaches that faith is not the absence of tears but the courage to voice them before the One who holds tomorrow.

1.3.3 The Spiritual Discipline of Complaint (Psalms of Lament)

The biblical Psalter devotes nearly one-third of its songs to lament—David's anguished cries in Psalm 13 ("How long, O Lord?"), the collective wail in Psalm 44, and the raw honesty of Psalm 88. These psalms model a "discipline of complaint" wherein frustration and faith collide on the page. Complaint here is not irreverent rebellion but the holy act of crying out to a God who welcomes our honesty (Psalm 62:8). Lament psalms move through stages: address, lamentation, petition, and trust, guiding us from pain toward praise. In our modern lifestyle, we often rush from pain to solution, bypassing the crucial middle ground where God meets us in sorrow. Introducing lament as a regular element in personal devotions—allocating time to voice hurts, questions, and cries—brings balance to a faith life otherwise dominated by thanksgiving. Group lament gatherings, where participants share laments and pray for one another, recreate the psalmist's communal honesty. Incorporating lament into liturgy, music, and prayer ensures that our faith communities embrace the full spectrum of human emotion. By practicing the spiritual discipline of complaint, we learn that God's ear is attentive not only to our praise but also to our pain.

1.3.4 Transforming Pain into Prayerful Dialogue

The journey from raw grief to rooted trust requires intentional practices that channel pain into prayerful dialogue. First, naming the hurt—whether through journaling, speaking it aloud, or creating art—acknowledges reality before God. Second, anchoring the lament in Scripture, such as praying Psalm 31:9-10 or Lamentations 3:22-23, connects personal pain to God's unchanging character. Third, petitioning God with specific requests (healing, comfort, justice) transforms passive suffering into active engagement with the divine. Fourth, listening in silence invites the Spirit to speak words of hope into our wounded places. Finally, concluding with an affirmation of trust—"Nevertheless, I will hope in You" (Psalm 43:5)—reorients the heart toward faith. In contemporary practice, setting aside a "lament hour" in daily devotions, using guided prayer apps that include lament liturgies, or leading "lament retreats" in churches can institutionalize this transformation. By systematically moving through these steps, we discover that pain need not be an endpoint but a portal to deeper communion with God. In this way, our modern lifestyle embraces lament not as weakness but as a vibrant pathway to the heart of the Father, whose sorrowing Son weeps with us even now.

1.4 Formation in the Waiting Room

1.4.1 Patience as a Fruit of the Spirit

Patience is listed among the fruit of the Spirit, marking it not as human achievement but as a gift cultivated by the Spirit's work within us (Galatians 5:22). In a world of instant gratification—one-click purchases, on-demand entertainment, rapid notifications—the virtue of waiting feels almost extinct. Yet Scripture invites us to develop patience through repeated experiences of delay, learning to rest in God's timing rather than our own. Just as the farmer waits for the harvest (James 5:7), we are called to trust that God is at work beneath the soil of our circumstances. In practice today, we can create "pauses" in our schedules—turning off devices for set periods, observing a weekly Sabbath rest, or deliberately spacing our commitments to avoid hurried living. Small acts of patience, like waiting an extra minute before responding to an email or holding silence in family devotions, become spiritual exercises that strengthen our capacity to trust. These intentional pauses train our hearts to resist anxiety-driven shortcuts and to embrace God's pace. Over time, the Spirit transforms our hurried impulses into steady confidence, enabling us to bear seasonal delays with grace. Thus, patience ceases to be a grudging endurance and becomes a joyful surrender to the God who "is slow to anger and abounding in steadfast love" (Psalm 103:8).

1.4.2 Testing vs. Temptation: How Waiting Shapes Character

The Bible distinguishes between tests that build endurance and temptations that entice us toward sin (James 1:2–4; 1 Corinthians 10:13). A test invites us to stand firm under trials, producing maturity, while temptation lures us to compromise our faith. In the Bethany narrative, the sisters' prolonged wait tested their trust in Jesus without presenting a moral pitfall— here the waiting room served as a place of formation, not seduction. In modern life, tests may come through job-hunting seasons, medical diagnoses, or relational estrangement; these trials can deepen our reliance on God's promises rather than prompt us to impulsive escapes. By recognizing waiting as a sanctifying test, we can reframe discouragement into opportunity, viewing each delay as a divine classroom for perseverance. Practical steps include keeping a "trial and testimony" journal to record how God sustains us, seeking accountability partners to pray through waiting periods, and memorizing promises like Romans 8:28 to affirm God's redemptive purpose. When temptation to "take matters into our own hands" arises—perhaps through cutting ethical corners at work or manipulating outcomes in relationships—these disciplines anchor us in godly integrity. In doing so, we emerge from tests not bitter or hardened but refined and compassionate, ready to testify to God's sustaining grace.

1.4.3 Avoiding Anxious Shortcuts (Saul, King Uzziah)

Biblical history records leaders like Saul (1 Samuel 13) and King Uzziah (2 Chronicles 26) who, when impatient, violated divine protocols with disastrous consequences. Their anxious shortcuts—burning unauthorized offerings or overstepping priestly boundaries—stemmed from a desire for quick fixes rather than faithfulness. Similarly, in our day, we are tempted to expedite God's work through pragmatic but ungodly means: cutting ethical corners in business, resorting to manipulative tactics in relationships, or bypassing prayer for frantic action. To avoid these pitfalls, we must learn to cultivate margin in our lives—time buffers that prevent rushed decisions—and to submit major choices to communal discernment. Practices such as a "24-hour rule" (waiting a full day before responding to crises), presenting big decisions to a small trusted group, and anchoring action steps in prayerful fasting all help guard against hasty maneuvering. By honoring God's processes, we affirm that His methods—though slower—yield lasting fruit. Over time, resisting anxious shortcuts shapes us into people of integrity, whose trustworthiness reflects the character of the One whose timing we learn to embody.

1.4.4 Practices for Perseverance: Fasting, Silence, and Journaling

Spiritual disciplines anchor our souls during seasons of suspense. Fasting—whether from food, media, or other comforts—teaches dependency and heightens spiritual sensitivity (Matthew 6:16–18). Silence and solitude create sacred space for God's voice to speak into the clamor of uncertainty (Psalm 46:10). Journaling turns swirling emotions into tangible records of God's faithfulness, fostering hope as we look back on answered prayers. In a modern lifestyle dominated by noise—constant notifications, 24/7 news cycles—intentionally cultivating these disciplines counters spiritual fatigue. For example, a monthly "quiet day" away from screens can refresh perspective, while a daily five-minute journal entry celebrating even small mercies helps retrain our hearts to notice God's hand. Churches and small groups can sponsor collective fasting periods and guided silence retreats, reinforcing community support. Over time, these rhythms of deprivation and reflection build resilience, so that waiting becomes not a trial but a sacred journey of deeper intimacy with Christ.

1.5 When God Seems Late: Lessons for Today

1.5.1 Recognizing Areas of Apparent Divine Delay (Healing, Provision, Justice)

Even believers today face circumstances that feel like divine silence—unanswered prayers for physical healing, open doors of provision that remain closed, or longings for justice that seem perpetually deferred. In such seasons, it's vital to discern whether we are truly in God's waiting room or if our own choices have complicated His timing. Reflective practices—such as mapping prayer requests alongside life changes—can reveal patterns of alignment or distraction. Engaging trustworthy mentors or pastors to review our spiritual walk provides external clarity, ensuring we haven't missed steps of obedience. When petitions for healing (James

5:14–15), financial breakthrough (Philippians 4:19), or social justice (Isaiah 1:17) remain unfulfilled, we can affirm that God's purposes transcend our limited frames. By comparing our real-time experience with scriptural promises, we cultivate patience and hope. Modern lifestyles often equate delay with denial; recognizing divine pacing invites us to cultivate a posture of expectancy rather than despair. In this way, perceived delays become stepping-stones to deeper faith and broader understanding of God's redemptive work.

1.5.2 Cultivating Expectant Gratitude Before the Answer Arrives

Thanksgiving in advance—offered before the miracle is visible—echoes Jesus' own prayer over Lazarus: "Father, I thank you that you have heard me" (John 11:41–42). Gratitude anticipates God's faithfulness, shifting our focus from lack to provision. Contemporary spiritual practices like maintaining a "gratitude jar," where each day's thank-you note is deposited, train our hearts to notice grace in small moments. Digital apps that prompt daily gratitude entries harness technology for spiritual formation rather than distraction. When we publicly testify to future breakthroughs—declaring "I will rejoice in God's deliverance" (Psalm 32:11)—we align our speech with divine promises. This anticipatory thanksgiving acts as a shield against discouragement, rewiring neural pathways toward hopefulness. Over time, a lifestyle of expectant gratitude fosters resilience, equipping us to rejoice even in the "not yet" phases of prayer.

1.5.3 Building Community Support in Seasons of Waiting

Waiting alone can breed isolation and doubt; by contrast, shared waiting creates solidarity. The early church devoted itself to "the apostles' teaching and the fellowship, to the breaking of bread and the prayers" (Acts 2:42), modeling communal endurance. Today's believers can form "waiting circles"—small groups committed to speaking encouragement, praying regularly for one another's specific needs, and celebrating small signs of God's movement. Practical expressions include meal trains during crises, virtual check-ins for those homebound, and public prayer boards in church foyers where ongoing petitions are displayed. Social media, often blamed for superficial connections, can be repurposed to broadcast honest prayer updates and rally intercessory teams. By bearing one another's burdens (Galatians 6:2), we reflect Christ's body and confirm that no one waits alone. Such networks keep hope alive and remind us that the resurrection power that raised Lazarus is the same power sustaining each of us today.

1.5.4 Crafting Testimonies of Past Faithfulness to Fuel Present Trust

Remembering God's past deliverances stokes our faith for current challenges. Psalm 66:16 invites us, "Come and hear, all you who fear God, and I will tell what he has done for my soul," modeling the power of testimony. In our modern context, we can create "faith folders"—digital or physical collections of answered-prayer stories, Scripture verses that comforted us, and notes from spiritual mentors. Periodically reviewing these compilations reminds our hearts that God is consistent even when He seems silent. Sharing testimonies in worship services, social media posts, or small groups not only strengthens our own trust but encourages others in their waiting. When we speak aloud God's faithfulness in one season, we prime our spirits to anticipate His goodness in the next. This lifestyle of reflective testimony anchors us in the unchanging character of the Resurrector, who, like in Bethany, turns delays into declarations of His glory.

1.6 Exegetical Insights and Key Word Studies

1.6.1 Greek Terms for "Love" (ἀγαπάω) and "Glory" (δόξα) in John 11

John's Gospel deliberately uses the verb ἀγαπάω ("to love") to describe Jesus' affection for Lazarus (John 11:3, 5), distinguishing it from φιλέω, the more familiar "brotherly love." This choice underscores a deep, covenantal bond, revealing that Jesus' actions flow from profound divine love. Likewise, the noun δόξα ("glory") recurs as the ultimate aim of signs—glories God's character through acts that transcend natural possibility (John 11:4, 40). In contemporary application, we can meditate on these terms by translating them into relational and artistic expressions: practicing ἀγαπάω through sacrificial service in our communities and pursuing δόξα by crafting worship art, music, or storytelling that reflects God's beauty. Small-group studies of the original Greek, using interlinear Bibles or free online resources, equip laypeople to appreciate these nuances. Journaling reflections on how divine love has personally met us, and creating visual "glory boards" that capture moments of God's splendor, bring these ancient words alive in twenty-first-century life. Through these exercises, the layered meaning of love and glory in John 11 informs not only our theology but our everyday expressions of faith.

1.6.2 Comparative Analysis of Chronological Markers in the Text

John 11 uses precise chronological markers—Martha's urgent message ("he whom you love is sick"), Jesus' two-day delay (v. 6), and the four days Lazarus lay in the tomb (v. 17)—to heighten suspense and underscore divine sovereignty over time. Noting the shift from "sick" to "dead" accentuates the climax of the sign. In modern "digital diaries," we can mirror this attentiveness by timestamping prayer requests and answers, creating a visible timeline of God's activity. Comparing our own calendars—when we first prayed, when we sensed God's guidance, and when outcomes manifested—helps us recognize His pattern of timing. Churches might develop "waiting wall" installations where members post prayer date cards and later pin answered cards beneath them, visually tracing God's faithfulness. By learning to read chronological markers both in Scripture and in our stories, we cultivate a narrative sensitivity that discerns God's hand in the intervals as well as the outcomes.

1.6.3 Chiastic Structure of John 11:1–16

A chiastic framework in John 11:1–16 (A: report of illness; B: Jesus' delay; C: disciples' objection; D: Jesus' purpose statement; C': disciples' misunderstanding; B': departure to Bethany; A': arrival announcement) highlights theological pivots within the narrative. This mirror-like structure draws attention to Jesus' central declaration that Lazarus's sickness "is for the glory of God" (v. 4). In twenty-first-century practice, we can apply chiastic study by structuring personal journal entries or prayer meditations in A-B-C-B'-A' patterns—beginning with need, reflecting on God's response, acknowledging misunderstanding, and concluding with testimony. Workshops in churches can introduce this method as a tool for worship planning or sermon preparation, fostering deeper engagement with biblical texts. Recognizing these literary patterns not only enriches our exegetical skills but offers creative templates for spiritual reflection, turning each Scripture reading into a choreography of confession, meditation, and praise.

1.7 Practical Discipleship Pathways

1.7.1 Developing "Trust Timelines" in Personal Devotions

Creating a "Trust Timeline" begins with recording the date and details of a current need or prayer request, much like Mary and Martha's initial plea (John 11:3). First, identify the verses or promises you're resting upon—perhaps Isaiah 40:31 or Philippians 4:19—and note them beside the date. Each week, revisit that entry to journal any developments, even small ones, such as a growing sense of peace or unexpected provision. Over time, these incremental updates reveal the trajectory of God's activity, reminding us that His timing often unfolds in subtle steps rather than dramatic leaps. Use colored pens or digital tags to mark answered prayers, partial answers, and areas still awaiting resolution, creating a visual map of faith in action. This practice trains your heart to look for God's fingerprints in daily life, from a friend's encouraging text to a sudden change in circumstance. At the end of each month, take fifteen minutes to reflect on what you've learned about God's pacing—did He answer sooner than expected? Later? And how did your own trust evolve as you recorded each phase? By making "Trust Timelines" a regular rhythm, you cultivate an expectancy that transcends calendar constraints, echoing Jesus' perfect synchronization with the Father's plan (John 5:19). Over the long haul, this discipline fosters resilience: when fresh needs arise, you instinctively reach for your timeline, confident that the God who has never failed will remain faithful.

1.7.2 Small-Group Exercises: Sharing Stories of God's Timing

In a small-group setting, begin by inviting each member to bring one written account of a past prayer answered in God's time. Allocate equal sharing time—five to seven minutes each—so everyone can tell their story without rush. As each testimony unfolds, others practice active listening by noting one insight and one question, fostering both affirmation and deeper reflection. After each sharing, pause for corporate prayer, specifically thanking God for that answered request and interceding for personal waiting seasons among the group. Rotate facilitators weekly so that each person learns to guide both testimony and intercession, building leadership skills alongside trust. Incorporate icebreaker activities that underscore waiting, such as a timed silence exercise or a "waiting line" where members physically pause in staggered intervals before speaking. Encourage the group to create a communal "Waiting Wall"—a display of index cards with current requests and dates, updated as answers arrive. Schedule quarterly "celebration gatherings" to look back over months of both answered and ongoing prayers, reminding everyone that even partial or delayed responses bear witness to God's character. This collective practice not only deepens relational bonds but also embeds the theology of divine timing into the fabric of community life. Through shared stories, believers learn that waiting is not a solo struggle but a collective pilgrimage toward greater trust.

1.7.3 Family Worship Ideas: Teaching Children to Wait on the Lord

Children live in a world of immediate gratification—video games, streaming cartoons, snack vending machines—making spiritual waiting countercultural. To teach them trust in God's timing, begin family worship with a simple "anticipation candle": light a candle and explain that just as the flame grows slowly, some of God's answers take time. Read a kid-friendly version of the Lazarus story (John 11), pausing to ask, "Why do you think Jesus waited?" Use a timeline poster with movable stickers: when a child prays for something, they place a sticker on today's date, then follow up weekly by moving a different-colored sticker to show progress or change. Incorporate age-appropriate crafts—like making paper clocks where each number represents a step of faith (pray, trust, hope, obey)—to reinforce that God's "clock" sometimes ticks differently than ours. Encourage children to keep a "God's-Got-This" jar: they draw a slip with a need written on it, pray, and revisit it when the slip is pulled again, seeing that God is always present even if the answer isn't instant. Sing worship songs about waiting—"Still" by Hillsong or "Even If" by MercyMe—to give them memorable melodies that echo the lesson. During bedtime prayer, model honest lament alongside trust: "God, I'm sad my friend is still sick, but I know You love her." Over time, these family rhythms help children grasp that faith is active, not passive, nurturing hearts that lean on God's promises rather than their own timelines. As they grow, they'll carry these habits into adolescence and beyond, equipped to navigate life's uncertainties with steadfast hope.

1.7.4 Pastoral Counseling Guidelines for the Delayed Miracle

When counseling individuals in prolonged waiting seasons, pastors should first affirm the reality of their pain, echoing Jesus' compassion in shedding tears (John 11:35). Listen attentively, resisting the urge to offer quick answers; let silence underscore your empathy. Gently guide counselees to articulate both their deepest hopes and their frustrations, normalizing doubt as part of the faith journey. Introduce journaling prompts focused on God's character—His faithfulness, sovereignty, and goodness—to counterbalance feelings of abandonment. Pray Scripture over them, selecting passages like Lamentations 3:22-23 and Romans 8:28, and encourage memorization to fortify their hearts in lonely hours. Arrange periodic check-ins where progress is evaluated, and adjust treatment plans to include spiritual disciplines such as fasting or silence retreats if impatience persists. Facilitate support groups comprising others in similar seasons, fostering peer encouragement. Provide resources—books on biblical waiting, guided lament liturgies, and online sermon archives on trust—that offer continued learning. Caution against "miracle chasing" ministries that promise instant results, steering instead toward a patient confidence anchored in Christ alone. By integrating empathy, Scripture, and structured spiritual practices, pastoral care becomes a ministry of presence mirroring Jesus' own compassionate accompaniment in Bethany.

Conclusion Having explored the textures of grief, the discipline of waiting, and the mysterious wisdom in God's delay, we arrive at a place of renewed hope. Trusting God's timing does not eliminate pain; rather, it transforms pain into partnership, teaching us to stand alongside our Savior in the waiting room. As you close this chapter, may you be encouraged to view every season of apparent silence as an invitation to grow in intimacy with Christ, confident that His delays are never denials but integral steps toward His greater glory.

May the lessons drawn from Bethany's dusty roads and a sorrowing family's plea resonate in your own life, equipping you to bear both lament and praise with equal grace. And as you press forward—holding fast to God's unchanging character amid shifting circumstances—remember that the One who finally called Lazarus forth from the tomb is the very same Lord who walks with you through every moment of anticipation. Let this truth sustain you, for in His perfect timing, you will discover not only deliverance but the lasting joy of a faith refined.

Chapter 2. Confident Faith in the Face of Loss

Loss severs us from the familiar, plunging our hearts into shadows of grief and uncertainty. Yet in the Bethany tomb, Martha's courageous declaration—"I believe that you are the Christ, the Son of God" (John 11:27)—reveals that faith can rise above the sting of death itself. This chapter invites you into the tension between raw sorrow and unwavering trust, showing how honest lament and steadfast confession become twin pillars that uphold the soul when all else seems lost. Drawing on the example of Abraham's "hopeless hope" (Romans 4:18) and the psalmists who cried out in anguish even as they anchored their souls in God (Psalm 13), we will explore how belief grounded in relationship with Christ transcends circumstances. Whether facing the death of a loved one, the collapse of a dream, or the ache of abandonment, confident faith does not deny pain but finds its strength in the One who commands life from the tomb.

2.1 The Pivotal Conversation at the Tomb

2.1.1 Martha's Bold Confession (John 11:21–22)

Martha's words to Jesus—"Lord, if you had been here, my brother would not have died"—carry both grief and unwavering conviction (John 11:21). In that moment, she does not question Jesus' identity; instead, she affirms His power over life and death. Her statement presumes two truths: first, that Jesus could have prevented Lazarus's death, and second, that He was uniquely worth appealing to. This confession arises from years of fellowship with Christ, rooted in experiences of His compassion and miracles (cf. Luke 10:38–42). By voicing her faith openly, Martha models courageous honesty before God, refusing to hide her pain or dilute her belief. In contemporary practice, believers can learn from her example by bringing raw emotions into prayer rooms without fear, trusting that God welcomes our lament alongside our faith. A bold confession may begin with hesitation—"I believe, help my unbelief" (Mark 9:24)—but it matures into declarations of trust even amid unanswered questions. Martha's confidence also challenges us not to compartmentalize our faith; grief and belief can coexist. Her words invite us to remember past evidences of God's faithfulness whenever we face fresh losses. Thus, Martha's confession stands as a foundational pattern for faith that speaks truth to both sorrow and hope.

2.1.2 Jesus' Transformative Question: "Do You Believe This?" (John 11:26)

After Martha's confession of Christ, Jesus responds with a probing question: "Do you believe this?" (John 11:26), inviting her to move from doctrinal assent to personal appropriation. The "this" encompasses two profound truths: that Jesus is the resurrection and the life, and that whoever believes in Him will never truly die. By asking rather than lecturing, Jesus honors Martha's freedom to respond and encourages active engagement with the promises He offers. His question also surfaces the gulf between head knowledge and heart conviction—a theme Jesus returns to throughout His ministry (cf. Matthew 16:15). In pastoral counseling or small groups, asking similar questions—"Do you trust that Christ's life overcomes your greatest loss?"—can help believers internalize gospel truths. This approach shifts faith from abstract theology into lived reality. Contemporary discipleship might use "belief journals" where respondents write narrative answers to Jesus' question, documenting how each promise applies to their story. Group discussions can incorporate reflective pauses: after reading John 11:26, participants silently wrestle with their own "this" before sharing insights. By embracing Jesus' method, faith communities foster deeper, personal appropriation of Christ's life-giving power, catalyzing transformation at the level of the heart.

2.1.3 From Mourning to Declaration: The Shift in Tone

In the span of one conversation, the tone at the tomb shifts from sorrowful lament to powerful declaration. Initially, Martha expresses grief: her words drip with the weight of death's finality. Yet by affirming Who Jesus is—"the Christ, the Son of God"—her language transitions from looking backward at loss to looking forward in hope (John 11:27). This pivot demonstrates that confession of identity precedes assured anticipation of action. The movement from mourning to declaration is neither instantaneous nor easy; it involves wrestling with pain, recalling God's past interventions, and choosing to speak faith over fear. Modern believers can replicate this shift by pairing lament with scripted declarations: after voicing sorrow, one might recite Romans 8:38–39 to affirm unstoppable divine love. Worship playlists can be structured similarly—starting with a lament song like "Psalm 42 (As the Deer)" before transitioning into a declaration anthem like "Resurrecting." Liturgically, churches might employ responsive readings that move from complaints (e.g., Psalm 10) to doxologies (e.g., Psalm 104). Over time, this practice wires the soul to pivot naturally from grief into gospel proclamation. Recognizing that confession alters atmosphere, believers carry a powerful tool for ushering hope into dark places—both their own hearts and the lives of those they serve.

2.2 Anatomy of Faith under Pressure

2.2.1 Rooted in Relationship, Not Circumstance

True faith springs from knowing Christ personally, not from favorable situations or outward success. When Martha confesses belief, she does so because of a relationship cultivated over time (John 11:27), not because Lazarus's condition was stable. Similarly, our confidence during trials must be anchored in intimacy with Jesus—listening to His voice, abiding in His presence (John 15:4). Circumstances will ebb and flow, but relational trust endures beyond the changing tides. Developing this root involves daily practices: Scripture meditation, unhurried prayer, and honest sharing in accountability partnerships. These habits deepen awareness of Christ's nearness even when life unravels. Over time, believers learn that faith is not a formula but a Person to whom they cling. When external circumstances threaten to topple hope, the relational foundation prevents collapse. Imagine the vine and branches analogy: apart from the vine, the branch withers; connected, it bears fruit regardless of weather (John 15:5). In practical terms, scheduling monthly "retreat afternoons" for extended prayer and listening can nourish this connection. Group retreats centered on experiencing God's presence—through guided silence or lectio divina—reinforce relational roots that sustain faith under any pressure.

2.2.2 Head Knowledge vs. Heart Trust (James 2:19–20)

James warns that mere intellectual assent—"You believe that God is one; you do well. Even the demons believe—and shudder" (James 2:19)—falls short of living faith. Head knowledge without heart trust produces no transformation; faith must move from cognition to conviction. In the tomb scene, Martha's confession transcends an academic statement; it issues from the depths of her heart, evidenced by her willingness to confront death with declaration. To cultivate such trust, believers need practices that engage emotion and will: journaling prayers that confess fears, weaving personal testimonies into daily devotions, and creating "faith playlists" of songs that stir the soul. Teaching contexts might employ dramatized readings of biblical narratives, inviting participants to "step into" the story emotionally. Psychological studies confirm that multisensory experiences deepen memory and commitment; spiritual formation can harness this insight. Over time, believers convert static propositions into dynamic, embodied trust. When temptations to doubt arise, heart-trust quickens the memory of God's presence, even when facts seem grim. Thus, the goal is not to abandon head knowledge but to anchor it in heart-level devotion that bears the weight of real-life trials.

2.2.3 Faith That Wrestles with Reality (Hebrews 11:17–19)

Abraham's near-sacrifice of Isaac—"accounting that God was able even to raise him from the dead" (Hebrews 11:19)—illustrates faith that engages hard realities without evasion. Wrestling with reality does not weaken faith; it refines it. Martha's dialogue shows this pattern: she acknowledges Lazarus's death even as she clings to Christ's power. Faith under pressure asks honest questions—"Why this delay?"—while refusing to settle for easy answers. This dynamic tension resembles Jacob's nighttime struggle with the angel (Genesis 32:24–30), resulting in blessing and a new identity. Believers today can practice wrestling by journaling tough doubts alongside prayers for revelation, then revisiting those entries when God provides clarity. Spiritual directors can invite counselees to bring their strongest objections or fears to session, treating them as sacred soil for growth. Integrating lament psalms with hope declarations captures this dialectic, acknowledging pain without surrendering hope. Over time, believers discover that God honors those who engage Him earnestly, producing a faith that is both realistic and resilient. As Hebrews testifies, such faith pleases God (Hebrews 11:6) and becomes the conduit for miracles that transcend human limitation.

2.3 Lament and Hope Woven Together

2.3.1 Biblical Laments as Faith Expressions (Psalm 13; 22)

Psalms of lament—like "How long, O Lord? Will you forget me forever?" (Psalm 13:1)—are not signs of weak faith but blueprints for honest dialogue with God. Each lament psalm moves from complaint to hope, modeling a trajectory for believers in loss. Psalm 22 begins with despair—"My God, my God, why have you forsaken me?"—yet ends in praise, forecasting God's ultimate deliverance (vv. 31–32). In our practices today, we can adopt these psalms as liturgical guides: pray the lament section during times of sorrow, then meditate on the hope section as an act of faith. Worship leaders might compose services that juxtapose lament hymns with resurrection anthems, embodying the psalmist's journey. In private devotions, reading and paraphrasing these psalms in journal form transforms ancient laments into personalized prayers. Small groups can hold "lament nights," where participants anonymously submit laments that are prayed through collectively, followed by declarations of hope drawn from the same psalm. By imitating this woven pattern, believers learn that true faith incorporates both grief's honesty and hope's endurance, reflecting the full spectrum of trust in a sovereign, compassionate God.

2.3.2 Hope as an Anchor in Sorrow (Hebrews 6:19)

Hebrews 6:19 proclaims hope as "an anchor for the soul, firm and secure," signifying that hope sustains believers amid life's storms. Unlike wishful thinking, biblical hope rests on God's unbreakable promises—Jesus Himself being the anchor that enters the inner sanctuary (Hebrews 6:20). In practical terms, anchoring hope involves memorizing covenantal assurances such as Lamentations 3:22–23 and Isaiah 54:10, reciting them in moments of discouragement. Visual reminders—anchors painted on journal covers or phone wallpapers—can redirect anxious thoughts toward divine constancy. Counseling contexts might employ anchored breathing exercises paired with repeated Scripture recitations, integrating mind, body, and spirit. Churches can design "Hope Stations" in worship spaces—interactive displays where individuals write down fears and then overlay them with promise verses, symbolically anchoring their souls. Over time, these habits shift the default response from despair to expectant hope, enabling believers to navigate sorrow without losing spiritual equilibrium. Thus, anchor imagery and practice become a lifeline for souls buffeted by the waves of loss.

2.3.3 "Hopeless Hope": Abraham's Example of Believing Against All Odds (Romans 4:18)

Romans 4:18 celebrates Abraham's "hope against hope," believing God would fulfill His promise despite human impossibility. This paradoxical posture—"hopeless hope"—embraces the tension between bleak reality and divine promise. Abraham's story challenges modern believers to hold covenantal truths more tightly than circumstantial evidence. Practically, one can create "promise journals" where each entry cites a specific biblical promise alongside the present difficulty, reminding the heart that God's word supersedes facts. Prayer partners might use "promise cards," exchanging verses that speak to each other's situations, fostering mutual encouragement in "hopeless" circumstances. Sermon series could explore Hebrews 11's heroes, emphasizing Abraham's example as a template for faith under loss. Workshops on "faith mapping" teach participants to trace God's unfolding promises across Scripture, equipping them to deploy those promises when despair looms. By cultivating "hopeless hope," believers learn that certainty resides not in data or deliverance but in the character and word of God, who brought life from Abraham's dead promise and who still speaks life into our most desperate winters.

2.4 The Dynamics of Spiritual Confession

2.4.1 Declaring Scripture over Circumstance (2 Corinthians 4:13)

Spiritual confession means speaking God's Word into the reality of our loss, not merely voicing personal wishes. 2 Corinthians 4:13 records Paul's affirmation: "Since we have the same spirit of faith according to what has been written, 'I believed, and so I spoke,' we also believe, and so we speak." By deliberately quoting Scripture in prayer—saying, for instance, "The Lord is close to the brokenhearted" (Psalm 34:18)—we align our voices with divine truth rather than our fluctuating emotions. In practice today, believers can keep a "confession list" of key verses (e.g., Isaiah 43:2, Romans 8:28, Psalm 23:4) and read them aloud each morning over their circumstances. When grief or fear threatens to dominate, reciting these declarations disrupts anxious thought patterns and reorients the heart toward hope. Worship playlists featuring songs that incorporate biblical promises also serve as powerful confessional means, embedding truth through melody. Small groups might create "confession walls" where participants post index cards with Scripture declarations they need to live by during loss. Over time, this habit transforms language itself: believers begin to speak life, peace, and assurance into situations that once felt hopeless. As our tongues practice divine confession, our inner convictions grow stronger, and God's promises become living realities.

2.4.2 Public vs. Private Confession: Witnessing in Community

Confession takes two complementary forms: private declarations in prayer and public testimonies before others. Private confession cultivates intimacy with God (Psalm 17:6), while sharing faith publicly builds corporate trust and encourages fellow believers (Hebrews 10:23–25). In small-group settings, individuals can be invited to share brief testimonies of how God sustained them through loss, modeling both vulnerability and victory. Public confession need not be elaborate—simply stating, "I'm trusting God for healing in my family; would you join me in prayer?"—yet it creates spiritual accountability and collective intercession. Churches can designate "testimony moments" during services or midweek gatherings, reinforcing that honest stories of struggle and faith bolster communal resilience. Online platforms offer additional avenues: prayer chains via messaging apps, livestream segments for sharing answers, and social media "faith posts" that declare God's work in real time. By normalizing public confession, congregations foster environments where people feel safe to express doubts and victories alike. This creates a ripple effect: when one person's confession bears witness to God's goodness, others gain courage to confess their own needs and hopes, knitting the body closer together in confident faith.

2.4.3 Confession as Spiritual Warfare (Mark 11:23–24)

Jesus taught that faith-filled words wield spiritual authority: "Truly, I say to you, whoever says to this mountain, 'Be taken up and thrown into the sea,' and does not doubt in his heart but believes … it will be done for him" (Mark 11:23). In seasons of loss, our "mountains" may be grief, financial strain, or relational rupture. Confessional warfare involves proclaiming God's sovereignty—"Though I walk through the valley of the shadow of death, I will fear no evil" (Psalm 23:4)—and rejecting the enemy's lies of abandonment or defeat. Believers can organize "confession drills," gathering in prayer teams to practice declaring specific promises over one another's circumstances, reinforcing both faith and community. Journaling these declarations alongside notes of spiritual resistance ("I rebuke despair," "I take captive anxious thoughts," cf. 2 Corinthians 10:5) sharpens awareness of spiritual dynamics. Incorporating confession into personal spiritual warfare also means speaking forgiveness over oneself and others, cutting off bitterness that so easily festers in loss. Over time, consistent confession trains believers to view their words as weapons of light—piercing darkness, surmounting fear, and ushering in God's redemptive power. As faith-filled speech becomes second nature, the practice of confession itself becomes a tangible expression of invincible hope.

2.5 Faith in Action amid Loss

2.5.1 Serving Others while Grieving (Galatians 6:2)

Even in our deepest sorrow, faith finds expression in love for others. Galatians 6:2 urges us to "bear one another's burdens," a call that transforms grief from inward fixation into outward compassion. Serving—preparing meals for those in hospital, writing notes of encouragement, or volunteering—shifts focus from personal pain to God's work in the lives around us. Practical acts of service do not diminish our own grief but invite God's presence in empathy and solidarity. Churches can establish "grief teams" that partner with those mourning, offering practical help like childcare, errands, or household chores. Small groups might rotate "care champions" who check in on hurting members through calls, texts, or visits. Serving in this way echoes Christ's incarnational love—He Himself came not to be served but to serve (Mark 10:45). In serving, we discover that giving becomes a balm for our own wounds, as the Spirit consoles and strengthens us through the very acts of compassion we extend. Thus, faith manifested in service bears witness to Christ's resurrection power, demonstrating that life flourishes even in the soil of loss.

2.5.2 Obedience Before Understanding (1 Samuel 3:7–9)

The call to obedience often comes before full comprehension, just as Samuel responded to the Lord's voice without knowing the full plan (1 Samuel 3:7–9). In our own seasons of waiting, God may prompt us to take faithful steps—reaching out in reconciliation, giving beyond our means, or sharing hard truths—long before we see the outcome. Such obedience reflects trust in God's wisdom, resisting the temptation to demand guarantees before acting. Practically, this might look like writing a letter of forgiveness to someone who has hurt us, volunteering even when energy is low, or tithing sacrificially despite financial uncertainty (Malachi 3:10). Believers can create "obedience checklists," noting promptings from Scripture or the Spirit and committing to act within specified timeframes. Pairing with an accountability partner ensures that promises to obey are honored, sustaining faith when fear whispers to delay. Over time, repeated acts of obedience build a repository of testimonies, reminding us that God's purposes often unfold beyond our sight. Such lifestyle of obedience cements the truth that faith is not passive waiting but active trust—stepping forward even into the unknown because we believe God holds the map.

2.5.3 Testimonies of Modern-Day 'Lazarus Stories'

Contemporary "Lazarus stories" abound: people healed after terminal diagnoses, marriages restored after long estrangement, finances provisioned in impossible budgets. Collecting and sharing these testimonies in church newsletters, social media feeds, or small-group meetings breathes life into weary hearts. Each account amplifies the reality that Jesus is still "the resurrection and the life" (John 11:25). When drafting these stories, emphasize both the delay and the deliverance, showcasing how faith endured and hope was vindicated. Churches might host annual "Lazarus Nights," featuring video interviews with individuals who experienced God's power in their darkest moments. Publishing these testimonies in print or online not only encourages readers but invites unbelievers to consider the supernatural dimension of Christian faith. Recording testimonies in a communal "Storybook"—a bound volume kept in the church lobby— offers a tangible legacy for future generations. In every modern miracle, the pattern repeats: pain, petition, pause, and proclamation. By foregrounding these narratives, communities reinforce that loss is not the final word—and that Jesus still calls forth life from places deemed beyond hope.

2.6 Contemporary Expressions of Confident Faith

2.6.1 Believing God for Healing in the Midst of Pandemic Loss

The global pandemic brought unparalleled grief—loss of loved ones, livelihoods, and normalcy. Yet amid the crisis, believers held fast to promises like Isaiah 53:5 ("By his wounds we are healed") and James 5:14–15's call to pray over the sick. Churches pivoted to offer virtual prayer rooms, 24/7 intercession streams, and online anointing services, demonstrating that faith transcends physical barriers. Individuals organized "healing chains," rotating teams that committed to continuous prayer for designated regions. Social media campaigns like "#JesusHeals" spread testimonies of recovery, fostering global solidarity in faith. Telehealth chaplaincy emerged, enabling pastors to counsel and pray with isolated patients, bringing compassionate presence through screens. These contemporary modes of seeking divine healing exemplify confident faith: they adapt methods without diluting the message that God is still at work in our bodies and communities. Even as medical treatments advance, spiritual intercession remains indispensable—faith and science collaborating in holistic restoration.

2.6.2 Financial Faith: Trusting God's Provision When Jobs Disappear (Philippians 4:19)

Economic downturns and layoffs can shatter security, yet Scripture reminds us, "And my God will supply every need of yours according to his riches in glory in Christ Jesus" (Philippians 4:19). Believers facing job loss have cultivated financial faith by establishing "provision budgets" that pair anticipated expenses with corresponding promises (e.g., Psalm 37:25). Churches have launched benevolence funds and micro-grant programs to meet acute needs while modeling God's generosity. Financial discipleship courses teach stewardship principles, emphasizing giving even in scarcity as an act of trust (2 Corinthians 8:2–3). Small groups host "trust dinners" where members bring minimal food items and share testimonies of how God multiplied their resources. Such tangible experiences reinforce that God's economy operates on multiplication rather than subtraction. Over time, families practicing this faith discipline report reduced anxiety and deeper gratitude, testifying that divine provision often arrives through unconventional channels—unexpected gifts, new job offers, or creative side ventures. Thus, financial faith becomes a lifestyle that acknowledges God as ultimate Provider, not merely a fallback in emergencies.

2.6.3 Emotional Resilience: Counseling and Community Support (Romans 12:15)

Emotional fallout from loss can include depression, anxiety, and isolation. Yet Romans 12:15 exhorts us to "rejoice with those who rejoice, weep with those who weep," modeling communal empathy. In response, many churches have established grief share groups and counseling ministries that offer biblical and professional support. Lay counselors trained in listening skills provide one-on-one care, while licensed therapists partner with pastors to address deeper trauma. Online support forums moderated by faith leaders allow for anonymous sharing and prayer. Congregations integrate mental-health checkups into pastoral visits, treating emotional well-being as an integral part of discipleship. Workshops on resilience teach coping strategies—mindfulness rooted in Scripture, breathing prayers (Psalm 46:10), and cognitive reframing aligned with Philippians 4:8's call to think on whatever is true and honorable. This holistic approach recognizes that confident faith does not dismiss emotional pain but surrounds it with grace, truth, and communal care. Over time, those engaged in such support networks develop robust emotional muscles, enabling them to stand firm in faith even as loss tugs at every fiber of their being.

2.7 Cultivating Steadfast Belief Today

2.7.1 Daily Practices: Declaring Promises in Prayer Journals

Begin each day by opening a dedicated prayer journal and selecting a promise from Scripture—such as Romans 8:28 ("And we know that in all things God works for the good of those who love him") or Isaiah 41:10 ("Fear not, for I am with you"). Write out the promise in your own words, then record the specific loss or trial you're facing. Following this, craft a short confession that fuses the promise with your need—e.g., "God, I trust that You will work this financial setback for my good." Throughout the day, revisit your entry during transitional moments—before meals, during breaks, or when anxiety resurfaces—to speak the promise aloud. At night, journal any evidence of God's faithfulness—even subtle shifts in perspective or unexpected moments of peace—and note how it aligns with the morning declaration. Over time, these journal entries form a chronological tapestry of God's activity, reinforcing that His Word does not return void (Isaiah 55:11). Use colored highlighters to mark entries where your trust deepened and outcomes you can now celebrate. Incorporate creative elements—stickers, sketches, or printed Scripture art—to engage both heart and mind. If you miss a day, resist guilt; simply pick up where you left off, trusting that consistency, not perfection, shapes faith. By making confession of Scripture a daily rhythm, you cultivate a personal habit that transforms your inner dialogue, anchoring belief in the bedrock of God's unchanging Word.

2.7.2 Small-Group Rituals: "Hope Circles" for Ongoing Encouragement

Form a "Hope Circle" of four to six believers committed to mutual support through seasons of loss. Meet weekly—either in person or virtually—for a structured time of sharing, prayer, and encouragement. Begin each gathering with a brief centering ritual: light a candle and read Hebrews 6:19 ("…hope as an anchor for the soul…"). Rotate facilitation so each member leads one segment—testimony of God's faithfulness, Scripture reading, or guided prayer—nurturing leadership skills and shared ownership. Incorporate a symbolic "passing of the anchor": each person holds an anchor-shaped token as they share their prayer request, signifying that their hope is held by the group. After sharing, partners pair off for five minutes of focused prayer, then reconvene for group declarations: aloud affirming God's promises over each other's needs. Between meetings, maintain a group chat where members post daily encouragement—Scripture verses, short reflections, or answered-prayer updates. Schedule quarterly celebrations to revisit answered requests and testify to God's work, reinforcing hope's trajectory. Encourage tangible acts of care—sending handwritten cards or small care packages—to embody gospel love beyond words. Through consistent "Hope Circle" rituals, small groups become spiritual lifelines, weaving confident faith into the fabric of communal life.

2.7.3 Memorizing Anchor Verses: John 11:25–26 and Hebrews 11:1

Identify two foundational verses—John 11:25–26 ("I am the resurrection and the life ...") and Hebrews 11:1 ("Now faith is the assurance of things hoped for, the conviction of things not seen")—to serve as anchors in loss. Write each verse on index cards and place them in high-visibility spots: your bathroom mirror, workspace, or car dashboard. Use the "verse-sandwich" method: recite the first half before breakfast, the second half before lunch, then say the full verse before dinner, embedding it through repetition. Pair memorization with movement—walk laps around your neighborhood while speaking the verses—to engage kinesthetic memory. Incorporate the verses into everyday routines: recite them during daily chores, use them as mantras during stressful moments, or sing them to simple tunes at bedtime. Enlist an accountability partner to quiz you weekly, celebrating milestones with small rewards—a favorite coffee or a new journal. Record yourself saying the verses and play the audio during commutes, harnessing downtime for spiritual formation. Periodically reflect in your journal on how these anchor verses reshaped your response to loss, noting moments where they surfaced in crisis. As these truths saturate your mind, your heart gradually internalizes the confidence they convey, equipping you to stand firm when circumstances threaten to shake your hope. Thus, memorization becomes more than an intellectual exercise—it is the embedding of life-giving truth into the core of your being.

Conclusion As we emerge from the darkness of loss, the light of Christ's resurrection casts a new vision across our broken landscape. Faith that endures is not a fragile flicker but a beacon fueled by God's own presence—one that carries us through lament into praise, from confession into action. May Martha's bold words echo in your heart when grief presses close, reminding you that belief in Jesus carries eternal power. And may the God "who comforts us in all our troubles" (2 Corinthians 1:4) infuse your soul with a peace that surpasses understanding, anchoring you in hope until the day when every tear is wiped away.

Chapter 3. "Jesus Wept" — The Compassionate Heart of God

In the briefest verse of Scripture, John captures one of the most profound revelations of Christ's character: "Jesus wept" (John 11:35). In that moment beside the tomb of his friend, our Lord showed us that divine power and divine tenderness are inseparable. His tears did not signal weakness but illuminated the depth of his solidarity with human suffering—an empathy so complete that he enters into our sorrow even as he conquers its ultimate consequence. This chapter will draw back the curtain on the heart of God, exploring why the Son of Man, fully divine yet fully human, allowed compassion to overflow in tears. As we trace the many dimensions of his empathy—from the incarnation to the heavenly high priest's ongoing ministry—we'll discover how Jesus' emotional integrity becomes a model for our own response to pain, loss, and injustice.

3.1 The Shortest Verse, the Deepest Emotion

3.1.1 Literary & Historical Context of John 11:35

John places "Jesus wept" at the emotional climax of his fourth sign, the raising of Lazarus, breaking the narrative tension built by his earlier two-day delay (John 11:6). In first-century Jewish culture, public mourning was highly ritualized—tearing garments, throwing dust, and audible wailing (Genesis 37:34; Job 2:12). Yet here the Messiah joins the mourners with his own tears, validating grief even as he prepares to reverse death's finality. Ancient readers would recognize that the shortest verse carries the weight of the entire Passion narrative to come: the God-man who wept beside a tomb would weep again in Gethsemane and on the cross. For twenty-first-century believers, "Jesus wept" shatters any notion that divine power negates human pain; instead, it sanctifies our tears. In our modern lifestyle, where stoicism and productivity often mask suffering, this verse invites us to reclaim lament as a sacred practice. We might begin meetings or worship gatherings with a moment of silent, collective weeping—an embodied acknowledgment that sorrow is not shameful. In personal devotions, journaling times of tears beside the digital screen can become an entry point to deeper prayer. Even workplaces can benefit: introducing "grief breaks" or designated prayer rooms allows employees to process loss under God's compassionate gaze. Thus, the context of John 11:35 both roots us in ancient ritual and propels us toward fresh expressions of godly empathy today.

3.1.2 Why "Jesus Wept" Is So Startling

At first glance, it seems counterintuitive that omnipotent Jesus would weep. Yet his tears reveal that empathy is not limited by power but empowered by it. Rather than maintaining divine distance, the Son of God chooses to share fully in human sorrow, demonstrating that true strength embraces vulnerability. In a culture that prizes self-sufficiency and emotional control, Jesus' open grief challenges us to disrupt the "keep calm and carry on" mentality. The startling softness of his tears uncovers the gospel's paradox: the King of kings stoops to be present in our suffering. Today, this calls us to cultivate "tear-friendly" spaces in our homes and churches— places where raw emotion is met with gentle presence rather than quick fixes. Pastors could model weeping in their preaching when recounting personal losses, signaling that tears are neither unspiritual nor unprofessional. In counseling, practitioners can affirm tearful release as a step toward healing, rather than hurriedly redirecting clients to "positive thinking." On a societal level, faith communities might host "Tears & Testimony" evenings, where people share grief and grace in tandem. By making room for the unexpected weeping of the divine, we learn that compassion begins when we stop trying to fix every wound and instead allow God's love to flow through our tears.

3.1.3 Comparing Gospel Accounts of Divine Emotion (Mark 3:5; Luke 19:41)

John is not the only evangelist to record Jesus' emotions. In Mark 3:5, Jesus looks around "in anger, grieved at their hardness of heart" before healing a man's withered hand, combining righteous indignation with mercy. In Luke 19:41, he weeps over Jerusalem, lamenting its impending judgment and the people's blindness to their Messiah. Together, these accounts reveal a spectrum of divine feeling—compassion, anger, sorrow—each rooted in love's refusal to abandon those in need. Recognizing this breadth invites modern believers to embrace their own emotional range as reflections of God's image. In our daily rhythms, we can adopt "emotion journals" that track how Scripture stirs joy, sorrow, or righteous concern, inviting God to refine each response. Worship leaders might design services that move through lament songs, prophetic lament prayers, and finally into anthems of God's comfort, mirroring Jesus' own emotional journey. Small groups can study these Gospel scenes side-by-side, discussing how each emotion propelled Jesus into action—healing hands, weeping tears, or pronouncing judgment. Pastoral training programs would do well to integrate emotional intelligence with theological formation, equipping leaders to discern when to weep with congregants and when to confront sin in love. By comparing these Gospel windows into Jesus' heart, we discover a rich template for our own emotional discipleship—one that refuses to compartmentalize feeling but sees every response as an opportunity to embody Christ's compassionate presence.

3.2 Theology of Divine Empathy

3.2.1 Incarnation: God's Identification with Human Suffering (Hebrews 2:14–18)

Hebrews 2:17–18 explains that Jesus "shared in their humanity" to become a merciful and faithful high priest who can sympathize with our weaknesses. His incarnation means he did not merely observe suffering from a distance but entered into our frail flesh, experiencing hunger, fatigue, rejection, and ultimately the agony of the cross. This deep identification assures us that no pain is foreign to him. In the modern context, healthcare chaplains and hospital volunteers can proclaim this truth explicitly: Christ knows the pain of illness firsthand. Support groups for chronic illness or trauma might begin sessions by reading Hebrews 2:14–18, grounding participants in divine solidarity. In personal devotions, believers can imagine speaking to the incarnate Christ about their deepest wounds, knowing he truly understands. Creative ministries—such as art therapy workshops in prisons or grief retreats—can frame the Incarnation as the foundation for empathy-driven care. By rooting our compassionate service in the theology of the Incarnation, we ensure that our outreach is not mere human sympathy but participation in the divine empathy that moves mountains and mends hearts.

3.2.2 Compassion (σπλαγχνίζομαι) as a Divine Attribute (Matthew 9:36)

The Greek word σπλαγχνίζομαι, often translated "have compassion," literally refers to the inward organs—gut-level emotions. Matthew 9:36 records that Jesus, seeing crowds like sheep without a shepherd, was moved with compassionate pity. This visceral compassion drove him to teach, heal, and restore. Recognizing compassion as a defining attribute of God challenges modern believers to develop what we might call "gut empathy." In practical terms, social workers and nonprofit staff can incorporate compassion training that includes both emotional attunement exercises and exposure to marginalized communities. Congregations can sponsor immersion experiences—short-term mission trips or local neighborhood walks—geared not toward fixing but toward listening and feeling with. Christian schools might include modules on compassion in their character development curricula, using role-play scenarios to help students inhabit the experience of those who suffer. Even everyday friendships can benefit: next time a friend shares pain, pause, place a hand on their shoulder, and allow yourself to feel alongside them before jumping to advice. By reclaiming σπλαγχνίζομαι as a gut-level practice, we align our ministries with the heart of God, ensuring that compassion is not an abstract ideal but a lived reality.

3.2.3 "Sympathetic High Priest" — Jesus' Empathy in Heaven (Hebrews 4:15–16)

Hebrews 4:15 assures believers that Jesus is "a high priest who in every respect has been tempted as we are, yet without sin." Having felt our sorrows, he continues to minister compassionately in the heavenly sanctuary. His empathy does not cease with his earthly ministry but flows eternally toward those who draw near. For twenty-first-century followers, this truth transforms our understanding of prayer: when we approach God's throne, we do so not before an aloof deity but a sympathetic advocate. Prayer ministries can emphasize this posture by creating "heavenly courtroom" prayer rooms, where participants speak their needs into the mercy seat with confidence that their High Priest understands intimately. In worship music, lyrics that celebrate Jesus as our empathetic intercessor help embed this doctrine in congregational hearts. Pastoral counseling can incorporate guided imagery exercises—inviting counselees to envision presenting their hurts to Jesus at the heavenly altar and receiving his compassionate embrace. By emphasizing Jesus' ongoing empathy in heaven, we dispel shame and isolation from suffering, replacing them with the certainty that our pioneer of faith walks every valley with us still.

3.3 Jesus' Tears—More than Grief, a Mirror for Our Souls

3.3.1 Tears for Lazarus vs. Tears for Jerusalem (Luke 19:41)

Jesus' tears over Lazarus and over Jerusalem (Luke 19:41) reveal that his compassion extends from personal loss to corporate judgment. In Bethany, his tears arose from love for an individual; on the Mount of Olives, they poured out as he foresaw the city's destruction and the people's refusal to recognize God's visitation. This duality invites modern believers to balance personal empathy with prophetic sorrow for systemic brokenness. In urban ministries, for example, leaders might schedule "city lament" gatherings—services devoted to confessing collective sins and interceding for neighborhoods plagued by violence or poverty. Churches in regions facing natural disasters could host "tear-in-the-sand" ceremonies, writing community names on beach sand and weeping over their needs before Christ. In personal reflection, journaling both individual hurts and corporate anxieties trains our souls to mimic Jesus' expansive compassion. When we weep for friends and for cities alike, our tears become a mirror of Christ's heart, moving us from private pity to public action. Thus, Jesus' dual weeping models a holistic empathy that refuses to separate the personal from the communal, calling us to intercede at every level of brokenness.

3.3.2 Tears as Protest Against Death's Power (Revelation 21:4)

Jesus wept because death—the last enemy—invades God's creation and distorts his design for life (1 Corinthians 15:26). His tears stand as a protest against mourning's rule over humanity, signaling his intent to overturn death's reign. Revelation 21:4 promises a day when God will wipe away every tear, yet until that consummation, tears themselves bear witness to hope—an embodied declaration that present

51

suffering will not have the final word. In modern "death-denying" cultures, we often sanitize end-of-life conversations and avoid funerals' grim realities. To reclaim tears as protest and proclamation, churches can incorporate lament into funeral liturgies—encouraging weeping as an act of faith in Christ's coming restoration. Art ministers might host "Tear Walls," installations where people post handwritten notes of grief and hope, creating a visual protest of death's intrusion. In pastoral care, training on death literacy—teaching families about grief's trajectory and tears' role—helps congregations embrace sorrow as a sacred act. By understanding tears as spiritual protest, we join Jesus in standing against death's tyranny, living in the tension between now and not yet until "death shall be no more."

3.3.3 Tears as Expression of Hope Deferred (Psalm 13:1–2; Lamentations 3:49–50)

Psalm 13 opens with David's anguished cry—"How long, O LORD? Will you forget me forever?"—yet he concludes by praising God's steadfast love (vv. 5–6). Lamentations 3 records Jeremiah's tears as he recalls Zion's ruin, yet he still proclaims God's mercies as new each morning (Lam 3:22–23). These tears of hope deferred model for us that lament and trust coexist. In contemporary life, where instant gratification reigns, believers can relearn patience by incorporating these psalms into corporate worship on the first Sunday of each month—a "lament and trust" service. Small groups might memorize Psalm 13 and recite it in unison, acknowledging doubt before singing a doxology. Individual discipleship could include "lament playlists" that alternate songs of sorrow with hymns of hope, guiding emotional transitions. Counseling programs can offer "lament retreats," immersive weekends where participants journal, pray, and worship through the stages of deferred hope. By practicing tears alongside trust, we affirm that the Christian life is not about bypassing sorrow but about weaving lament into the very fabric of hope. In this way, our tears become declarations that, though answers tarry, our confidence rests in a God whose faithfulness endures all delays.

3.4 Emotional Integrity in Ministry

3.4.1 Balancing Compassion and Strength in Pastoral Care

Pastoral caregivers must steward both empathy and resilience, avoiding the extremes of emotional detachment or total emotional immersion. Scripture commends servants who "weep with those who weep" (Romans 12:15) while also urging leaders to "shepherd the flock... exercising oversight" (1 Peter 5:2), a balance of heart and hand. In today's context, pastors and lay counselors can schedule regular debriefs with peers or supervisors, creating "emotion check-ins" that allow them to process burdens without offloading onto congregants. Implementing boundaries—such as designated "office hours" for visitation and clear guidelines around digital availability—protects against burnout while ensuring the hurting receive timely care. Training programs can include role-play scenarios that teach when to offer comforting silence and when to deliver strong biblical truth, modeling Jesus' own mix of tears and commands. Including self-care modules—regular Sabbath rest, physical exercise, spiritual retreats—reinforces that caretakers must themselves be cared for (Mark 6:31). Churches might incorporate "pastor peer groups" that meet monthly for mutual encouragement, prayer, and accountability. By embracing both compassion and strength, ministry leaders reflect the heart of Christ—tender yet tenacious—ensuring their empathy is sustainable and their counsel effective.

3.4.2 Avoiding "Compassion Fatigue" through Spiritual Disciplines

Compassion fatigue arises when constant exposure to others' suffering dulls our empathy or leads to emotional exhaustion. Jesus avoided fatigue by retreating to solitary prayer (Mark 1:35), modeling the necessity of replenishment. Modern caregivers can adopt daily rhythms of solitude—brief periods of silent listening to God—to recalibrate their hearts. Regular engagement in spiritual disciplines such as fasting, solitude, and Scripture meditation replenishes emotional reserves

(Psalm 46:10). Integrating breath prayers—brief invocations like "Lord, have mercy"—throughout the day creates micro-pauses that help process accumulated stress. Group retreats or half-day quiet days offer extended breaks from ministry demands, allowing leaders to reconnect with God's presence. Journaling emotional responses to pastoral encounters helps externalize burdens, preventing internalization that leads to fatigue. Churches can provide subscription access to guided prayer apps focused on renewal, making spiritual disciplines accessible amid busy schedules. Peer support networks— "compassion cohorts"—can meet regularly to share struggles and encourage disciplined rest. By prioritizing personal renewal through spiritual practices, ministers sustain vibrant empathy, ensuring their service remains life-giving rather than depleting.

3.4.3 Modeling Vulnerability: When Leaders "Weep with Those Who Weep" (Romans 12:15)

True leadership in the church does not demand unfeeling stoicism but models honest vulnerability. When leaders share appropriate personal struggles—financial anxieties, family tensions, or health challenges—they normalize the full range of human emotion before God. Scripture invites this openness: "My grace is sufficient for you, for my power is made perfect in weakness" (2 Corinthians 12:9). In practice today, leaders might begin staff meetings with brief testimonies of recent trials and lessons learned, fostering a culture where honesty is valued over performance. During pastoral visits, sharing a prayer of lament alongside the congregant's own tears demonstrates solidarity with suffering. Training workshops can include exercises in storytelling, equipping leaders to craft testimonies that balance authenticity and hope. Including short "vulnerability moments" in sermons—where pastors acknowledge their own need for grace—reinforces that empathy is rooted in shared humanity. Leadership teams can establish annual "ladder retreats," set aside for transparent sharing and mutual encouragement. By modeling vulnerability, church leaders create safe spaces where congregants feel free to weep, knowing their tears are met with genuine compassion rather than quick fixes.

3.5 Spiritual Formation through Shared Sorrow

3.5.1 Corporate Lament as a Path to Healing (Nehemiah 8:9–10)

Nehemiah led Israel in public fasting, confession, and weeping until they understood that "the joy of the LORD is your strength" (Nehemiah 8:10). Corporate lament transforms private sorrow into communal solidarity, offering healing beyond individual coping mechanisms. Contemporary churches can dedicate one Sunday per quarter to a "Lament Service," featuring Psalms of lament, open-mic expressions of grief, and guided confession prayers. Incorporating art stations—where participants paint or draw their sorrow—provides non-verbal pathways for expression. Worship playlists should balance lament hymns (e.g., "God of Grace and God of Glory") with anthems of hope, guiding the congregation from grief into praise. Small groups might hold "lament dinners," where members share burdens over a simple meal of bread and water, echoing ancient fasts. Pastoral teams can curate liturgies that interweave confession, intercession, and thanksgiving, modeling the flow of lament psalms. Online congregations can host virtual lament rooms, enabling global participation through live chat and worship streams. Through corporate lament, churches embody Nehemiah's example—moving from collective weeping into the strengthening joy of the Lord, fostering deep communal healing.

3.5.2 Small-Group Rituals for Expressing Grief and Comfort

Small groups provide intimate contexts for shared sorrow, where confidentiality and trust can flourish. Begin meetings with a simple ritual: lighting a candle for each person's current loss, naming it aloud before God. Incorporate guided exercises such as "Memory Mapping," where participants chart significant losses and milestones, then pray over each point. Facilitators can introduce tactile practices—such as tearing paper to symbolize brokenness and then weaving the pieces into a collage of hope—to engage body and spirit. Groups should balance lament time with comfort time, reading Romans 15:13 and praying for joy and peace to fill weary hearts. Establish norms that permit silence, tears, and mutual holding of hands, communicating that grief is welcome rather than taboo. Rotate leadership so every member experiences the dual roles of mourner and comforter. Encourage group members to send follow-up cards or texts mid-week, reinforcing that sorrow doesn't wait for scheduled gatherings. By embedding these rituals into small-group life, congregations create micro-cultures of compassion where participants learn that God's comfort often arrives through the shared sorrow and care of his body.

3.5.3 Personal Practices: Journaling Tears, Articulating Longings

Individual spiritual formation in sorrow benefits from intentional practices that give shape to emotion. Begin a "Tear Journal" where each entry describes a moment of grief—what triggered the tears, what thoughts surfaced, and how God's presence felt amidst pain. Pair this with "Longing Letters," addressed to God, articulating deep desires—healing, justice, reconciliation—and inviting dialogue rather than monologue. Incorporate artistic expression: sketching, poetry, or songwriting that captures the texture of sorrow and hope. Use guided prompts based on lament psalms—"What have you forgotten, O Lord?" (Psalm 13:1) or "How long must I bear pain in my soul?" (Psalm 38:17)—to structure journal sessions. Schedule regular "grief hours" in your calendar—30 minutes of uninterrupted mourning before transitioning into praise or gratitude practice. Technological tools, such as voice-memo prayers, allow for spoken lament when writing feels inadequate. Over time, review journals and letters to trace God's faithfulness and growth in resilience. By giving tears a tangible form and longings a voice, individuals engage sorrow as an active path toward deeper intimacy with God, learning that personal lament is both honest petition and sacred spiritual formation.

3.6 Practical Ministries of Compassion

3.6.1 Hospital Visitation Ministries: Presence over Protocol

While hospitals often emphasize procedural efficiency, Christ's compassion calls us to prioritize presence over mere protocol. Volunteer teams trained in "companion ministry" visit patients for scheduled time blocks, offering listening ears rather than quick prayers before departure. Training equips visitors in HIPAA-compliant confidentiality, active listening skills, and basic spiritual care (e.g., using 2 Corinthians 1:3–4 to comfort grief). Churches can partner with chaplaincy departments to coordinate visit schedules, ensuring consistent support rather than sporadic drop-ins. Providing visitors with small "comfort kits"—including Scripture cards, a soft blanket, and a journal—demonstrates practical love. Following visits, teams hold debrief meetings to process emotional weight and pray for ongoing care. Virtual visitation—video calls for home-bound or immunocompromised patients—extends compassion beyond hospital walls. Feedback loops with medical staff inform ministry improvements and identify critical patient needs. By centering presence, hospital ministries mirror Jesus' own bedside compassion, reminding patients they are cherished beyond their medical charts.

3.6.2 Community Bereavement Support: Structuring Grief Groups

Structured grief groups offer ongoing support beyond the initial funeral services. Effective groups run 8–12 week cycles, each session focusing on themes such as anger, guilt, hope, and spiritual questions (cf. Psalm 34:18). Facilitators receive training in grief psychology and biblical lament to guide conversations safely and respectfully. Sessions blend teaching—exploring passages like Ecclesiastes 3:1–4—with personal sharing, prayer, and coping skills workshops (journaling, breathing prayers). Peer "grief buddies" are paired for one-on-one check-ins between meetings, deepening relational care. Incorporating occasional guest speakers—

bereaved volunteers, counselor professionals, or pastors—provides diverse perspectives and testimonies. Celebrating milestones, such as six months or one year since a loss, acknowledges that grief is a non-linear journey. Churches host annual remembrance services—lighting candles and reading aloud names of the departed—to renew hope in community. Resources—books, podcasts, online forums—are curated and shared, offering continuity outside group meetings. Well-structured bereavement support embodies Christ's comfort, helping mourners journey toward wholeness.

3.6.3 Digital Compassion: Online Prayer Rooms & Virtual Support

In a digitally connected world, online platforms can facilitate compassion for those isolated by distance or circumstance. Churches can establish "24/7 Prayer Rooms" via video-conference or chat apps, where trained volunteers offer immediate prayer, Scripture reading, and listening. Clear guidelines—confidentiality protocols, referral pathways for crisis situations, and volunteer rotation schedules—maintain quality and sustainability. Virtual support groups, hosted on secure platforms, allow participants to share testimonies, pray, and lament together from home. Short video devotionals—scripture reflections filmed by pastors—can be posted daily, providing ongoing encouragement. Mobile apps that prompt users to "Check on a Friend" integrate compassion into everyday life, reminding believers to reach out with calls or messages. Social media ministries can livestream prayer times, encouraging live chat intercession and real-time healing testimonies. Accessibility features—closed captioning, language subtitles—ensure inclusivity. By leveraging digital tools with the same pastoral heart, churches extend Jesus' weeping compassion into the cyber-corridors where many now dwell, proving that no distance hinders divine empathy made manifest in human care.

3.7 Jesus' Tears as Catalyst for Action

3.7.1 From Weeping to the Miracle: Timeline of Jesus' Response

Jesus' emotional response at Lazarus's tomb was not an end in itself but the prelude to decisive action (John 11:38–44). First, his tears signified deep compassion; then, with a loud voice, he commanded the stone to be removed—inviting human participation in divine work. This sequence—emotion, command, collaboration, miracle—models a rhythm for compassionate ministry today. In practical terms, a church responding to community loss might begin with a "weeping vigil," gathering to pray and lament together (cf. Psalm 126:5–6). Next, leadership prays for specific guidance and identifies concrete needs—food distribution, counseling, financial aid—then mobilizes volunteers. Clear communication ("Come, let us remove the stone of isolation") and logistical planning follow, ensuring that compassionate feeling translates into effective service. Finally, the community witnesses restored lives—healed relationships, renewed hope—testifying to the power of God working through human hands (James 2:14–17). Documenting this timeline in newsletters or on bulletin boards reinforces the pattern of emotion leading to action. By tracing our own "weeping-to-miracle" stories, congregations learn to trust that sensitive hearts spur obedient feet, and that God's compassion always propels us into service.

3.7.2 Compassion that Moves: The Link between Emotion and Obedience (James 2:14–17)

James insists that faith without works is dead, and compassion without action is mere sentiment (James 2:14–17). When Jesus wept, his tears moved him to speak and act on behalf of Lazarus. Likewise, our empathy must culminate in tangible help—comforting words, practical assistance, or advocacy. Modern ministries can harness this principle by pairing empathy training with volunteer placement: after attending a "heart-awareness" workshop, participants commit to a specific service role—visiting nursing homes, serving at shelters, or mentoring youth. Weekly debriefs allow volunteers to share emotional takeaways and celebrate lives touched. Incorporating "compassion pledges" into worship services—where congregants publicly commit to a ministry of mercy—cements the link between feeling and doing. Churches can track volunteer hours as a community metric of faithful obedience, reminding everyone that tears without follow-through starve the body of Christ. By embedding James's call into church culture, compassion becomes a verb rather than an adjective. This approach ensures that our shared sorrow over suffering moves us beyond lament into life-giving action, reflecting the dynamic compassion of our Savior.

3.7.3 Everyday "Tear-Triggered" Service: Identifying Needs in Your Neighborhood

Jesus' tears were triggered by seeing Lazarus's plight; likewise, believers can cultivate a "tear-triggered" sensitivity to suffering around them. Begin by developing spiritual eyes: during daily routines, ask, "Who is hurting here?"—in the coffee line, on the playground, or at the bus stop. When you notice a single mom struggling with groceries, offer to carry her bags or pray for provision. If you see a neighbor's yard overgrown—a sign of illness or loss—drop off a gift card for lawn care with a note of encouragement. Workplace compassion might mean checking in privately on a coworker who seems withdrawn, offering a listening ear (Romans 12:15). Form "compassion clusters" of three to four friends who commit to weekly "sorrow walks"—walking through the neighborhood praying for needs and noting actionable opportunities. Use mobile apps or shared spreadsheets to coordinate these spontaneous acts of service. Over time, the habit of responding in the moment to visible need transforms neighborhoods, making God's tears tangible through human touch. In this way, everyday "tear-triggered" service becomes a lifestyle, bridging divine empathy and grassroots ministry.

3.8 Cultivating a Compassionate Heart Today

3.8.1 Developing "Empathy Exercises" in Daily Prayer

Compassion can be trained through intentional prayer "exercises" that stretch our hearts toward others' suffering. Begin each day with a "Compassion Scan": spend five minutes in silence imagining the faces of friends or strangers in pain—refugees, hospitalized patients, grieving families— and invite the Holy Spirit to fill you with genuine concern (Romans 12:12). Record one name or demographic group in a "Compassion Notebook," then pray specifically for their needs. Midday, practice a "silent lament breath prayer": inhale the anguish of another's suffering, exhale a plea for God's comfort (Psalm 61:2). In evening reflections, journal any emotional stirrings—tears shed, grief felt—and ask how God might want you to respond. Monthly, incorporate "Hearts Aloud" gatherings in small groups: participants share brief stories of those they've prayed for, fostering mutual empathy. Use guided resources—apps or printed devotionals—that include daily exercises focused on compassion. These spiritual workouts expand our capacity to reflect Christ's empathy, ensuring our prayers are not abstract but deeply connected to human need.

3.8.2 Volunteering with the Vulnerable: Putting Tears into Action

Hands-on service to vulnerable populations channels our compassion into concrete blessing. Identify local partners— homeless shelters, refugee resettlement agencies, hospice centers—and commit to regular volunteer shifts. Before service, convene a short "heart alignment" prayer, reflecting on Jesus' tears and asking for a compassionate spirit (Matthew 9:36). During interaction, practice "compassionate listening": give undivided attention, validate emotions, and resist the urge to "fix" immediately. After each session, debrief with fellow volunteers, sharing emotional highs and lows to foster resilience. Track service hours in a "Compassion Log," noting personal reflections alongside actions taken. Annually, host a church-wide "Service Fair" where members sign up for varied compassionate initiatives, from prison ministry to eldercare visitation. Encourage post-volunteering care packages—handwritten notes or simple gifts—to maintain relationships with those served. By embedding volunteering into the rhythm of church life, we ensure our tears find avenues for sustained, life-changing action.

3.8.3 Memory Verses & Liturgical Prayers on Divine Compassion

Anchoring compassion in Scripture and prayer deepens our emotional formation. Select key verses—such as Psalm 145:9 ("The Lord is good to all, and his mercy is over all that he has made") and Colossians 3:12 ("...clothe yourselves with compassion, kindness, humility, meekness, and patience")— and memorize them using daily repetition and verse-mapping techniques. Incorporate these into communal liturgies: begin services with responsive readings of these texts, having leader and congregation alternate lines. Develop brief "compassion collect" prayers—following the Anglican tradition—that succinctly petition God's mercy for the suffering world. Use artwork in worship spaces—banners or screens displaying compassion verses alongside images of service— to reinforce themes visually. Encourage families to place compassion verse cards in common areas, prompting spontaneous prayer throughout the day. By embedding divine compassion into both private memory work and public worship, believers internalize God's heart for the hurting, ensuring that our lifestyles reflect the tears and mercy of Christ.

Conclusion By standing with us in our deepest grief, Jesus transforms tears into testimonies: proof that God's love meets us not from afar but from within our sorrows. His tears beside Lazarus' tomb become a lens through which we view every broken heart—calling us to bear one another's burdens with genuine vulnerability and to let empathy fuel our service. As you close this chapter, may the portrait of Christ weeping alongside suffering humanity awaken within you a compassionate resolve: to lament with the oppressed, to serve the hurting, and to mirror the tender heart of your Savior in every place of need. In doing so, you bear witness that the God who wept is the same God who wipes away every tear (Revelation 21:4), leading his people from sorrow into the joy of resurrection life.

Chapter 4. Miracles for the Father's Glory

From the water turned wine at Cana to the final, climactic raising of Lazarus, Jesus' miracles are far more than displays of power—they are carefully crafted revelations designed to disclose the character and purposes of His Father. Each sign in the Gospel of John invites us beyond mere amazement, beckoning us into an encounter with the divine glory that dwells in Christ. In this chapter, we will explore how these miraculous acts function as theological lenses, focusing our attention on God's authority over creation, His compassion in suffering, and His ultimate victory over death. As we trace the pattern from astonishment to belief and onward into worship, we discover that every miracle both magnifies God's glory and invites our faith to take deeper root.

4.1 The Purpose Statement in John 11:4

4.1.1 Jesus' Explicit Aim: "This illness is not to end in death but for the glory of God"

In John 11:4, Jesus reframes Lazarus's sickness from a mere medical crisis into a divine opportunity: "This illness is not to end in death but for the glory of God." This declaration overturns human expectations—what appears as tragedy becomes the stage for God's supreme display of power. The Greek phrasing οὐ εἰς θάνατον ("not to death") emphasizes the illness's temporary nature in light of the resurrection miracle. In first-century Judea, equating sickness with divine judgment was common; Jesus instead presents suffering as a vehicle for divine honor. By speaking of "glory" (δόξα), he anticipates not only Lazarus's restoration but the broader revelation of the Father's nature. Early readers of John's Gospel would recall that glory in Johannine usage often points to the cross and resurrection (John 12:23–24). Today, believers can adopt this same lens: rather than seeing setbacks as endpoints, we discern arenas where God intends to reveal his worth. When a terminal diagnosis, financial collapse, or relational rupture strikes, asking "How might God be glorified?" aligns our perspective with Jesus'. Praying this question brings hope: even the darkest valley may become a corridor to divine praise. By internalizing Jesus' purpose statement, we learn to move beyond mere petition for relief into participation in God's glory project.

4.1.2 Defining "Glory" (δόξα) in Johannine Theology

In the Gospel of John, δόξα (glory) denotes both the visible manifestation of God's presence and the intrinsic worth of his character. Early in John, the glory of the Father shines through Jesus at Cana, Capernaum, and ultimately on the cross (John 2:11; 12:23). This glory is paradoxical: it appears in humble acts—washing feet, dying on a cross—yet unveils divine majesty. In John 11, the raising of Lazarus offers the clearest window into this paradox: the One who weeps wields power to reverse death. The term conveys relational intimacy as well—God's glory is shared with his Son and, through Christ, with believers (John 17:22). Modern readers encounter glory in worship gatherings when Scripture, song, and Spirit converge to reveal God's presence. Theological education programs can emphasize glory's dimensions: as God's radiant beauty, his communicable attributes (love, holiness), and the eschatological hope of sharing in that glory (Rom. 8:17). In personal devotion, meditating on passages like Isaiah 6:3 and Revelation 4:11 expands our grasp of glory's scope—from heaven's throne room to resurrected life. Understanding glory in its Johannine fullness transforms our vision: miracles cease to be wonders for wonder's sake and become invitations into the eternal fellowship of Father, Son, and Spirit.

4.1.3 Miracles as "Signs," Not Mere Wonders (σημεῖα vs. τέρατα)

John deliberately uses σημεῖα (signs) rather than the more generic τέρατα (wonders) to describe Jesus' miracles, signaling their instructive function. A sign both points beyond itself and beckons a response—Martha's confession "I believe" follows the raising of Lazarus (John 11:27,45). The first sign at Cana invites faith in Jesus' identity (John 2:11), while the Lazarus event culminates in explicit belief in him as life itself (John 11:25). Unlike mere spectacular acts, signs form a cohesive narrative arc: they disclose Jesus' divine prerogatives over nature, disease, and death. For contemporary faith, this distinction remains vital: miraculous accounts in church history or personal testimony ought to direct hearts toward Christ, not toward curiosity or sensationalism. Preachers can structure sermons on modern "sign experiences" by emphasizing how each led to deeper trust or transformed community worship. Likewise, Christian publishers can label testimonies as "God's signs" when they genuinely foster faith, avoiding sensational headlines that prioritize shock value. Recognizing miracles as signs helps guard against anemic spirituality that craves spectacle over substance. By tracking the trajectory "sign → belief → glory," believers cultivate discernment, embracing wonders that foster lasting transformation and rejecting those that merely entertain.

4.2 Miracles as Windows into Divine Identity

4.2.1 Authority over Creation: Water into Wine (John 2:1–11)

At Cana, Jesus' first recorded sign, water becomes wine—an act that reveals his sovereign authority over the created order (John 2:1–11). Wine in Jewish culture signified joy, covenant blessing, and Messianic abundance (Amos 9:13). By transforming ordinary water jars used for purification, Jesus teaches that purification itself will now be accomplished through his person and work. This sign foreshadows a new creation wherein Christ's presence fulfills and surpasses old rituals. In modern "creation care" initiatives, Christians can connect ecological stewardship to this miracle: honoring the Creator by preserving water, soil, and biodiversity reflects recognition of Jesus' authority over all creation. Worship events might celebrate God's artistry in nature with outdoor communion services, acknowledging that the same power that changed water into wine sustains forests, oceans, and wildlife. Christian educational programs can incorporate the Cana sign into curriculum on environmental ethics, showing that divine authority invites human responsibility. Thus, the first sign at Cana continues to guide believers in honoring God as sovereign Lord of cosmos, culture, and covenant joy.

4.2.2 Authority over Disease: Healing the Official's Son (John 4:46–54)

In Capernaum, a royal official appeals to Jesus for his dying son, and Jesus' word alone brings healing at a distance (John 4:46–54). This miracle demonstrates Christ's authority over infirmity and his prerogative to transcend space and time. The official's faith in Jesus' spoken promise models the posture of trust that undergirds every sign (John 4:50). In our modern era of telemedicine and remote support, this narrative inspires faith in Christ's transcendent capacity: he attends our deepest needs even when physical proximity is impossible. Churches can host "virtual prayer rooms" echoing this dynamic, offering online intercession for those who cannot attend in person. Pastoral teams might study this sign to develop guidelines for remote pastoral care—using video calls, phone visits, and prayer apps to bring spiritual healing across distances. Healthcare ministries can integrate biblical reflection on this miracle into chaplaincy training, equipping staff to pray confidently for patients worldwide. By viewing the healing of the official's son as a template for distant compassion, believers learn that no illness or location limits the reach of Christ's restorative power.

4.2.3 Authority over Death: Raising Lazarus as Climax

Lazarus' resurrection stands as the apex of Jesus' authority over death itself (John 11:38–44). The four-day interval after Lazarus's burial accentuates the finality of death, heightening the sign's impact. Jesus' command, "Lazarus, come forth," echoes God's creative word in Genesis, underscoring his power to call life out of lifelessness. At the same time, his tears reveal that even in triumph he shares our sorrow over death's intrusion. New Testament theology interprets this sign as both foretaste and guarantee of Christ's own resurrection (1 Corinthians 15:20–22). Contemporary pastors might frame funerals and memorial services around this miracle, pointing mourners to the living hope found in Jesus' victory over death. Funeral liturgies can include reenactments or symbolic "uncapping of the stone" rituals, allowing congregations to experience hope. In discipleship contexts, believers can be taught to anchor their final hope in Christ's authority over the grave, reducing fear of death and reinforcing evangelistic urgency. Thus, the raising of Lazarus remains the definitive sign that death is conquered and eternal life secured for all who believe.

4.3 Suffering and Glory Interwoven

4.3.1 Redemptive Reversal: From Grave to Glory

The Lazarus narrative exemplifies redemptive reversal: mourning is met with joy, death with life, loss with restoration.

This overturning pattern echoes throughout Scripture—from Joseph's descent into the pit to his rise in Egypt (Genesis 37–41) and from Christ's crucifixion to his resurrection (Luke 24). By locating glory in reversal, John teaches that God transfigures our darkest valleys into stages of divine splendor. Contemporary ministries can mirror this redemptive pattern through "restoration programs" for those who have fallen into addiction, poverty, or prison. Testimony events entitled "From Grave to Glory" invite individuals to share how God reversed their stories, creating powerful corporate worship experiences. Counseling centers might design intake forms that catalog "dead ends" in clients' lives, then track subsequent milestones of recovery as evidence of God's glory. In everyday spirituality, believers can adopt a "reversal journal," noting moments when God transformed disappointment into delight. Embracing redemptive reversal fosters resilience: we learn to expect divine surprises that magnify God's glory in places of deepest need.

4.3.2 The Paradox of Delay: Timing that Maximizes Glory

Jesus' intentional wait to go to Bethany (John 11:6) illustrates that God's delays are not mistakes but strategic timing devices. By delaying, Jesus ensures Lazarus is truly dead, so the miracle's magnitude is undeniable—glory is maximized through the most desperate circumstances. This paradox overturns human impatience: we expect quick fixes, yet often divine glory emerges most brightly when hope seems extinguished. In personal spiritual formation, believers can practice "holy waiting" exercises—calendar periods of silence and expectancy—paired with journaling insights and observed answers. Corporate worship can mark seasons of waiting—Advent or Lent—as opportunities to rehearse trust when God seems silent. Leadership training for nonprofits might include sessions on "strategic waiting," teaching staff to discern when delayed action will yield more transformative results. By embracing the paradox of delay, we come to valorize seasons of silence and sow them with seeds of future praise, knowing that divine glory often waits just beyond our momentary frustrations.

4.3.3 Participating in God's Suffering for Eternal Praise (Romans 8:17)

Paul declares that believers are "co-heirs with Christ, provided we suffer with him in order that we may also be glorified with him" (Romans 8:17). The cross-connection of suffering and glory means that sharing in Christ's afflictions is preparatory for sharing in his triumph. Jesus' own path—from tears at Lazarus's tomb to triumph over death—models this journey. Contemporary discipleship can integrate this truth through small-group curricula on "redemptive suffering," exploring biblical case studies (Paul's imprisonment, Stephen's martyrdom) alongside personal narratives. Spiritual retreats might offer guided meditations on the cross, inviting participants to lay down their pains in the shadow of Christ's glory. Pastoral counseling can reassure those enduring chronic illness or persecution that their sufferings are temporary preludes to eternal celebration. Worship services could incorporate responsive readings of Romans 8:18–39, reminding congregations that our present sufferings pale compared to the glory awaiting us. By participating in God's suffering, we become living epistles of hope—our scars testifying that the same power that raised Lazarus will raise us into eternal praise.

4.4 The Johannine "Seven Signs" Framework

4.4.1 Overview of John's Seven Miracles

John structures his Gospel around seven key "signs" that progressively unveil Jesus' identity and mission. The first sign at Cana (water into wine, John 2:1–11) introduces Jesus as the source of new covenant joy. The healing of the royal official's son (John 4:46–54) displays his power over illness—even from a distance. Cleansing the temple (John 2:13–22) asserts authority over worship and foreshadows his body's resurrection. Healing the paralytic at Bethesda (John 5:1–9) highlights compassion and the Sabbath's renewal. Feeding the 5,000 (John 6:1–14) reveals his ability to satisfy deepest needs and points to the Bread of Life. Walking on water (John

6:16–21) confronts natural law, inviting disciples to trust beyond sight. Finally, the raising of Lazarus (John 11:1–44) climaxes this sign sequence, demonstrating mastery over death itself. Early readers would recognize this chiastic arrangement as pointing from social joy to cosmic resurrection. In modern preaching, outlining these seven signs helps congregations trace the Gospel's narrative arc, from anticipation at Cana to culmination at Bethany. By viewing each miracle as an integral frame in John's mosaic, we discern how Jesus systematically invites belief (John 20:30–31) through progressively weighty revelations of the Father's glory.

4.4.2 Lazarus as the Culminating Sign of Resurrection Life

The raising of Lazarus stands at the pinnacle of John's sign sequence, embodying the very theme of resurrection life. John alone records the four-day delay that underscores death's finality (John 11:17), making the miracle's reversal all the more astonishing. Jesus' declaration "I am the resurrection and the life" (John 11:25) serves as both introduction and interpretation of the sign. The sequence—compassionate weeping, command to roll away the stone, voice that echoes creation's call—unmistakably mirrors the Genesis narrative, portraying Jesus as the agent of new creation. Early Christian communities used this account to assert Christ's victory over Hades, grounding the doctrine of bodily resurrection (1 Corinthians 15:20–22). In contemporary teaching, couples preparing for marriage might study Lazarus as a sign of Christ's power to bring dead relationships to life. Funeral services can pivot around this miracle, offering mourners concrete hope that death is not final. Seminary courses on Johannine theology often highlight this sign as the hinge between life and eschatological promise. By treating Lazarus as the culminating sign, we see that all prior miracles prepared the way for this ultimate demonstration of Father-glory, inviting belief that transcends earthly limits.

4.4.3 Flow from Belief (πιστεύω) to Doxology (δόξα)

John's seven signs are carefully calibrated to move readers from initial astonishment to active belief (πιστεύω), culminating in doxology (δόξα)—the praise that God deserves. Each sign features a narrative arc: miracle → reaction of witnesses → confession or increase of belief → doxological affirmation (e.g., John 2:11, 11:4, 12:28). This structure trains the community to recognize that true faith issues in worshipful response. In liturgical planning, worship leaders can mirror this flow: introduce a testimony or video "sign," provide time for personal reflection and confession of faith, then lead into corporate praise songs. Small-group studies might chart each sign's impact on disciples (John 2:12; 11:45), discussing how belief deepened and how glory was proclaimed. Digital devotionals can use interactive timelines, prompting readers to log their own "signs" of God's work and record doxologies in response. By coupling belief and doxology, John invites us into a dynamic cycle: seeing God's work leads to deeper trust, which overflows in worship—and this worship in turn sensitizes us to further signs. Thus, the Johannine framework guides the church to live continually between revelation and response, ensuring that miracles never become mere curiosities but catalysts for sustained praise.

4.5 Community Witness and Evangelistic Impact

4.5.1 Disciples as Firsthand Witnesses (John 11:45–46)

Immediately after Lazarus' resurrection, John notes that "many of the Jews… believed in him" because of this sign (John 11:45). Yet we also see resistance—some report to the Pharisees, sparking the plot against Jesus (John 11:46). The disciples function as primary witnesses, carrying the testimony from Bethany into Jerusalem's power centers. Their eyewitness accounts lend credibility to the claim that Jesus is the Messiah and Son of God (John 20:30–31). In modern church planting, this principle translates into "story teams" that gather and verify baptismal testimonies, medical healings, or life-change narratives. Training laypeople to share first-person accounts ensures authenticity and safeguards against rumor. Churches can host "Witness Nights" where local believers recount how God acted in their lives, followed by invitations to explore faith. In digital evangelism, short video testimonials amplify the disciples' role, broadcasting firsthand encounters to global audiences. By centering disciples as witnesses, the community builds a ripple effect: individual faith becomes collective testimony, strengthening the church's evangelistic impact.

4.5.2 Ripple Effect: Many Believed Because of Lazarus (John 12:17–18)

John explicitly describes a ripple effect: those who saw Lazarus raised "went away and told the people" how Jesus had raised him from the dead (John 12:17–18). This chain of testimony created momentum, drawing large crowds to meet Jesus during his triumphal entry. It demonstrates that a single sign, when effectively communicated, can mobilize widespread interest and belief. Contemporary ministries can harness this principle by equipping members to "share one story this week," turning local encounters into global ripples via social media. Church communications teams should curate and package testimonies—short written blurbs, video clips, social graphics—to facilitate sharing across networks. Discipleship classes can include modules on storytelling techniques, emphasizing clarity, brevity, and authenticity. Community events like block parties or open-air worship services become modern equivalents of Bethany's buzz, inviting neighbors to experience signs of God's active presence. By stewarding testimonies strategically, churches emulate the ripple effect, ensuring that miracles for the Father's glory propagate faith far beyond initial witnesses.

4.5.3 Testimony as Doxology: Proclaiming God's Glory

Testimony inherently functions as doxology—praise that extols God's character and deeds. When Mary and Martha shared Lazarus' resurrection, they were not merely reporting facts; they were glorifying God (cf. John 2:11: "and his disciples believed in him"). In Paul's letters, believers are urged to "declare the works of the Lord" so that he may be glorified (Psalm 107:2; 1 Peter 2:9). Modern discipleship programs can integrate "Testify & Praise" segments into weekly gatherings, where members offer short praises based on personal signs of God's work. Worship teams might structure services around testimonies interspersed with congregational responses of "Praise God!" Digital platforms can host "Glory Blogs" where stories of transformation are published, each ending with a liturgical doxology prayer. Small groups can practice "testimony circles," encouraging everyone to articulate one moment of God's glory each meeting. Elevating testimony to doxology ensures that signs lead naturally into worship, reflecting the Johannine pattern and magnifying the Father's glory in every generation.

4.6 Miracles, the Cross, and Ultimate Glory

4.6.1 Lazarus as a Foreshadowing of Christ's Death and Resurrection

The Lazarus miracle not only demonstrates Jesus' power over death but prefigures his own entry into death and subsequent resurrection. John records Jesus' intent "to glorify God" (11:4) through Lazarus, and that same purpose is realized supremely on the cross and empty tomb (John 12:28). Early Christians saw in Lazarus a typological shadow: just as the stone was rolled away from Lazarus's tomb, so was the tombstone rolled away from Jesus's grave (Matthew 28:2). In theological education, this typology underscores how signs prepare the way for the ultimate sign: Christ's victory over death (Colossians 2:12). Churches can develop cross-centered sermon series linking Lazarus to Good Friday and Easter, tracing the motif of stone-rolling and life-calling. Visual arts ministries might create installations that juxtapose a bound Lazarus figure with an empty cross tomb, prompting congregational reflection. By seeing Lazarus as foreshadowing, believers connect discrete miracles into a unified redemptive narrative culminating in the glory of the risen Christ.

4.6.2 Glory Revealed through the Suffering Servant (Isaiah 52:13–53:12)

Jesus' miracles anticipate the suffering servant of Isaiah 52–53, whose ultimate "sign" is his vicarious suffering and atoning death. The prophet declares that God's Servant will "sprinkle many nations" and "bear the sins of many" (Isaiah 52:15; 53:12), bringing redemption and revealing God's glory through woundedness. Lazarus' resurrection illustrates this paradox: glory emerges through a journey into the tomb. Contemporary preaching can weave Isaiah's prophecy into miracle narratives, showing that physical resurrections point to spiritual restoration achieved on the cross. Worship liturgies during Lent might intersperse readings from Isaiah 53 between Gospel sign passages, reinforcing the link between sign-miracles and the glorified suffering of Christ. Small groups studying prophecy and Gospel together gain a holistic understanding of how suffering and glory coalesce in the Messiah. By aligning signs with servant-suffering, the church embraces a theology of redemptive pain that honors both resurrection power and cross-borne compassion.

4.6.3 The Empty Tomb: Glory's Final Sign (Matthew 28:1–7)

The resurrection morning accounts in Matthew 28:1–7 record the angel's announcement: "He is not here, for he has risen, as he said." This final sign confirms Jesus' own power over death and inaugurates the age of the Spirit-empowered church. The empty tomb shifts the focus from individual revivals to cosmic renewal—God's glory filling heaven and earth (Isaiah 6:3; Revelation 21:23). In modern Easter celebrations, churches can reenact the empty tomb narrative through dramatic presentations or interactive "tomb trails," inviting participants to discover the emptiness for themselves. Sunrise services held outside reinforce the theme of new creation dawning. Pre-Easter "watch nights" that mirror vigil in the garden connect believers to the tension of waiting before glory's revelation. The empty tomb becomes the final sign that seals the Johannine trajectory: from water to wine, from sickness to healing, from death to resurrection. Every believer, having encountered these signs, is commissioned to carry the news—"He is risen!"—as living testimony, ensuring that the Father's glory continues to echo through every generation.

4.7 Contemporary Implications: Miracles for God's Fame Today

4.7.1 Miracles and Spiritual Formation: Cultivating Expectant Faith

Cultivating expectant faith begins by intentionally remembering past acts of God's power, whether biblical or personal, and reflecting on them daily (Psalm 77:11–12). Believers can keep a "Signs Journal" to record answered prayers, providential coincidences, and moments of unexpected provision, reviewing it each week to spur their confidence. Prayer retreats focused on "expectation" teach participants to pray with anticipation rather than mere petition, echoing Jesus' invitation to believe for a greater harvest (John 4:36). Spiritual directors can guide counselees through contemplative exercises that imagine encountering Jesus in familiar routines, opening eyes to "small signs" of his nearness. Christian formation curricula might include modules on the history of missions and revival movements, showing how God's spectacular interventions fueled spiritual awakening. Personal disciplines such as lectio divina on miracle passages—Cana, Bethesda, Lazarus—immerse souls in the narrative rhythm of seeing, believing, and praising. Fasting seasons dedicated to "waiting for a sign" sharpen hunger for divine revelation, aligning our wills with God's timing (Matthew 17:21). Mentoring relationships can pair mature believers with novices to encourage eyewitness testimonies and mutual prayer for signs. Online devotional platforms might feature daily "sign prompts" that challenge readers to look for God's handiwork in news headlines, ecology, or technology. Over time, these practices weave expectancy into the fabric of everyday life, so that faith becomes poised not on human ability but on the Father's glorious power.

4.7.2 Miracles in Public Worship: Shaping Corporate Awe

Public worship provides a canvas to display God's miracles as invitations to corporate awe and doxology. Services can incorporate "Sign Spotlights," brief testimonies read aloud before a worship song that thematically connects to the miracle shared—e.g., closing water jars at the start of a song on new creation. Liturgical elements such as processions with unlit lamps that are later ignited symbolize the transition from darkness to light, mirroring Jesus' authority over death (John 8:12). Visual arts—live painting or projection of creative responses to miracle texts—invite congregants to experience the narrative visually and emotionally. Sermon series structured around the seven signs engage the entire Body, encouraging small groups to study each sign in depth. Responsive readings drawn from miracle passages bind the congregation's voice to the biblical narrative, echoing the disciples' confession after each sign (John 2:11; 4:53). Communion liturgies can be preceded by reminders of how Christ's body and blood represent the ultimate sign of redemption (Luke 22:19–20). Architectural design—such as placing a "Sign Wall" in a foyer with artifacts symbolizing each miracle—immerses attendees in a constant reminder of God's glory. Worship teams might integrate original compositions based on sign texts, fostering fresh expressions of adoration. By infusing public worship with layered references to miracles, churches cultivate a culture where awe becomes the default posture before a God who continually reveals his glory.

4.7.3 Miraculous Testimonies in Digital Evangelism

Digital platforms multiply the reach of testimonies, turning local signs into global invitations to faith. Churches can create short, high-quality video vignettes that recount modern "sign stories," ending with a clear gospel bridge and invitation (Mark 16:15). Podcast series interviewing individuals about life-changing miracles—healing, restoration, deliverance—offer in-depth narratives that sustain listener engagement beyond the five-minute scroll. Social media campaigns centered on a unifying hashtag (e.g., #GodStillWorks) encourage users to post bite-sized testimonies, creating an online mosaic of divine glory. Digital prayer walls enable believers worldwide to submit requests and report answers in real time, fostering collective intercession and visible sign-tracking. Training webinars teach lay evangelists to craft and share testimony content that is culturally sensitive, theologically sound, and emotionally compelling. Email devotionals that pair Scripture with a curated testimony help subscribers witness God's ongoing activity in diverse contexts. Live-streamed "Sign Nights," where a panel of believers shares and prays over miracle reports, combine immediacy with communal engagement. Websites dedicated to archiving testimonies provide searchable archives—by type of sign, location, or date—offering a resource for seekers and researchers alike. By leveraging digital tools with pastoral oversight and theological clarity, the church amplifies the Father's glory to every corner of the internet, inviting millions to believe.

4.8 Discerning Authentic Signs from Spectacle

4.8.1 Biblical Criteria for Genuine Miracles (Deuteronomy 13:1–3)

Scripture provides guardrails to discern true divine signs from deceptive wonders. Deuteronomy 13:1–3 warns that even if a sign or wonder occurs, it must align with God's revealed will—leading hearts to exclusive allegiance to Yahweh. Genuine signs corroborate God's character as revealed in Scripture (Numbers 23:19; Hebrews 13:8) and never contradict his moral commands. The early church tested prophetic signs by measuring them against apostolic teaching and ethical fruit (1 John 4:1–3; Matthew 7:15–20). In practice, churches can establish "Sign Review Committees" of pastors and lay theologians who evaluate claimed miracles for theological consistency and community impact. Training sessions on discernment equip members to ask critical questions: Was Scripture central to the testimony? Did the event lead to repentance, worship, and love? Were there any unaccounted-for financial motives? Spiritual directors can mentor emerging leaders in weighing signs against biblical patterns, emphasizing humility and caution. Publishing evaluations—balanced and respectful—of public miracle claims fosters transparency and trust. By rigorously applying biblical criteria, the church safeguards its witness and honors the Father's glory rather than human sensationalism.

4.8.2 Guarding against Sensationalism and Profit Motive

The allure of financial gain or celebrity status can corrupt miracle ministries, shifting focus from God's glory to human acclaim. Acts 8:18–24 records Simon the sorcerer's misguided attempt to purchase the gift of the Spirit, a cautionary tale against merchandising the miraculous. Contemporary ministries should adopt accountability structures—independent oversight boards, audited financial reporting, and clear policies forbidding "miracle fees." Conferences or healing crusades must ensure offerings support kingdom work rather than enrich organizers under the guise of spiritual gifting. Educational workshops on ethical fundraising and marketing help leaders recognize and resist the temptation to hype signs for attendance. Testimonies should highlight God's work, not the personality of the minister, and avoid staging emotional manipulation through scripted responses or selective editing. Denominational networks can develop best-practice guidelines that promote integrity, including third-party verification of healing claims when appropriate. Congregational teaching on the perils of "prosperity prophets" strengthens lay discernment, encouraging believers to value substance over spectacle. By proactively guarding against profit-driven sensationalism, the church ensures that miracles remain conduits of divine glory rather than commodities for sale.

4.8.3 Rooting Signs in Love and Truth (1 Corinthians 13:1–3)

Paul's exposition in 1 Corinthians 13 reminds us that even the most spectacular spiritual gifts, including signs and wonders, are hollow without love. Authentic miracles emerge from a foundation of self-sacrificial service and truthful proclamation (Galatians 5:13–14). When signs heal or restore, they must also foster compassion, justice, and community transformation—miracles that advance the kingdom of love (Micah 6:8). Ministries can embed "Love Checks" into sign-related activities: assessing whether the event prioritized the welfare of marginalized participants and addressed their ongoing needs. Preaching on the primacy of love alongside miracle accounts prevents spiritual narcissism and fuels genuine ministry. Training programs for sign-gifted individuals should include modules on pastoral care, ethics, and relational integrity. Testimony protocols can require sign recipients to share not only the miracle but also how they are supported by the church afterward. By anchoring every sign in the twin pillars of love and truth, the church honors the Father's heart and ensures that glory flows exclusively to him.

4.9 Personal and Corporate Response Pathways

4.9.1 Worshipful Awe: Practices for Doxological Living

Encountering miracles should overflow into doxology—lives marked by continual praise and gratitude (Psalm 150:6). Personal practices such as "Sign Sabbaths," where individuals spend the entire day praising God for his acts, cultivate a lifestyle of worship beyond Sunday services. Journaling prompts that pair each recorded sign with a prayer of thanksgiving reinforce the connection between miracle and praise. Churches can introduce doxology-focused small groups that begin meetings with shared miracles from the week and close with spontaneous worship. Congregational worship guides might include "Sign Psalms," curated selections from the Psalter that directly reference God's wondrous deeds (Psalm 77, 98, 107). Daily breath prayers—short phrases like "Hallelujah, He is mighty"—kept in pocket diaries, help embed awe into routine moments. Liturgical calendars can mark annual "Glory Days," celebrating historical revivals and local testimonies with extended praise services. Visual reminders—wall art displaying miracle quoter—turn homes and offices into constant reminders of God's power. By intentionally weaving worship into every response to signs, believers live doxological lives that magnify the Father's glory in both private and public spheres.

4.9.2 Testimony Sharing: Small-Group and Public Platforms

Testimony remains one of the church's most potent evangelistic tools, transforming abstract doctrine into lived reality. Small groups provide safe environments where members learn to craft concise, impactful testimonies that highlight God's glory, the crisis encountered, and the transformative sign (Acts 4:20). Public platforms—Sunday morning services, midweek gatherings, or evening "Testimony Evenings"—equip believers to share their stories before larger audiences. Training workshops on "Storytelling for the Kingdom" teach narrative arc, emotional authenticity, and gospel clarity. Digital testimonies—edited video clips of 2–3 minutes—can be integrated into sermon slides, church websites, or social media feeds. Outreach events like community fairs or health clinics benefit from live testimony booths, where attendees record brief accounts to encourage onlookers. Celebrating "Testimony Sundays" quarterly ensures regular exposure to God's ongoing miracles. Encouraging children and youth to share age-appropriate stories fosters intergenerational faith transmission. By valuing testimony as corporate currency, the church amplifies the Father's glory and invites skeptics to consider the reality behind the words.

4.9.3 Service as Response: Demonstrating God's Glory in Compassion

Miracles call forth practical service that echoes God's compassionate action, fulfilling Jesus' command to love our neighbors (Matthew 25:35–40). Mercy ministries—food banks, free clinics, tutoring centers—become extensions of divine signs, tangible proof of God's heart for the marginalized. Churches can organize "Sign Serves," volunteer days where participants recall a miracle and then serve in its honor, linking gratitude with action. Long-term partnerships with local nonprofits ensure that service responses are sustained beyond one-off events. Training in "compassion evangelism" equips volunteers to combine practical help with gospel conversation. Periodic "Impact Reports" track how service projects mirror the glory of God by transforming communities, fostering accountability and vision. Vision-casting sermons on the connection between signs and service inspire congregational buy-in and resource commitment. Youth ministries can adopt neighborhood blocks for ongoing clean-ups and care visits, training the next generation to respond to signs with action. By aligning service initiatives with the narrative of miracles, the church embodies the Father's glory, proving that divine power always flows through hands and hearts of willing servants.

Conclusion Having surveyed the tapestry of signs that culminate in Lazarus' resurrection, we come to see that true wonder always serves a higher purpose: to reflect God's splendor, to draw hearts into steadfast belief, and to catalyze worship that transforms communities. These miracles, though ancient, still speak with fresh relevance today—calling us to cultivate expectant faith, to discern genuine signs from empty spectacle, and to live lives that mirror the compassion and power we have witnessed. As you move forward, may your eyes remain open to the everyday wonders God orchestrates, and may your heart continually echo the doxology they inspire: "To Him be glory forever and ever."

Chapter 5. "I Am the Resurrection and the Life" — Christological Centerpiece

When Jesus stood before the tomb of Lazarus and proclaimed, "I am the resurrection and the life," he unveiled the very heart of his identity and mission. This claim transcends all other "I am" statements in John's Gospel, for it addresses humanity's deepest need: victory over death itself. In this chapter, we will explore how this confession both fulfills Old Testament hopes and inaugurates a new reality for all who trust in him. From the promise of abundant life here and now to the assurance of bodily resurrection in the age to come, Christ's words anchor our faith in his power over the grave and his gift of eternal communion with the Father.

5.1 Context and Declaration at Bethany

5.1.1 Martha's Statement of Faith (John 11:25–26)

Standing at the threshold of death and life's frontier, Martha articulates a confession born of both grief and conviction: "I know that he will rise again in the resurrection on the last day, and I believe that you are the Christ, the Son of God" (vv. 24–27). In declaring Jesus not only as Messiah but as the source of resurrection, she bridges present mourning with future hope. Her words reveal two tiers of resurrection: the corporate eschatological rising and the immediate, personal deliverance Jesus now offers. Martha's faith is informed by covenant promise (Daniel 12:2; Isaiah 26:19) and shaped by prior encounters with Jesus in Galilean villages. In the dust of Bethany, she rehearses ancient hopes, yet personalizes them in her present crisis—an exemplar of faith that roots future expectation in present relationship. This confession does not emerge in doctrinal isolation but in the crucible of loss, showing that true Christology is forged in lament as well as in praise. Jesus' gentle affirmation, "Your brother will rise again," echoes her hope before unveiling a deeper reality as Savior over death itself. Martha's statement models for us the gospel's dialectic: we hold fast to future promise even as we lean on Christ's present person. In pastoral care today, counselors can invite mourners to echo Martha's dual confession—acknowledging bodily resurrection while declaring faith in Jesus' pastoral presence. By centering our belief on Christ's person rather than circumstances, we adopt a faith capable of sustaining us through life's darkest hours.

5.1.2 Immediate Reaction of Those Present

Martha's declaration reverberates among the gathered mourners—disciples, Mary, and onlookers—shifting the emotional atmosphere from despair to expectant wondering. Prior to Lazarus's resurrection, debates about Jesus' delay and divine timing had dominated the scene (John 11:6–16); now, theological reality pierces through tears. Some disciples respond with curiosity, recalling Jesus' earlier "I am" sayings and anticipating a new revelation. Mary, arriving only moments later, echoes Martha's confession with her own weeping that births deeper revelation (vv. 32–33). The crowd's reaction oscillates between skepticism—"Could not he who opened the eyes of the blind have kept this man from dying?" (v. 37)—and amazement as Jesus commands life from the tomb. The Jews present, steeped in Mosaic law regarding purity and death (Numbers 19:11), watch as divine authority trumps ritual uncleanness. When Lazarus emerges bound in grave-clothes, the assembly's astonishment crescendos into belief—though some would carry that belief only so far (vv. 45–46). This mixed response mirrors modern congregations where signs elicit faith in some and questions in others. Small-group leaders can use this scene to discuss the interplay of personal confession, communal lament, and collective amazement. By examining these reactions, church communities learn to create spaces where doubt and wonder can coexist, moving together toward deeper trust.

5.1.3 Contrast with Earlier "I Am" Sayings

Jesus' self-declarations in John's Gospel form a progressive Christological mosaic: "I am the bread of life," "the light of the world," "the gate," "the good shepherd," "the way, the truth, and the life," and "the true vine." Each earlier saying addresses an aspect of spiritual need—hunger, darkness, exclusion, vulnerability, direction, and vitality—inviting hearers into relational dependence. By the time we reach Bethany, the climax arises: "I am the resurrection and the life" (v. 25), integrating and surpassing all prior metaphors. Whereas the "bread" sustains and the "vine" nourishes ongoing growth, the "resurrection and life" restores the dead to vibrant existence. The progression reveals Jesus not just as provider or guide but as sovereign over the greatest human boundary: death. This summit statement reframes every other "I am" in light of eternal triumph—light dispels even the shadow of the grave, and shepherd care includes leading home from the sheepfold of death. In preaching series, pastors can trace this ascending sequence, allowing congregations to ascend with Jesus from daily sustenance to cosmic redemption. Educators might invite learners to map each metaphor's contribution to the crown imagery of the resurrection statement. When we contrast earlier sayings with this centerpiece, we recognize that all of Christ's ministries hinge on his authority to confer life unto death's victims. Thus, the Bethany declaration stands as the theological keystone, binding the arch of John's Christology in the glory of life over death.

5.2 The Seven "I Am" Sayings: A Theological Panorama

5.2.1 "Bread of Life" — Sustainer of Spiritual Hunger (John 6:35)

In the synagogue at Capernaum, Jesus explains that just as God provided manna in the wilderness, he is the "bread of life"—the unparalleled sustenance for spiritual hunger (John 6:35). This metaphor emphasizes ongoing nourishment: believers must continually "eat" of Christ through faith and communion (John 6:56). The crowd initially misunderstands, seeking physical bread, but Jesus redirects them to the invisible sustenance that results in eternal life. His claim subverts temple sacrificial systems by locating ultimate purification not in ritual offerings but in personal participation in his life. Contemporary applications include emphasizing spiritual disciplines—Scripture intake, prayer, Eucharist—that feed souls daily. Church educational programs can teach "feeding classes," integrating biblical nutrition analogies with practical guidance for developing consistent devotional rhythms. Digital platforms might offer "daily bread" devotionals via email or apps, reminding users to feast on Christ first thing each morning. By exploring this "I am," congregations learn to distinguish between physical cravings and the deeper, God-centered hunger only Christ can satisfy. As the foundation for subsequent metaphors, the bread theme underscores that resurrection life springs from continual dependence on the living Christ.

5.2.2 "Light of the World" — Illuminator of Darkness (John 8:12)

At the Feast of Tabernacles, a festival of light, Jesus proclaims, "I am the light of the world" (John 8:12), claiming authority to illuminate moral and spiritual darkness. Light in Jewish imagery evokes God's presence (Exodus 13:21) and the dawning of redemption (Isaiah 9:2). Jesus' self-revelation announces the eclipse of sin and ignorance, inviting followers to walk in clarity rather than stumble in shadows. The dual promise—no believer walking in him will ever walk in darkness—encompasses both ethical transformation and eschatological assurance. Modern worship services often feature candles or lighting dramas to symbolize Christ's illuminating work; small groups can follow with "light walks" around neighborhoods, praying for spiritual awakening. Bible studies on darkness themes—fear, deceit, unbelief—should anchor responses in Jesus' light, teaching members to replace anxious thoughts with scriptural illumination (Psalm 119:105). Children's ministries can craft simple "flashlight lessons" that demonstrate the power of a small light in vast darkness, echoing the gospel's reach. Through this saying, believers learn that resurrection life includes newfound vision—seeing God, self, and world in divine clarity—and are empowered to shine Christ's light into dark places.

5.2.3 "Gate" — Guardian and Access Point (John 10:7–9)

Jesus casts himself as the "gate" for the sheepfold, asserting that only through him can one enter safely into the pasture of God's presence (John 10:7–9). This metaphor combines access and protection: the gatekeeper's role in first-century flocks was to open the pen by day and lock it by night, guarding animals from predators. Through Christ, believers gain entry into abundant life, while the gate's threshold acts as a barrier against false shepherds and harmful influences. The invitation to "enter through me" underscores exclusivity—no parallel path exists to divine provision. Contemporary church architecture can incorporate "gate motifs" at entrances, reminding attendees of Christ's protective welcome. Pastoral care teams might refer to counseling sessions as "gate consultations," guiding individuals through the threshold from bondage into freedom. Small-group leaders can enact symbolical gate-opening rituals—singing a short refrain as someone confesses opening their heart to Christ—fortifying communal entry into safe spiritual space. This "I am" affirms that resurrection life begins at the gate of faith, inviting each soul to step beyond death's enclosure into green pastures of God's abiding care.

5.2.4 "Good Shepherd" — Tender Guide and Protector (John 10:11–15)

Building on the gate image, Jesus declares himself the "good shepherd" who lays down his life for the sheep. Unlike mercenary hirelings who flee at danger, he remains steadfast amid wolves, epitomizing sacrificial love (John 10:11–13). His intimate knowledge—knowing each sheep by name—speaks of personal relationship rather than anonymous mass care. This shepherd-sheep motif resonates with Davidic and Ezekielic promises of shepherding restoration (Psalm 23; Ezekiel 34). Resurrection life thus includes relational depth: secure identity and unceasing guidance under Christ's vigilant watch. In pastoral ministry, elders can adopt shepherd-care training, learning to "know by name" each congregant's needs and struggles. Small-group contexts become "sheep pens" where members share burdens, pray, and follow the shepherd's voice through Scripture. Missionary care often uses "pastoral calls" to reenact the shepherd's rounds, checking spiritual and practical needs in far-flung fields. Worship leaders might insert sheepfold imagery into litanies, asking Christ to guide and guard his flock. This "I am" assures that resurrection life thrives under the tender protection of the shepherd who sacrifices all for our well-being.

5.2.5 "Way, Truth, and Life" — Exclusive Path to the Father (John 14:6)

In his farewell discourse, Jesus identifies himself as the exclusive "way, the truth, and the life," asserting that no one reaches the Father apart from him (John 14:6). "Way" conveys movement and direction—Jesus as the trajectory to God's presence. "Truth" (ἀλήθεια) signifies both factual reality and constancy—Christ embodies divine revelation that sets free (John 8:32). "Life" reiterates his resurrection-giving power, now framed as the ongoing quality of relationship with the Father. This triad compresses the gospel into a succinct formula: Jesus is the path, the content, and the vitality of salvation. Discipleship classes can explore each term through guided Bible study, contrasting worldly philosophies with Christ's path, truth, and life. Evangelistic training equips believers to articulate this exclusive claim lovingly, explaining why pluralistic alternatives cannot replace Christ's unique role. Digital evangelism campaigns might feature graphics highlighting each attribute, inviting seekers into a deeper exploration. Christian education curricula could assign projects where students map "the way" through New Testament narratives, assess "truth" in apologetic contexts, and research "life" in spiritual formation disciplines. In a culture enamored with many paths, this "I am" reorients seekers to the single road that leads to resurrection life in the Father's presence.

5.2.6 "True Vine" — Source of Spiritual Vitality (John 15:1–5)

Jesus portrays himself as the "true vine" and believers as branches, emphasizing organic union and mutual sustenance (John 15:1–5). The choice of "true" (ἡ ἀληθινή) contrasts with Israel's history of wild vines producing sour fruit (Hosea 10:1). By abiding in the true vine, branches participate in divine sap—nourishment that yields enduring fruit of character and witness. Pruning seasons—periods of discipline and hardship—serve to increase fruitfulness, not to punish. Spiritual formation programs can integrate "vineyard retreats," where participants reflect on pruning in their own lives and journal resultant growth. Home groups might conduct "abiding exercises," laying down agendas to simply rest in Christ's presence for fixed intervals. Worship teams can incorporate metaphors of sap and fruit into songs and visuals during communion or healing services. Christian counseling incorporates vine-abide metaphors, helping counselees identify unfruitful attachments and cooperate with God's pruning work. As branches bear fruit in community, they join the vine's collective glory—demonstrating the resurrection-life power that flows from Christ into his people.

5.2.7 Summation in Lazarus: "Resurrection and Life" as Climax

All preceding "I am" images converge at Lazarus's tomb where Christ reveals his ultimate identity: the one who grants resurrection and life itself. This climactic saying recapitulates bread, light, gate, shepherd, way, and vine—bringing together sustenance, illumination, access, protection, direction, and vitality into the singular promise of overcoming death. Ancient readers recognized this summit as the keystone of John's theological structure, the apex where God's glory shines most brightly. In liturgical rhythm, Easter's focus on the empty tomb echoes this climactic "I am," while other "I am" sayings inform Holy Week's progression. Preaching series can culminate in a Bethany sermon, tying together each earlier metaphor to this final, life-giving declaration. Small-group studies might conclude their "seven signs" module with shared testimonies of new life in Christ, symbolically reenacting Lazarus's walk from the tomb. Theologically, this summit asserts that Christ's person and work cannot be separated—the one who nourishes, guides, and protects is the same who conquers death. As readers, we stand at the apex of revelation, invited to place our faith in the resurrection-and-life-giver and thereby participate in the Father's eternal glory.

5.3 Christ as the Resurrection

5.3.1 Resurrection in Old Testament Typology (Isaiah 25:8; Ezekiel 37)

The prophet Isaiah foretells a day when the Lord "will swallow up death forever, and the Lord God will wipe away tears from all faces" (Isaiah 25:8), laying groundwork for understanding resurrection as divine reversal of death's effects. This promise echoes in Ezekiel's vision of the valley of dry bones (Ezekiel 37), where God's breath revives lifeless skeletons into a living army. These Old Testament types prepare Israel to receive a Messiah who confers not merely physical restoration but participation in God's own life. By declaring "I am the resurrection," Jesus anchors his identity in this rich prophetic tradition, fulfilling and surpassing ancient hopes. In rabbinic expectation, resurrection was associated with the end of days; Christ inaugurates that age here and now, yet consummates it in final glory (1 Corinthians 15:20). In personal devotions, believers can study these typologies side by side with Gospel narratives, tracing the continuity of God's redemptive plan. Preachers might weave Ezekiel's valley and Lazarus's tomb into a single sermon to underscore continuity of promise and fulfillment. Small groups can dramatize Ezekiel's vision and then read John 11 aloud, emphasizing how Jesus embodies the living word. Even art ministries can depict dry bones transforming into Lazarus emerging, reinforcing theology visually. Thus, Old Testament typology grounds our confidence that resurrection is not an abstract doctrine but rooted in God's long-standing covenant faithfulness.

5.3.2 Firstfruits of Resurrection: Christ's Empty Tomb (1 Corinthians 15:20)

Paul calls Christ the "firstfruits of those who have fallen asleep" (1 Corinthians 15:20), affirming that Jesus' resurrection is the guarantee and model for the faithful's future rising. In agricultural terms, the firstfruits offering consecrated the harvest to God, symbolizing both thanksgiving and assured provision. Jesus as firstfruits indicates that his resurrection is both the initial and the pledge of the full harvest of redeemed humanity. The empty tomb, then, transcends mere historical fact; it is a cosmic inauguration of new creation (Revelation 21:1–5). Early believers centered their preaching on this firstfruits event, empowering missionary outreach across the Roman Empire (Acts 2:32). Contemporary Easter liturgies can highlight the firstfruits theme by lifting bread samples at Communion—symbolizing both Christ's body given and our coming resurrection bodies. Theology seminars might dissect first-century Jewish harvest festivals to deepen understanding of Paul's metaphor. Personal reflection exercises—writing "resurrection firstfruits" prayers—allow believers to name areas of life where they already experience resurrection power. Youth ministries can stage "firstfruits celebrations," offering creative arts inspired by gratitude for Christ's rising. By embracing Christ as firstfruits, we stand in the stream of resurrection life, assured that our future hope is already secured in his victory.

5.3.3 Future Hope: Believers' Resurrection Body (Philippians 3:20–21)

Paul affirms that our "citizenship is in heaven," and we eagerly await a Savior who "will transform our lowly body to be like his glorious body" (Philippians 3:20–21). This promise speaks to both continuity and transformation: our identity as believers carries into the resurrection life, yet our bodies will be gloriously renewed. In John's Gospel, Christ's resurrection body—pierced hands, tangible presence—anticipates the physical reality of our own resurrection (John 20:19–29). Early Christians penned creedal statements declaring belief in the "resurrection of the body," solidifying hope beyond metaphor. Modern funeral rites rooted in this confession assure mourners that death's sting is but a threshold into embodied communion with Christ (1 Thessalonians 4:16–17). Pastoral care for the terminally ill can integrate Philippians 3:20–21 into prayers, shifting focus from suffering bodies to resurrected ones. Art ministries might invite congregants to sketch "glorious bodies," fostering imaginative hope. Small groups can study the nature of resurrection bodies—incorruptible, luminous, recognizable—exploring implications for identity and relationships beyond death. Scientific discussions on the continuity of personal identity reinforce that resurrection is not loss of self but its highest fulfillment. Thus, the future hope of our resurrected bodies anchors present faith, empowering us to live courageously in the face of mortality.

5.4 Christ as the Life

5.4.1 Life Defined Biblically: From Creation through Covenant (Genesis 2:7; Deut. 30:20)

Life in Scripture begins with God breathing into Adam's nostrils, making him "a living being" (Genesis 2:7), indicating that true life is divine gift and breath. Within the Sinai covenant, God warns Israel to "choose life, that you and your offspring may live" (Deut. 30:19–20), tying obedience to the Torah with flourishing existence. These Old Testament anchors frame Jesus' later claim: as Life itself, he embodies the divine breath that animates both creation and covenant community. By affirming "I am the life," Christ situates himself at the nexus of creation and redemption, granting not only biological animation but covenantal vitality. In catechism classes, teachers can trace "life" from Eden through Exodus to the Gospels, showing continuity of divine intention. Congregational worship can include readings from Genesis and Deuteronomy before Gospel proclamation, underscoring that Christ fulfills ancient life-giving promises. Personal prayer practices—guided by breath prayers invoking the Spirit as breath of life—connect individuals to the creation account. Environmental stewardship ministries can frame ecological care as honoring the Source of life, integrating conservation with covenant fidelity. By defining life biblically, we recognize that Christ's life-giving power extends from atoms to nations, from breath to eternity.

5.4.2 Abundant Life Now: Spiritual, Emotional, Relational (John 10:10)

Jesus clarifies that he came "that they may have life and have it abundantly" (John 10:10), indicating a quality of life that exceeds bare existence. Abundance here includes spiritual union with God, emotional wholeness in God's love, and relational flourishing within the community of faith. The "good shepherd" motif underscores that under Christ's care, sheep lack nothing essential—they enjoy pasture, protection, and purpose. Contemporary discipleship can map "abundant life inventories," inviting believers to assess spiritual health, emotional well-being, and relational vitality. Counseling ministries might incorporate John 10:10 into their vision, offering holistic care that addresses soul, mind, and community integration. Young adult ministries can structure workshops on "abundant relationships," exploring authentic friendship and accountability. Worship music playlists can include songs that celebrate fullness of joy in Christ, anchoring emotional life in divine presence. Congregations can host "abundance festivals"—community fairs that showcase stories of transformed lives, from addiction recovery to restored marriages. Environmental and social justice efforts further embody abundant life by addressing systemic barriers to human flourishing. By embracing abundant life now, we testify that resurrection life is not solely future promise but a present reality empowered by Christ's ongoing work.

5.4.3 Eternal Life: Quality and Duration (John 17:3; 1 John 5:11–13)

Jesus defines eternal life as knowing the only true God and Jesus Christ whom He has sent (John 17:3), stressing relational knowledge over mere endless duration. This relational dimension distinguishes eternal life from mere immortality; it is life with depth and intimacy. John reaffirms this in 1 John 5:11–13, assuring believers that they already possess eternal life and need confidence in their standing before God. Early catecheses instructed converts that eternal life begins at conversion ("now") and continues beyond death ("forever"). Pastoral counseling for grief can emphasize that loved ones in Christ now enjoy unbroken fellowship with God, offering solace in sorrow. Marriage prep courses can ground covenant vows in eternal life metaphors, underscoring that Christian unions participate in divine relationship. Children's ministries can teach eternal life through relational language— knowing God as friend and maker—rather than abstract temporal concepts. Devotional writings might include "eternal life prayers" that celebrate present knowledge of God while longing for consummation. By clarifying eternal life's quality and duration, Christians gain assurance and motivation to cultivate deeper knowledge of God now, anticipating fullness in the age to come.

5.5 Union with Christ: Participating in Resurrection Life

5.5.1 Baptism as Identification with Death and Resurrection (Romans 6:3–5)

Paul explains that through baptism, believers are baptized into Christ's death and raised to walk in newness of life (Romans 6:3–5), making the rite both sacrament and symbol. Immersion illustrates burial and burial in water echoes participation in his death, while emerging symbolizes resurrection. Early church practice involved catechumenate instruction, preparing candidates to grasp the theological weight of baptism's union with Christ. In contemporary liturgy, pastors can deepen understanding by solemnly unpacking each stage—kneeling, immersion, rising—and linking to Romans 6's promises. Baptism preparation classes might include testimonies from long-time believers recounting how their baptismal union empowered new patterns of life. Photography or videography of baptisms can be edited into "resurrection reels," showing testimonies synchronized with water and worship. Small groups can celebrate baptisms as community landmarks, hosting meals and prayer gatherings to welcome new members. Infant baptism contexts can incorporate age-appropriate affirmations as children grow, reinforcing union with Christ as lifelong identity. By emphasizing baptism's union with resurrection, the church instills profound appreciation for the gift of participatory life Christ secures.

5.5.2 Indwelling Spirit as Life-Giver (Romans 8:11)

Paul promises that the same Spirit who raised Jesus from the dead dwells in believers, giving life to their mortal bodies (Romans 8:11). This indwelling is both immediate—empowering prayer, worship, and service—and eschatological—guaranteeing future resurrection. In the

Upper Room, Jesus breathes the Spirit upon the disciples (John 20:22), echoing God's creative breath in Eden (Genesis 2:7). Contemporary spiritual formation can include Breath of Life sessions—guided breathing prayers linking physical breath to Spirit's life-giving work. Healing ministries can invoke Romans 8:11 in prayer for bodily renewal, acknowledging the Spirit's power over infirmity. Small groups might practice "Spirit-led worship," inviting members to share spontaneous expressions as evidence of the indwelling life. Theological education can explore the Spirit's role in sanctification, linking resurrection reality to daily transformation (2 Corinthians 3:18). Worship team rehearsals might begin with invocation of the Spirit's presence, setting the tone for Spirit-empowered performance. Evangelistic teaching on the Spirit's indwelling distinguishes Christian experience from mere moralism, highlighting relational empowerment. By recognizing the Spirit as life-giver, the church lives in the dynamic reality of resurrection life, sustained moment by moment.

5.5.3 Daily "Walking in Newness of Life" (Colossians 2:6–7)

Paul urges believers to "walk in him, rooted and built up in him" (Colossians 2:6–7), capturing the ongoing nature of resurrection participation. This daily walk involves obedience, prayer, and engagement with the Word—practices that manifest the new identity we have in Christ. Spiritual disciplines—daily Bible reading, journaling, solitude—serve as "walking sticks" supporting our journey in resurrection life. Churches can sponsor "Newness of Life Challenges," encouraging members to adopt a new spiritual habit for 40 days, celebrating growth collectively. Small groups might walk together—literally, as "faith walks"—discussing weekly Scripture and prayer insights along the way. Workplaces can host brief "walk-and-pray" breaks, integrating faith into routine activity. Counseling programs might encourage "life-walk logs," where clients record daily reflections on how they experienced newness of life. Preachers can illustrate walking metaphors with local hiking trails, inviting congregations on pilgrimage experiences. By emphasizing daily walking in newness, believers avoid treating resurrection life as a one-time event, embracing it instead as an ongoing vocation of transformation and growth.

5.6 Empowering Presence: Overcoming Death in Daily Experience

5.6.1 Freedom from Fear of Death (Hebrews 2:14–15)

The author of Hebrews explains that Christ "shared in their humanity" so that, by his death, he might "destroy him who has the power of death, that is, the devil, and deliver all those who through fear of death were subject to lifelong slavery" (Hebrews 2:14–15). By breaking death's dominion, Jesus frees his people from constant dread of mortality. This empowerment is lived out in daily courage—believers can face serious illness or accident without panic because Christ has already triumphed. In practical pastoral care, funerals and hospital visits should emphasize this victory, offering Scripture like Romans 8:38–39 to counter death anxiety. Support groups for the terminally ill can incorporate workshops on "dying well," teaching that fear need not dominate one's final days when grounded in Christ's victory. In Christian counseling, therapists might use narrative therapy to replace death-fear stories with testimonies of resurrection hope. Personal devotions can include memorizing Hebrews 2:14–15, turning it into a breath prayer when anxiety spikes. Preachers can reinforce this freedom by preaching through the "last enemy" texts (1 Corinthians 15:26), helping congregations envision death as a defeated foe. Youth groups can host "No Fear Nights" where teens discuss questions about death candidly, anchored in Christ's victory. In all these settings, the reality that Jesus has conquered death empowers believers to live boldly, unshackled by fear, every day.

5.6.2 Comfort in Mourning: "Blessed Are Those Who Mourn" (Matthew 5:4)

Jesus pronounces a blessing on mourners—"Blessed are those who mourn, for they shall be comforted" (Matthew 5:4)—

including resurrection's promise in the comfort offered. Mourning is not a sign of weak faith but an invitation for Christ's presence to enfold our grief. In grief ministries, facilitators can begin sessions by reading Matthew 5:4, then inviting participants to share how they have already experienced God's comfort. Pastoral counseling might teach mourners to pray the Beatitudes back to God, personalizing each promise. Worship services can include corporate lament songs paired with assurance hymns, modeling the mourning–comfort flow. Support groups might meet at dawn or dusk—times of heightened emotion—praying Psalm 30:5 ("weeping may tarry for the night, but joy comes with the morning") together. Personal prayer practices can involve writing laments in a dedicated "mourning journal," followed by writing comfort notes from Scripture (e.g., 2 Corinthians 1:3–4) as God's reply. In funeral liturgies, clergy can offer symbolic comfort gestures—laying hands on the casket or grave—visibly manifesting Christ's blessing on mourners. Seminaries should train ministers in grief theology, ensuring that comfort is offered theologically and pastorally. By embracing mourning as blessed, the church becomes a sanctuary of resurrection comfort for all who grieve.

5.6.3 Witnessing Amid Persecution: Martyr's Confidence (Revelation 2:10)

Revelation 2:10 exhorts believers to "be faithful unto death, and I will give you the crown of life," linking resurrection hope to steadfast witness amid persecution. Martyrs throughout church history—from Stephen (Acts 7:59–60) to modern-day believers—have faced death with the confidence that Christ's resurrection renders death powerless. Contemporary discipleship programs can include "Crown of Life" case studies, examining how faith in resurrection sustained persecuted Christians. Church mission agencies should prepare cross-cultural workers with training in both local context and resurrection theology, equipping them for the possibility of martyrdom. In worship, singing hymns like "Because He Lives" in contexts of oppression reinforces the certainty of life beyond death. Small groups can host "Martyr Testimony Nights," where expatriate or refugee believers share how resurrection hope upheld them under threat. Theological education must integrate eschatological confidence into leadership formation, preventing fear-driven retreat. In prayer gatherings, reading Revelation 7:9–17 gives a foretaste of that vast multitude crowned in white, inspiring present endurance. Youth ministries addressing radicalization and identity can root young Christians in proclamation of resurrection life, countering extremist narratives. By linking persecution and resurrection confidence, the church affirms that Christ's empowering presence sustains faithful witness even unto death.

5.7 Liturgical and Sacramental Reflections

5.7.1 Eucharist as Proclamation of Resurrection (1 Corinthians 11:26)

Paul affirms that by eating the bread and drinking the cup, believers "proclaim the Lord's death until he comes" (1 Corinthians 11:26). In Johannine perspective, the Lord's Supper also signifies participation in his resurrection life (John 6:54). Liturgies can underscore this dual proclamation: brief catechesis before Communion explains that each Eucharistic celebration is both remembrance of the cross and anticipation of resurrection. Worship leaders might incorporate responsive readings from 1 Corinthians 15, connecting Christ's death to his risen life. The bread can be distributed first to emphasize remembrance, then the cup served with the acclamation "He is risen!" to celebrate resurrection presence. Visual art— communion banners depicting empty tomb imagery— reinforces the festive aspect of the Eucharist. Small group celebrations of the Supper can allow for extended sharing of resurrection testimonies between the breaking of bread and drinking of the cup. In homes, families observing "family communion" on resurrection Sundays can teach children the unity of the Lord's death and life. Seminary liturgics courses should explore the sacramental theology of resurrection in the Lord's Supper. By making the Eucharist a weekly declaration of resurrection glory, the church lives into its Christological centerpiece in community.

5.7.2 Funeral Rites Rooted in "Resurrection and Life"

Funeral liturgies present opportunities to proclaim the Lord's victory over death through word and symbol. Clergy should begin services by reading John 11:25–26 and John 5:24, affirming trust in Christ's promise. The service order can include the "Resurrection Acclamation" from 1 Corinthians 15:20 ("Christ has indeed been raised from the dead..."), recited by congregation. Music selections—Isaac Watts's "When I Survey the Wondrous Cross" followed by Charles Wesley's "Thine Be the Glory"—guide mourners from the cross into triumph. During committal, the minister might uncap the casket lid briefly, symbolizing the empty tomb that awaits all believers. Video tributes can intersperse personal memories with Scripture graphics of resurrection promises. Condolence cards distributed at the reception may feature Philippians 3:20–21, encouraging grieving families. Grief counselors should incorporate "resurrection grief" models that distinguish healthy mourning from despair, fostering hope rather than denial. Training for funeral volunteers includes instruction on comforting language that draws on resurrection life. By weaving the "I am the resurrection and the life" theme throughout funeral practices, the church demonstrates its commitment to life beyond the grave.

5.7.3 Festal Celebrations: Easter and Baptism Services

Easter Sunday is the annual apex of resurrection proclamation, yet baptism services throughout the year echo this centerpiece. Easter liturgies should be steeped in Johannine theology: Easter Vigil readings can include John 20:1–18 and John 11:25–26, linking Lazarus's resurrection to Christ's own. Lighting the Paschal candle symbolizes Christ as the light of the risen age (John 8:12). Baptismal services can be scheduled on Easter, allowing candidates to be baptized into new life in the context of the resurrection festival. During baptism, the congregation can sing "Thine Be the Glory" as each candidate emerges from the water, proclaiming participation in Christ's triumph. Church-wide events—such as resurrection morning potlucks—encourage communal celebration of baptismal life. Children's pageants can dramatize Lazarus's story alongside Easter narratives, teaching young ones the continuity of resurrection themes. Adult classes held during Lent can prepare participants for Easter baptisms, grounding them in the semantics of death-and-resurrection union (Romans 6:4). Music ministries can commission original anthems on "Resurrection and Life," premiering them each year at Easter. By centering both Easter and baptisms on this "I am" statement, the church embeds Christological identity deeply into its sacramental rhythms.

5.8 Contemporary Applications: Living Resurrection Now

5.8.1 Healing Ministries: Signs of Life in Broken Bodies

Healing ministries bring resurrection life into the realm of physical brokenness, echoing John's signs. Prayer teams trained in Scripture-based intercession (James 5:14–15) minister to those with chronic illness, expecting God to demonstrate life over infirmity. Healing services incorporate testimonies of past recoveries, reinforcing faith that God still responds. Hospitals partnered with churches can establish "healing chaplaincy" programs where volunteers pray and read John 11 for patients. Seminaries can offer courses in biblical healing theology, equipping ministers to discern spiritual versus medical dimensions of illness. Small-group "Healing Circles" meet regularly to support members in health crises, combining prayer, Scripture, and practical assistance. Digital healing networks use video calls to extend prayer across distances, reflecting the official's son healing. Care packages with comforting Scriptures and anointing oil kits accompany volunteers, giving tangible signs of God's life-giving presence. Encouraging medical professionals within the congregation to join healing teams bridges faith and science. Through these ministries, resurrection life touches broken bodies today, manifesting Christ's power over sickness.

5.8.2 Social Justice: Bringing Life to Marginalized Communities

Resurrection life extends beyond individuals to communities marginalized by poverty, racism, and violence. Gospel-centered social justice initiatives—food pantries, homelessness outreaches, prison ministries—embody Christ's resurrection compassion. Churches can adopt neighborhoods marked by systemic death—gang violence or environmental injustice—to invest long-term in holistic renewal. Training on the seven "signs" model helps activists see each program as a sign pointing to God's glory, not as self-promotional charity. Advocacy teams educate congregations on policy change for fair housing or criminal justice reform, reflecting Christ's care for the least of these (Matthew 25:40). Faith-based organizations can partner with local governments, mirroring the official's remote healing approach by leveraging resources and influence without seeking personal gain. Community art projects—murals of Lazarus rising—visually proclaim hope in spaces of despair. Educational workshops on structural sin help believers move from sympathy to systemic action. By bringing resurrection life into social structures, the church testifies that Christ's victory over death inaugurates justice, dignity, and flourishing for all people.

5.8.3 Environmental Stewardship: Renewing Creation

The resurrection motif encompasses cosmic renewal—"Behold, I make all things new" (Revelation 21:5)—calling believers to care for creation as stewards of resurrection life. Environmental ministries adopt practices like community gardens, tree plantings, and river clean-ups, embodying new creation in ecosystems. Sermon series on the "seventh sign" can explore creation's own longing for liberation from decay (Romans 8:19–21). Churches can install solar panels or rainwater-harvesting systems, demonstrating resurrection innovation. Eco-theology workshops teach congregants how Genesis's dominion mandate connects to Christ's work of cosmic reconciliation. Creation care teams organize "Earth Day Celebrations" with lectures, prayer vigils, and indigenous land acknowledgments. Children's programs weave resurrection themes into environmental lessons—singing about new life in soil and streams. Interfaith coalitions on climate justice reflect the universal scope of resurrection hope. By stewarding earth's resources responsibly, believers participate in the consummation of new creation, testifying that "resurrection and life" extends to every corner of God's handiwork.

Conclusion As we reflect on Jesus' declaration, we discover that resurrection life is neither an abstract doctrine nor a distant hope but a present reality to be embraced and embodied. In union with Christ, we participate in his triumph over death through baptism, the indwelling Spirit, and daily walks of faith. This truth shapes our worship, our sacraments, and our service—calling us to bear witness to life in every sphere of brokenness. May this centerpiece of Christian confession inspire you to live boldly in the power of Christ's resurrection, confident that the One who spoke life into Lazarus still speaks life into you today—and into all creation until that final, glorious morning when death is forever swallowed up in victory.

Chapter 6. "Take Away the Stone" — Obedient Partnership with God

When Jesus stood before the sealed tomb of Lazarus, he didn't step forward alone—he called Martha and the bystanders into the work of resurrection. His command to "take away the stone" transforms a passive audience into active partners in God's miracle. This moment shatters the illusion that divine power unfolds solely by celestial decree; instead, it reveals a God who invites our hands, our faith, and even our doubts into his redemptive work. As we explore this compelling scene, we will discover how obeying seemingly irrational commands becomes the gateway to experiencing God's life-giving presence. Whether the barrier is fear, cultural taboo, or deeply ingrained habit, our obedience positions us to witness the glory of God breaking through the strongest resistance.

6.1 The Command to Obey: Rolling Away Resistance

6.1.1 Jesus' Directive to Martha: "Did I Not Tell You…" (John 11:39)

When Jesus looks at the sealed tomb and says, "Did I not tell you that if you believed you would see the glory of God?" (John 11:40), he reminds Martha—and all of us—that faith often precedes full understanding. This question reframes the obstacle not as Lazarus' death but as the disciples' lack of trust. By issuing a gentle rebuke, Jesus calls Martha out of passive lament into active partnership. Her faith had affirmed the resurrection (v. 24), yet she hesitated at the stone. Jesus' command highlights that belief must move from head to hands—trust becomes tangible action. In our own lives, we may have heard God's promises but stalled when called to obey. This directive invites us to ask, "What has Jesus already told me that I'm refusing to do?" Obedience thus becomes the soil in which God's glory springs forth. Preachers can use John 11:39 to challenge congregations: real faith doesn't wait for perfect conditions but moves forward on divine word. When we roll away our "stones," we position ourselves to witness a display of God's power far beyond our own capacity.

6.1.2 Symbolism of the Stone: Barriers of Doubt and Fear

The stone sealing Lazarus' tomb symbolizes every barrier that confines life—doubt, fear, guilt, and entrenched sin. In first-century Palestine, tombstones were heavy rock slabs designed to prevent scavengers and deter the living from entering death's domain. Spiritually, these stones represent the walls we erect around our hearts: self-protection that ultimately imprisons us. Facing a "stone" in prayer might mean confronting past trauma, admitting sin, or risking vulnerability. Like Martha, we might know Jesus' power yet demur at the smell of change (John 11:39). In therapy and counseling, identifying one's "stone" is often the first breakthrough moment. Faith communities can facilitate "stone-mapping" exercises—naming the fears that keep them from God's promises. Once a stone is identified, the next step is to call out Jesus' command and take the first act of faith. Rolling away a stone never eliminates the odor immediately, but it reveals God's power to breathe new life. By treating our barriers as removable, we learn that obedience unlocks resurrection hope.

6.1.3 Human Participation in Divine Action

The instruction to remove the stone underlines that God's miracles often require human cooperation. Jesus does not simply snap his fingers; he invites Martha and the mourners to engage physically in the process of resurrection. This divine-human partnership echoes creation itself: God speaks the world into being and commands Adam to cultivate the garden (Genesis 2:15). Our willingness to act demonstrates trust—"faith without works is dead" (James 2:17). In missional communities, this principle translates into serving neighborhoods, not waiting for missionaries to parachute in but rolling stones of neglect aside ourselves. In personal discipleship, it looks like obeying a prompt to forgive before feeling forgiven. Every act of obedience, however small, co-laborers with God's Spirit, setting the stage for his greater works (Philippians 2:12–13). Training programs can help believers recognize the spark of God's initiative and respond with concrete steps—prayer, hospitality, or advocacy. Over time, the church becomes a collective force that both listens for and enacts divine directives. In this way, obedience is not drudgery but joyful collaboration in God's redeeming mission.

6.2 Risking Ridicule: Obedience Despite Social Stench

6.2.1 Cultural Taboo of Graveyards and Decomposition (Numbers 19:11–12)

In Jewish law, contact with a corpse rendered one ritually unclean for seven days, requiring elaborate purification rites (Numbers 19:11–12). Graveyards were avoided and mourners kept at a distance to maintain communal purity.

When Jesus calls for the stone's removal, he asks his followers to ignore social taboos and embrace the stench of death. This radical hospitality modeled divine compassion that trumps ritual propriety. Today, cultures erect different taboos: mental health, addiction, domestic violence. Yet the gospel calls us into the very places we dread—hospices, homeless encampments, prisons—bearing Christ's presence into decay. Ministries that train volunteers to enter "unclean" spaces reflect this obedience. Seminary courses on urban ministry often emphasize the need to overcome social disgust to serve marginalized populations. Churches can host "stink nights," artifacts of societal fears, to rehearse stepping into discomfort for the sake of love. By embracing the stench, we echo Jesus' willingness to sacrifice social standing to roll away stones of separation and usher in resurrection life.

6.2.2 The Fear of Shame Versus the Call to Faith

Obedience can demand risking reputation. Martha and Mary knew neighbors would balk at handling a dead body; unrolling grave-clothes would be scandalous. Yet their fear of shame had to yield to faith in Jesus' command. In modern contexts, believers risk social ridicule when they publicly confess faith, advocate unpopular justice causes, or extend mercy to enemies. High-profile examples include church leaders standing for racial reconciliation or advocacy for the unborn despite backlash. Personal discipleship groups can create "courage circles" where individuals share their stones of potential shame and pray for boldness. Role-playing exercises in church workshops help members practice speaking gospel truth amid skepticism. The call to faith often clashes with fear of exclusion, but Jesus promises that those who lose their lives for his sake find true life (Matthew 16:25). Obedient partnership requires reframing shame as participation in Christ's own shame-bearing on the cross (Hebrews 12:2). In this way, the Christian community becomes a countercultural cohort that prioritizes God's approval over human applause.

6.2.3 Modern Stones: What Keeps Us from God's Power?

While ancient barriers were stones of tombs, today our stones include busyness, cynicism, and self-reliance. The relentless pace of modern life often leaves no room to hear Jesus' prompt to remove a stone. Doubt and spiritual apathy also operate like heavy lids, sealing off possibilities for divine breakthrough. Addictions and habitual sins tighten the stone's seal, making it harder to roll away. Congregations can identify common contemporary stones—technology addiction, consumerism, fear of vulnerability—and address them through teaching and small-group accountability. Spiritual retreats or digital sabbaths offer structured breaks, creating space to detect and move these stones. Counseling ministries might integrate spiritual assessments to uncover hidden obstacles to faith. Prayer gatherings that focus on "stone identification" followed by corporate actions—fasting, confession, service—model communal stone removal. By naming and confronting these modern stones, the church reawakens its expectancy for signs and wonders, ready to partner with God in rolling away the barriers to his power.

6.3 Obedience Before Understanding: Faith's Leap

6.3.1 Martha and Mary's Hesitation and Ultimate Compliance

Initially, Martha hesitates to move the stone—"Lord, by this time there will be a stench" (John 11:39)—while Mary remains at home until Jesus arrives. Their delay illustrates the tension between knowing Jesus' power and grasping its application. Yet both sisters ultimately join in rolling away the barrier (v. 41), demonstrating that obedience often follows hesitation. In our lives, we frequently wait for circumstances to make sense before acting, yet faith requires stepping out ahead of clarity. Parenting ministries teach that obedience to God's call—say, to foster care—may involve entering a messy, uncertain situation. Marriage counseling might ask couples to take a faith step—publishing wedding vows or moving in together—before they feel fully ready. Retreat leaders often encourage participants to respond to a naked prompt—saying "yes" to a specific ministry role—even without full details. As Martha and Mary discovered, the moment of obedience itself brings understanding and reveals the miracle. Churches can collect "hesitation-to-obedience" testimonies, encouraging others that when we act in faith, God expands our vision. This pattern teaches that faith's leap precedes full sight, yet yields the clarity we seek.

6.3.2 Biblical Examples of Obedience in the Dark (Abraham at Moriah)

Abraham's journey to Mount Moriah illustrates obedience without clear understanding (Genesis 22). God commanded him to offer Isaac, his promised son, as a sacrifice. Though he could not see the outcome, Abraham moved forward in blind worship. At the last moment, an angel intervenes, substituting a ram and revealing God's deeper purpose (vv. 11–12). This narrative echoes the Bethany story: human hands act to prepare for divine revelation. In discipleship contexts, studying Abraham encourages believers to trust God's voice even when the path seems contradictory to promise. Mission teams often adopt a "Moriah prayer," entrusting long-term projects to God without visible fruit, expecting his intervention. Sermons on Abraham's faith can culminate in a commitment moment, where congregants write down a "dark obedience" they sense God calling them to. The parallel between Abraham and Martha highlights that obedient partnership is a hallmark of covenant faith. As Abraham believed God could raise Isaac from the dead (Hebrews 11:19), so Martha rolled away the stone in hope of resurrection. Through this example, the church learns that obedience in the dark aligns us with God's redemptive trajectory.

6.3.3 Practices for Obedience in Uncertainty

Developing a lifestyle of bold obedience requires intentional spiritual practices. Begin with daily "small-step obedience" exercises—identifying one minor prompt from the Holy Spirit and acting immediately, whether sending an encouraging text or offering a cold cup of coffee to a neighbor. Journaling can document these steps, tracking patterns of divine guidance. Prayer partners provide accountability: committing to one obedience action and then reporting back fosters collective courage. Periodic "Obedience Sabbaths" set aside a half-day for silent listening, reviewing God's prompts without distraction. Incorporating Scripture memory—verses like Proverbs 3:5–6—anchors heart trust when clarity is lacking. Small groups can hold "Yes, Lord" nights where participants share next-step obediences before praying for each other. Retreat programs might include obstacle courses, symbolizing stones to be moved, culminating in an act of symbolic obedience. Pastors can model obedience by sharing their own "uncertain step" stories during sermons. Over time, these practices rewire the spiritual life so that the initial shock of God's call gives way to a reflexive "Yes" that moves stones and unlocks glory.

6.4 Partnership in Resurrection: God's Invitation to Co-Labor

6.4.1 Divine Initiative Meets Human Agency (Philippians 2:12–13)

Paul exhorts believers to "work out your own salvation with fear and trembling, for it is God who works in you" (Philippians 2:12–13). This dynamic confirms that while God initiates every good work—including resurrection life—he calls us to participate actively. Just as the Spirit prompted Jesus to call Lazarus forth, the same Spirit prompts our steps of faith. In practice, this means discerning God's leading in prayer and then taking tangible steps—sending that reconciliation letter, responding to a call to serve, or boldly sharing one's testimony. Church leadership teams can foster this partnership by integrating "action planning" into sermons: after preaching on a promise, invite congregants to write down and commit to one obedience task. Discipleship groups can keep "co-labor journals," tracking both God's prompts and the steps taken in response, then sharing outcomes weekly. Missions training emphasizes that God's power for revival often flows through believers' willingness to go, speak, and serve in his name. Workshops on spiritual gifts remind Christians that each gifting is an invitation to co-labor with divine power (1 Corinthians 12:4–7). In pastoral care, counselors encourage clients to list next-step actions alongside prayer requests, reinforcing that God's work unfolds in tandem with human agency. By embracing partnership, the church moves from passive spectators of miracles to active participants in God's redemptive mission.

6.4.2 "Work Out Your Salvation": Cooperative Grace (Ephesians 2:10)

Ephesians 2:10 declares that we are "created in Christ Jesus for good works, which God prepared beforehand." This verse underscores that salvation is not a reward for works but a foundation for them—grace undergirds our cooperative obedience. Rolling away stones of resistance often looks like stepping into pre-arranged "good works" that God has tailored for us. Churches can help believers discover these works by offering spiritual gift assessments and ministry placement days. Volunteer coordinators might assign newcomers to roles that align with their passions and talents, modeling Ephesians 2:10 in action. Small groups can undertake community projects—tutoring, elder visits, neighborhood clean-ups—viewing each assignment as part of the good works God prepared. Testimonies from those stepping into unexpected service roles illustrate how grace empowers cooperation. Leadership development programs train members to spot and equip others for these works, creating a relay of obedience. Pastors can regularly remind congregations that doing good is not optional but is intrinsic to our identity in Christ. As we "work out" our salvation, we see that grace and obedience dance together, producing the fruit of resurrection life in the world.

6.4.3 Equipping the Church for Hands-On Faith

Obedient partnership flourishes in communities intentionally equipped for faith in action. Leadership teams should offer regular training in spiritual disciplines—prayer, fasting, discernment—that prepare members to hear and obey God's prompts. Equipping workshops can include practical sessions:

how to host a prayer station, facilitate a small-group Stone-Mapping exercise, or organize a neighborhood "Take Away the Stone" action day. Mentorship programs pair mature believers with novices, walking alongside them through their first obedience steps. Resource libraries stocked with books on practical theology, evangelism methods, and justice initiatives provide ongoing support. Quarterly "Faith in Action" conferences bring in guest speakers who have seen God move mountains in various contexts. Tech teams can develop mobile apps that send weekly "stone removal" challenges, prompting users to act on faith. Volunteer fairs connecting church ministries with local nonprofits help members find tangible outlets for their obedience. By investing in equipping, the church ensures that when Jesus issues his call—"Take away the stone"—believers are ready and confident to obey, unlocking fresh demonstrations of God's glory.

6.5 Stones We Encounter Today: Identifying and Removing Obstacles

6.5.1 Personal Stones: Habits, Hurts, and Hang-Ups

Personal stones are the internal barriers—addictive habits, unresolved trauma, self-condemnation—that prevent us from experiencing fullness of life. Habits like chronic anger or compulsive behavior often feel immovable until confronted by God's word (Psalm 139:23–24). Hurts from past wounds—parental rejection or betrayal—can harden the heart, making faith steps terrifying (Hebrews 12:15). Hang-ups such as perfectionism or fear of failure keep us in spiritual paralysis. Identifying personal stones requires honest self-examination, perhaps aided by trusted counselors or accountability partners. Journaling prompts—"What area of my life feels most stuck?"—help surface hidden obstacles. Prayer practices like the Examen encourage noticing daily moments of resistance. Small groups can conduct "stone-mapping" retreats, combining worship, silence, and group discernment to name stones. Once identified, personal stones are removed through targeted disciplines: setting specific repentance goals, enlisting pastoral support, and celebrating every small step of obedience. As these stones roll away, we witness the power of Christ to breathe new life into every corner of our being.

6.5.2 Relational Stones: Barriers in Families and Friendships

Relational stones manifest as grudges, miscommunication, or broken trust that hinder love's flow. Family feuds—unspoken offenses or long-standing resentments—can seal relationships off like a tombstone. Friendships suffer when pride or fear prevents confession and reconciliation (Matthew 18:15–17). Identifying relational stones means asking: "What relationships feel lifeless, and why?" Role-playing exercises in safe small-group settings teach skills for initiating difficult conversations. Couples' retreats often include guided "stone removal" dialogues where partners share hurts and then pray for courage to forgive. Family ministries can provide "reconciliation kits"—scripture prompts, guided questions, and symbolic acts like breaking a plate to represent letting go. Workshops on active listening and empathy strengthen relational resilience. After relationships are reopened, ongoing commitments—regular check-ins or joint service projects— prevent stones from reforming. Church leadership can model this by publicly resolving conflicts, demonstrating grace in action. As relational stones are removed, communities experience the resurrection life of restored fellowship.

6.5.3 Corporate Stones: Structural Injustices and Institutional Sins

Corporate stones are systemic barriers—racism, poverty, environmental degradation, or institutional hypocrisy—that choke collective flourishing. These "stones" demand corporate repentance and collective action. Churches can launch "Justice Audits," examining policies and practices that perpetuate inequality. Scripture prompts such as Micah 6:8 ("Do justice, love kindness, walk humbly") guide audit criteria. Equipping sessions on advocacy train members to engage local government, support affordable housing, or campaign for criminal-justice reform. Inter-church coalitions amplify impact, as multiple congregations roll away large stones together.

Communal confession liturgies address institutional sins—past complicity in oppression or negligence toward the poor—opening the way for healing. Joint service initiatives, like community food forests or free healthcare clinics, act as living stones removal. Transparent reporting on outcomes maintains accountability and prevents reformation of corporate stones. By confronting structural evils, the church embodies the gospel's resurrection power on societal scales.

6.6 Tools for Stone Removal: Spiritual Disciplines as Instruments of Obedience

6.6.1 Prayer and Fasting: Power to Overturn Stubborn Resistance (Matthew 17:21)

Jesus indicates that some stones yield only to "prayer and fasting" (Matthew 17:21, KJV). Fasting intensifies prayer focus, dethroning idols of appetite and releasing spiritual breakthrough. Corporate fasts—24-hour or Daniel fasts—unite congregations in seeking God's mercy on communal stones. Personal fasts—food, media, even comfort—can precede critical obedience steps, sharpening sensitivity to God's leading. Prayer guides specifically designed for fasts help participants intercede for identified barriers. Small-group "fasting pods" provide accountability and mutual encouragement. Prayer vigils at sunrise or midnight dramatize spiritual urgency. Spiritual directors teach "fasting stages," from physical detox to emotional renewal to spiritual empowerment. Testimonies of breakthroughs post-fast galvanize faith for future struggles. Through prayer and fasting, believers leverage divine resources to roll away the most stubborn stones.

6.6.2 Confession and Repentance: Breaking the Hard Heart (Psalm 51:17)

Psalm 51:17 assures us that "the sacrifices of God are a broken spirit; a broken and contrite heart, O God, you will not despise." Confession cracks open the hard soil of pride and self-justification, preparing it for God's life-giving seed.

Structured confession practices—writing sins on paper and burning them, public confession services, or guided confession prompts in prayer journals—help believers face and release inner stones. Pastoral counseling uses confession to liberate clients from guilt-stone accumulation. Liturgical traditions incorporate confession liturgies before Communion, symbolizing pre-emptive stone removal. Small groups can hold "confession circles," maintaining confidentiality while experiencing collective grace. Annual "Day of Repentance" events invite the whole church to confess corporate and personal sins. Follow-up accountability pairs ensure ongoing repentance and restoration. By practicing confession and repentance, we open pathways for God's mercy to roll away stones of sin and shame.

6.6.3 Scripture Meditation: Hearing God's Voice for Next Steps

Meditatio on Scripture aligns our hearts with God's voice, revealing which stones to remove and how. Lectio divina's four steps—read, meditate, pray, contemplate—invite the Spirit to illuminate obstacles and next-step obedience. Daily scripture meditation on life-giving texts (e.g., Psalm 119:105; John 15:5) fosters sensitivity to personal stones. Church apps offering daily verse prompts can steer members into targeted meditation. Retreat centers often include "Scripture labyrinths," where participants walk and reflect on specific passages. Sermon series might distribute meditation guides alongside each message, encouraging reflection on how the text compels stone removal. Personal scripture memory of promises related to obstacles—Isaiah 43:19, Philippians 4:13—equips believers to stand firm when resistance returns. Small groups can begin meetings with shared meditation experiences, inviting fresh insights and planned obedience. By anchoring our steps in God's Word, we roll away stones with divine wisdom rather than mere human will.

6.7 Community Stones: Rolling Them Away Together

6.7.1 Small-Group Accountability in Acts of Obedience

Small groups provide a safe context in which believers can name their stones and commit to removing them together. Each member might share a specific barrier—fear of evangelism, a toxic habit, a broken relationship—and then articulate one obedience step they will take before the next gathering. Accountability partners within the group check in midweek, offering prayer and encouragement, modeling Galatians 6:2's "bear one another's burdens." Tracking progress on a shared "stone-roll chart" allows visible evidence of God's work in real time. Groups can celebrate each removal with a brief testimony and a moment of corporate praise— echoing Nehemiah's wall-building team that "read from the Book of the Law" then "celebrated with great rejoicing" (Nehemiah 8:12). When one person falters, the group prays earnestly, demonstrating 1 Thessalonians 5:11's call to "encourage one another and build each other up." Over months, these accountability rhythms cultivate an ethos of obedience and trust. Leaders should model vulnerability by sharing their own stones and next steps. Periodic "stone resets" allow members to reassess and redirect commitments, ensuring accountability remains dynamic. Through small-group partnership, individual faith steps become momentum for community transformation.

6.7.2 Corporate Liturgy: Public Confession and Shared Next Steps

Corporate gatherings can integrate confession and commitment into the worship liturgy, transforming Sunday services into communal stone-removal events. Begin with a responsive reading of Psalm 32:5 ("I acknowledged my sin to you… and you forgave the iniquity of my sin"). Offer a time of silent self-examination, then invite volunteers to stand and briefly name a "stone" they are called to remove, publicly committing to specific actions. Pastors or worship leaders pray over each confession, reminding the congregation of Jesus' promise: "Whoever confesses me before men, I will also confess before my Father" (Matthew 10:32). Liturgical elements—burning written stones in a fireproof bowl or placing stones at the foot of the cross—provide symbolic closure. Following the service, small-group facilitators distribute "next-step cards" where attendees write down their personal action and prayer support needs. Corporate liturgy ties confession to shared steps, reinforcing Ephesians 4:25's call to "each one speak truth." Quarterly "Stone Sunday" services can focus the entire congregation on removing a single corporate barrier—such as fear of evangelism or racial division—through coordinated prayer and pledge drives. Music selections echo themes of surrender ("I Surrender All") and commitment ("Take My Life and Let It Be"). By publicly confessing and committing, the church embodies transparent partnership with God and one another.

6.7.3 Social Action: Removing Stones of Injustice as the Body of Christ

When communities identify systemic stones—homelessness, human trafficking, environmental harm—the church can mobilize large-scale social action. Begin with a "Stone Summit," gathering leaders, social justice experts, and affected neighbors to map structural barriers and plan collective responses (Isaiah 58:6). Action teams then roll these stones by organizing food distribution for the hungry, legal clinics for immigrants, or habitat restoration projects. Training workshops on biblical justice (Micah 6:8) equip volunteers with theological grounding and practical skills. Partnering with NGOs and local agencies multiplies impact and provides accountability. Advocacy campaigns petition policymakers, echoing Amos 5:24's cry, "Let justice roll down like waters." Regular "impact reports" in services and newsletters keep the congregation informed and motivated. Storytelling events featuring beneficiaries of these initiatives celebrate victories and spur further investment. Social media hashtags (#RollAwayStones) and community fairs expand awareness beyond the church walls. As the body of Christ addresses corporate stones, it incarnates the gospel's power to bring resurrection life into entire neighborhoods and systems.

6.8 Testimonies of Stones Taken Away

6.8.1 Biblical Case Studies: Naaman's Cleansing (2 Kings 5)

The story of Naaman the Syrian general illustrates stone removal through obedience in humility. Stricken with leprosy—a living stone of shame—Naaman initially balks at Elisha's simple command to wash seven times in the Jordan (2 Kings 5:10–11). His resistance reflects the pride that often bars us from the most straightforward cures. Yet when he submits, his flesh "was restored like the flesh of a little child" (v. 14), demonstrating God's power to remove the most entrenched barriers. Naaman's story teaches that divine instructions may seem beneath our dignity, yet obedience unlocks healing. In discipleship settings, this case study encourages participants to name personal "pride-stones" that must be lowered. Interactive workshops can reenact Naaman's journey—walking to a local stream and symbolically washing away pretense. Pastors might preach a series on biblical cleansings, inviting congregants to consider what God calls them to humble themselves before obeying. By reflecting on Naaman's transformation, believers gain courage to roll away stones of pride and self-reliance.

6.8.2 Contemporary Stories: Confronting Cancer, Addiction, and Curiosity

Modern testimonies abound of individuals who, through a step of obedience, experienced God's power over seemingly insurmountable stones. A cancer survivor might recount how saying "yes" to an aggressive treatment plan—despite fear—led to a clear diagnosis and remission, viewing it as God's guiding hand. Those freed from addiction often describe hitting "rock bottom" before obeying an invitation to rehab and faith community, illustrating how obedience precedes deliverance. Similarly, a skeptic who obeyed a friend's invitation to church discovered insights that transformed doubt into conviction. Churches can collect these stories via video interviews, compiling a "Stone-Removal" testimony library. Small-group evenings can feature live testimonies followed by prayer for participants' own stones. Social media "Testimony Tuesdays" highlight one story each week, offering hope and illustrating obedience's fruit. Pastoral newsletters might publish written accounts with before-and-after snapshots of lives changed. Healthcare chaplains use patient testimonies to comfort those still wrestling with illness stones. These contemporary stories bridge ancient narratives and present realities, showing God's consistent invitation to partnership in stone removal.

6.8.3 Stories from Your Congregation: Celebrating Community Obedience

Every congregation has its own history of stones removed through collective faith. Whether it's revitalizing a failing ministry, paying off building debt, or halting neighborhood blight, these local narratives deserve celebration. Designate a "Stone Sunday" twice a year for laypeople to share short testimonies of community obedience. Prepare a bulletin insert or digital slideshow featuring "then and now" photos—showing a repurposed facility or cleaned-up park. Invite groups responsible for specific initiatives—youth mission trips, food pantry teams—to give firsthand accounts of God's power through their obedience. Host a community "stone removal fair" after service, with interactive booths illustrating each project's impact. Offer "thank you" certificates to volunteers as tangible recognition of their co-laboring with God. Incorporate these stories into sermon illustrations, reinforcing that churchwide obedience yields resurrection results. Publishing a yearly "Stone-Removal Report" fosters ongoing vision and gratitude. By celebrating these local obedience milestones, congregations reinforce the culture of faith-in-action and encourage future stone-rollers to answer the call.

Conclusion As the stone rolled aside and Lazarus emerged bound no more, we see the potency of faith in motion— obedience that collaborates with, rather than replaces, divine initiative. Our own "stones" may not be tomb entrances but the habits, fears, and injustices that confine life's fullness. Yet every act of faithful compliance—however small—becomes the pivot for God's power to flow. May this chapter inspire you to heed Christ's call to move whatever stands between you and the miracle waiting on the other side. In stepping forward, you become a living proof that the Author of resurrection life still writes his story through willing hands.

Chapter 7. Prayer That Thanks Before It Sees

In the stillness before the miracle, Jesus stood at the tomb of his friend, lifted his eyes to heaven, and gave thanks—though Lazarus lay dead and the world saw only stone and silence. This counterintuitive act of gratitude, uttered before any sign of resurrection, reveals a posture of faith that trusts God's heart more than human circumstances. In this chapter, we will explore how praying thanksgiving in advance aligns our souls with the purposes of heaven, shifts the atmosphere around our greatest needs, and invites the Father's glory into the darkest moments of life. Whether you face stalled dreams, persistent pain, or unanswered petitions, learning to thank God before you see the answer empowers you to walk in partnership with him, confident that he is at work even when the evidence seems hidden.

7.1 The Model in Bethany

7.1.1 Jesus' Thanksgiving over the Tomb (John 11:41–42)

Before calling Lazarus from the tomb, Jesus pauses and "lifted up his eyes and said, 'Father, I thank you that you have heard me'" (John 11:41–42). In uttering thanks prior to any visible sign of life, he demonstrates that gratitude precedes manifestation. This thanksgiving acknowledges the Father's attentive love, not the apparent silence of circumstances. By thanking God for hearing him—before Lazarus responds—Jesus models trust in God's faithfulness rather than in human timetables. His prayer occurs publicly, with mourners watching, reinforcing that anticipatory praise is a corporate act, inviting communal faith. Theologically, this thanksgiving reframes the narrative: what looks like a tragedy is refracted through praise into opportunity for divine glory. Practically, believers can learn to begin requests with thanksgiving—"Thank You, Lord, for hearing me, even though I don't yet see the answer." In small groups, you might read John 11:41–42 aloud, then share "thank-you" statements for unanswered prayers. Prayer meetings can incorporate this model by beginning intercession times with collective gratitude for God's unseen work. By following Christ's example, our thanksgiving becomes the opening chord in the symphony of resurrection hope.

7.1.2 Public Praise as a Prelude to Power

Jesus' act of thanksgiving took place before "they took away the stone" (John 11:41), in full view of onlookers carrying burial spices and tears. Public praise declares faith before friends, family, and skeptics, binding communal expectation to divine action. In Old Testament precedents, the people sang at the Red Sea's edge before the waters parted (Exodus 15:1–2), and priests marched around Jericho, sounding trumpets before the walls fell (Joshua 6). Such corporate praise sets the spiritual atmosphere, signaling to heaven that earthbound hearts are ready for breakthrough. Contemporary worship services can replicate this pattern by opening with thanksgiving declarations before moving into petition. Testimony nights that begin with "Let's thank God for what He's about to do" prime hearts for encounter. Community praise gatherings in public spaces—parks or courtyards—invite neighbors into expectancy, mirroring Bethany's open-air tomb scene. Corporate praise also guards against discouragement, as communal voices reinforce individual faith. By praising in view of all, the church forms a living cue for God's power to follow, turning public witness into prayerful preparation.

7.1.3 Anticipatory Faith Rooted in Relationship

Jesus' thanksgiving arose from intimate communion with the Father: "Father, I thank you…" He did not begin with a theological lecture but from relational connection. Anticipatory faith flows from knowing God personally, not merely from abstract promises. Martha's earlier confession—"I believe that you are the Christ" (John 11:27)—and Jesus' ongoing dialogue reveals a conversation of mutual knowledge and trust. When we thank God before seeing, we lean on relational history—past deliverances, answered prayers, and moments of guidance. Personal prayer journals can trace these moments, providing relational fuel for future thanksgiving. Spiritual formation groups might encourage members to share relational memories of God's faithfulness before asking for current needs. Devotional time that begins with recalling God's character—His goodness, sovereignty, compassion—grounds anticipatory praise. In pastoral counseling, inviting counselees to articulate personal encounters with God warms hearts toward bold thanksgiving. Thus, anticipatory faith is less a technique and more an overflow of friendship with God, in which thanks is natural even when sight is dim.

7.2 Biblical Foundations of Anticipatory Thanksgiving

7.2.1 Old Testament Examples: Hannah's Song (1 Samuel 2:1–2) and Moses (Exodus 15:1–2)

Hannah's prayer of thanksgiving following Samuel's birth begins, "My heart exults in the Lord; my horn is exalted in the Lord" (1 Samuel 2:1). Though she had endured years of barrenness, her song proclaims God's reversal of circumstances before she could see Samuel grown. Similarly, after crossing the Red Sea, Moses and the Israelites broke into a song of praise: "I will sing to the Lord, for he has triumphed gloriously" (Exodus 15:1). Their thanksgiving came at the very threshold of deliverance, waters still rippling where the Egyptian army had pursued. These Old Testament models show that praising God in advance shapes understanding of His past and present work. Liturgical traditions often include the Song of Moses (Exodus 15) and Hannah's prayer in festival readings, reminding the community of anticipatory praise. Hebrew poetry encourages early praise—Psalm 22:22 turns from lament to praise mid-psalm. By embedding these songs in teaching, faith communities learn that thankfulness before fulfillment is rooted in the Word. Personal devotions can include reading Hannah's and Moses' songs and then responding with one's own "anticipatory psalm."

7.2.2 New Testament Precedents: Feeding the Five Thousand (John 6:11) and Paul in Prison (Philippians 1:3–6)

When Jesus fed the five thousand, John notes he "gave thanks" (εὐχαριστήσας) for the loaves before distributing them (John 6:11), demonstrating thanks in anticipation of multiplication. The crowd received far more than expected; the meal became a sign pointing to Christ's identity. Similarly, Paul writes from prison, "I thank my God in all my remembrance of you" (Philippians 1:3), expressing gratitude for the Philippians' partnership even while confined. His thanksgiving fueled continued confidence that God would complete His good work in them. Pauline letters consistently pair prayer and thanksgiving (Colossians 1:3; Ephesians 1:16), modeling thankful intercession before outcomes are visible. Churches can incorporate these New Testament precedents by reading John 6:11 in communion services, encouraging gratitude before partaking. Mission organizations might share Paul's prison example in supporter updates, thanking partners in advance for provision. Faith formation curricula teaching Pauline gratitude invite students to compose thank-you prayers for their own "prison" situations— waiting jobs, healing, reconciliation. These precedents show that anticipatory thanksgiving is a New Covenant inheritance, actionable in both miraculous provision and relational perseverance.

7.2.3 Psalms of Thanksgiving Before Deliverance (Psalm 22:22–24; 40:1–3)

Psalm 22 begins with a cry of abandonment—"My God, my God, why have you forsaken me?"—yet by verse 22 transitions: "I will tell of your name to my brothers; in the midst of the congregation I will praise you." The psalmist moves from lament into anticipatory praise, declaring God's future faithfulness. Likewise, Psalm 40 recounts upward rescue: "For he drew me up from the pit... he put a new song in my mouth, a hymn of praise to our God" (vv. 1–3). The psalmist sings of a deliverance he has not yet fully experienced, trusting in God's past record. These psalms serve as liturgical models for worship services that blend lament and praise. Small groups can study Psalms 22 and 40, observing the shift from petition to promise, then compose modern "anticipatory psalms" based on personal needs. Music ministries might craft worship sets that begin in minor keys of lament before resolving into major-key anthems of praise. Prayer gatherings can include responsive readings of these psalms, reinforcing that anticipation of rescue is as biblical as retrospection on past deliverance. Thus, the Psalter teaches the church to lift its voice in gratitude even before the crescendo of salvation swells to fullness.

7.3 The Theology of Thankful Prayer

7.3.1 Thanksgiving as an Act of Trust (Hebrews 11:1)

Hebrews 11:1 defines faith as "the assurance of things hoped for, the conviction of things not seen." Offering thanksgiving for unseen answers constitutes a concrete act of that assurance: we speak as if the promise is already secured. This act of trust differs from mere optimism; it rests on God's character—His faithfulness, power, and love. When we thank God before answers arrive, we posture our hearts to receive rather than complain. Prayer ministries can teach that thanksgiving is the initial step of faith's journey, subsequent to confession and petition. In discipleship, participants practice writing "thank-you prayers" for promises they claim from Scripture. Worship teams might intersperse spontaneous thanksgiving declarations during intercession, modeling faith in action. Counselors can use "faith statements" to help clients replace anxious self-talk with scripture-based thanksgiving. By defining thanksgiving as faith, we shift prayer from transactional requests to relational trust, deepening our dependence on God's promises.

7.3.2 Revealing God's Character through Praise (Psalm 100:4)

Psalm 100:4 exhorts worshippers to "Enter his gates with thanksgiving, and his courts with praise! Give thanks to him; bless his name!" Thankful prayer reveals and magnifies God's attributes—His goodness, mercy, sovereignty, and grace—turning attention from self to God. As we thank him in advance, we declare confidence in those attributes, reinforcing our understanding of his nature. Theological education can incorporate praise catalogs—lists of God's names and attributes—so congregants have language for anticipatory gratitude. Family devotions might include rotating focus on different divine names—Jehovah Jireh for provision, Jehovah Rapha for healing—pausing to offer thanks in advance. Liturgies that place praises of God's character before individual petitions cultivate the priority of God over need.

Prayer card decks featuring a name and a prayer prompt assist individuals in praising God's nature daily. By making God's character the centerpiece of prayer, we ensure thanksgiving aligns with divine reality rather than fickle feelings.

7.3.3 Thanksgiving in Suffering: Light in Darkness (1 Thessalonians 5:18)

Paul instructs believers to "give thanks in all circumstances; for this is the will of God in Christ Jesus for you" (1 Thessalonians 5:18). Thanksgiving amid suffering is a radical trust that God is working good even through pain. Martyrs and persecuted churches throughout history have embodied this, singing hymns in prisons and writing letters of gratitude despite hardship. In pastoral counseling, encouraging clients to name "gifts in the trial"—strengths acquired, relationships deepened—offers tangible starting points for gratitude. Support groups for chronic illness or grief can start each session by sharing one thing they can thank God for, reframing focus toward divine presence. Journaling prompts like "Today I thank You, Lord, for..." invite mourners to practice gratitude muscles. Worship songs that recount God's faithfulness—"It Is Well with My Soul"—provide language for praise in darkness. Teaching 1 Thessalonians 5:18 in youth groups equips young believers to develop resilience through gratitude. By thanking God in suffering, we shine light into darkness, affirming that God's hands hold both our wounds and our praises.

7.4 Power Dynamics: How Thanks Shifts Atmosphere

7.4.1 Spiritual Warfare through Praise (2 Chronicles 20:22)

In 2 Chronicles 20, King Jehoshaphat appointed singers to lead the army into battle, declaring "Give thanks to the Lord, for his steadfast love endures forever" before any arrows flew (v. 21). As they praised, God routed the enemy without their raising a sword, demonstrating that praise can precede and effect victory. Thanksgiving disarms the enemy's schemes by affirming God's sovereignty, turning our focus from fear to faith. In spiritual warfare prayer, opening with communal thanksgiving—"Thank You, Lord, that You have already won this battle"—creates a protective hedge around intercession (Psalm 149:6–9). Worship teams can intersperse adoration songs within deliverance prayers, echoing Jehoshaphat's strategy. Deliverance ministries often begin sessions with declarations of God's unchanging love and power, releasing peace into anxious hearts. Testimonies of breakthroughs shared mid-prayer time reinforce collective confidence in God's triumph. Personal prayer warriors are encouraged to memorize 2 Chronicles 20:22 as a "battle hymn," singing it mentally when facing spiritual attacks. By engaging praise as warfare, the church wields thanksgiving not as passive sentiment but as an active weapon that shifts the spiritual atmosphere toward victory.

7.4.2 Physiological and Emotional Benefits of Gratitude (Philippians 4:6–7)

Paul urges believers, "Do not be anxious about anything, but in everything by prayer and supplication with thanksgiving let your requests be made known to God. And the peace of God, which surpasses all understanding, will guard your hearts and your minds in Christ Jesus" (Philippians 4:6–7). Contemporary research confirms that expressing gratitude lowers cortisol levels, reduces blood pressure, and improves sleep quality— physical manifestations of God's promised peace. Emotionally, thanksgiving rewires neural pathways, shifting from threat-focused to hope-focused cognition. Prayer groups can incorporate guided gratitude exercises—listing three things to thank God for before sharing prayer requests—to activate these benefits. Christian counseling integrates gratitude journals into therapy plans, helping clients manage anxiety and depression through regular thankfulness. Worship leaders can explain Philippians 4:6–7 in teaching moments, linking scientific findings with spiritual truths. Congregations might host "Peace Nights," combining gratitude meditation with prayer for personal concerns. Youth ministries can create "Gratitude Challenges," incentivizing teens to text daily thank-you notes to God and observe resulting emotional shifts. By embedding gratitude into prayer, believers experience the physiological peace that mirrors the spiritual peace Paul describes.

7.4.3 Creating a Culture of Expectancy

A church that expects God to move cultivates anticipation through routine thanksgiving. Leaders can invite congregants to begin each service by sharing one "thank-you-before-it's-seen," training hearts to expect answers. Bulletin boards or digital walls listing ongoing prayer requests and pre-thanksgivings reinforce community expectancy. Monthly "Expectant Prayer Retreats" guide participants through silence, Scripture, and anticipatory praise, deepening corporate hunger for breakthroughs. Teaching series on "Faith that Sees the Invisible" can pair Bible study with personal gratitude practice, weaving expectancy into discipleship. Small groups can adopt "Thank-You Drills," where each member names a promised answer they're thanking God for, fostering mutual encouragement. Leadership should model expectancy by publicly celebrating "stones about to be moved" alongside testimonies of past answers. Visual cues—like an empty tomb sculpture in the foyer—remind all that God delights to honor anticipatory praise. Over time, gratitude becomes the air the congregation breathes, sustaining a culture where faith rises, not from circumstances, but from confident expectation in God's character.

7.5 Practices for Anticipatory Thanksgiving

7.5.1 Gratitude Journaling with Future Promises (Psalm 119:49–50)

Psalm 119:49–50 reads, "Remember your word to your servant, in which you have made me hope. This is my comfort in my affliction, that your promise gives me life." A gratitude journal that pairs today's struggles with specific Scripture promises—"I'm thanking You for provision (Philippians 4:19) even before I see it"—anchors hope in God's written word.

Each entry begins with naming the promise, followed by a heartfelt "Thank You, Lord, for..." and space to record any small signs of movement. Over weeks and months, these journals become living chronologies of God's faithfulness, reinforcing expectancy. Faith formation groups can integrate guided journaling workshops, teaching participants to select promises relevant to their needs. Digital journal apps with Scripture tagging enable searchable records, so believers can revisit entries when doubt resurfaces. Retreat centers might offer printed "promise journals" with curated verses and writing prompts. Celebrating journal milestones—like filling a book—at church gatherings fosters collective thanksgiving. By scripting anticipatory gratitude alongside promises, we cultivate the habit of thanking God in advance and watching Him fulfill His word.

7.5.2 Declarative Prayers: Speaking God's Word Aloud (Romans 4:17)

Paul affirms that God "calls into existence the things that do not exist" (Romans 4:17), inviting believers to speak faith over voids. Declarative prayer involves proclaiming Scripture promises as present reality—"I speak healing over my body, for by his wounds I am healed" (Isaiah 53:5)—before symptoms subside. In prayer gatherings, leaders can guide the congregation in corporate declarations, using call-and-response formats to reinforce collective voice. Recording audio or video of these declarations allows members to replay and internalize God's word. Training on voice and posture shows how bold speech, backed by Scripture, carries spiritual weight. Small groups might practice "Word and Worship" nights, alternating declaration with song until hearts align with spoken truth. Christian schools can introduce daily "declaration time," where students recite foundational verses over campus needs. Integrating declarations into crisis prayer—instead of only lament—shifts the dynamic from pleading to partnering. Through speaking God's word aloud, believers activate the creative power behind Romans 4:17, aligning speech with divine initiative.

7.5.3 "Thank-You" Rituals: Candles, Stones, or Symbols (Joshua 4:1–7)

In Joshua 4, twelve stones erected at Gilgal served as memorials of God's faithfulness in crossing the Jordan. Similarly, "thank-you" rituals create tangible reminders of promised answers. Lighting a candle each time you give thanks for a future promise symbolizes the dawn of anticipated breakthrough. Writing prayer requests on stones and stacking them by your bedside marks the physical removal of barriers in time. Churches can provide "symbol kits"—small candles, stones, or cards—during prayer events for congregants to take home. Family devotions may include placing "thank-you stones" in a jar, then exchanging them on Watch Night to celebrate fulfilled promises. Creative arts ministries can host workshops where participants craft personalized symbols of gratitude—woven bracelets, painted tiles—to anchor anticipatory thankfulness. Prayer rooms with symbolic stations engage all senses, reinforcing thanksgiving in the body, not just the mind. Over time, these physical reminders train our reflex to respond with thanks when God moves, and to trust when He seems silent. Through ritual, anticipatory thanksgiving becomes a multi-sensory practice that imprints faith on our everyday environments.

7.6 Thanksgiving in Intercession

7.6.1 Mapping Prayer Requests with Scriptural Anchors (Ephesians 6:18)

Ephesians 6:18 calls believers to "pray at all times in the Spirit, with all prayer and supplication. To that end keep alert with all perseverance." Mapping prayer requests alongside relevant Scriptures transforms lists into faith-filled intercession. Create a "prayer map" chart: column one lists needs, column two records corresponding promises (e.g., John 14:27 for peace), column three holds "thank-you" statements anticipating each promise's fulfillment. Prayer teams use these maps to guide sessions—first reading the need, then the anchor verse, then giving thanks for the outcome. Digital tools like shared spreadsheets or prayer apps can host these maps for collective use. Pastors can teach mapping in prayer workshops, demonstrating how to weave promises into petitions. Intercessory retreats can include guided sessions on creating and reviewing prayer maps, ensuring numbers of requests don't obscure the necessity of anchored thanksgiving. As requests shift from vague pleas to promise-based petitions, intercession deepens in expectancy. Mapping thus fuses thanksgiving with intercession, enabling Ephesians 6:18's Spirit-led vigilance to bear fruit in answered prayers.

7.6.2 SOAP Method Enriched by Gratitude (Psalm 145:7)

The SOAP (Scripture, Observation, Application, Prayer) meditation method gains power when suffused with gratitude. After reading Scripture, one notes Thanksgiving observations: "I thank God for..." before noting applications. Using Psalm 145:7 ("They shall celebrate your abundant goodness and shall sing aloud of your righteousness"), participants record specific "goodness" moments even within their prayer focus. For application, one writes "Because of this promise, I will..." followed by a declaration of thanks in the prayer section: "Thank You, Lord, that I will be strengthened to obey." Small groups can practice SOAP together, sharing gratitude insights before praying. Journals with dedicated "Thanksgiving" sections alongside each SOAP entry keep thanksgiving front and center. Digital devotionals might integrate a gratitude prompt into each day's SOAP guide. Training on reflective practice emphasizes that gratitude reveals God's character and motivates obedience. By enriching SOAP with thanksgiving, prayer becomes not only structured but saturated with faith that thanks before it sees.

7.6.3 Testimony Breaks: Celebrating Small Answers Mid-Prayer

Long intercession sessions can lose momentum without punctuated reminders of God's faithfulness. Incorporating "testimony breaks"—short interjections where participants share even minor answers—rekindles gratitude and renews expectancy. After a set time of petition, pause to invite quick testimonies: a changed heart, a timely provision, a scripture suddenly meaningful. Each testimony is followed by a brief collective "Thank You!" or singing a line from a gratitude hymn. Prayer leaders can schedule testimony segments at regular intervals—every 15 minutes in intensive prayer gatherings. Digital prayer forums can encourage participants to post real-time testimonies in chat, keeping the atmosphere charged with praise. Small groups might use a "prayer wheel," rotating the focus and inviting a fresh testimony each turn. These breaks prevent discouragement, anchor prayer in past faithfulness, and model Luke 17:15–16's grateful leper returning to give thanks. By celebrating small answers mid-prayer, the church sustains joy and vigilance, affirming that even partial breakthroughs warrant gratitude and fuel continued intercession.

7.7 Liturgical and Corporate Expressions

7.7.1 Responsive Thanksgiving Litanies (Revelation 11:17)

Responsive litanies invite congregations into active participation, alternating leader and assembly rejoicing in God's character and promises. Revelation 11:17 models this form: "We give you thanks… because you have taken your great power and begun to reign." Crafting a Thanksgiving Litany begins with cataloging divine attributes—faithfulness, mercy, sovereignty—and pairing each with a corporate response: "Leader: We thank you, O Lord, for your steadfast love; Congregation: Your mercy endures forever." Litanies can draw on biblical poetry—Psalm 100's calls to "enter his gates with thanksgiving"—and include modern testimonies as inserted responses. Seasonal litanies align with church calendar themes: Advent expectations of the Messiah, Lent's trust amid trial, Easter's triumphal thanks in advance of the empty tomb. Worship planners schedule these litanies early in service, setting an anticipatory tone before readings or sermons. Training lay leaders to read litany parts fosters shared ownership of corporate praise. Including moments of silent sung responses—using a single chord or "Amen"—accentuates the communal heartbeat of expectancy. Musicians can support litanies with soft instrumental beds, allowing voices to carry the weight of thanksgiving. Regularly rotating litany texts prevents rote repetition, ensuring fresh engagement with God's manifold goodness.

7.7.2 Incorporating Psalms of Praise into Services (Psalm 136)

Psalm 136, with its repeated refrain "for his steadfast love endures forever," serves as an ideal corporate thanksgiving tool. Worship teams can teach the congregation to sing or recite each verse-refrain pair, anchoring praise in God's enduring mercy. To deepen engagement, break the psalm into sections—creation (vv. 4–9), deliverance (vv. 10–22), and provision (vv. 23–25)—and rotate between chant, spoken word, and congregational singing. Visual projections of psalm texts paired with evocative imagery—sunrises over mountains, parting seas—reinforce thematic connections. Choirs and small ensembles might present motet-style settings of the refrain interspersed with instrumental responses. During Thanksgiving or Harvest services, Psalm 136 can underscore testimonies of seasonal provision, leading into altar calls of anticipatory praise. Sermons on corporate gratitude can unpack the psalm's theology, highlighting how each act of creation and redemption elicits thanksgiving. Children's choirs can learn simplified refrains, inviting all ages into the practice. Midweek services called "Psalms & Praise" can focus exclusively on singing multiple Psalms of thanksgiving. By embedding psalms of praise into liturgy, the church rehearses biblical patterns of anticipatory gratitude and aligns its voice with generations of worshippers.

7.7.3 Feast Days Focused on Anticipatory Praise

Feast days—biblical celebrations mandated by God—offer rhythms for anticipatory thanksgiving. The Feast of Ingathering (Deuteronomy 16:15) taught Israel to rejoice at harvest's start, thanking God in advance for completed gathering. Churches can establish modern "Feast Days" for prayer initiatives: a monthly "Feast of Faith" where the community fasts, prays, and thanks God for breakthroughs yet to come. On such days, worship services center on anticipatory liturgies—reading prophetic promises (e.g., Joel 2:25–26) and giving thanks for their fulfillment. Communal meals following the service reinforce the feast motif, with prayers of thanksgiving before and after each course. Integration with global church calendar—World Communion Sunday, Thanksgiving Sunday—unites local congregations with the wider body. Small groups can hold home-based feasts, inviting neighbors to share food, testimony, and anticipatory praise. Digital gatherings on these days use virtual breakout "feast rooms" where participants light candles and share pre-thanksgivings. Churches might create symbol-laden "feast altars" with harvest produce, candles, and written promises for people to place on the altar as anticipatory offerings. By reclaiming feast days for anticipatory praise, communities embed gratitude into a liturgical architecture that transcends seasons, anchoring hope in God's unfolding story.

7.8 Small-Group and Family Rhythms

7.8.1 "Gratitude Circles" for Shared Expectation

Gratitude Circles are small-group gatherings structured around mutual thanksgiving for future promises. Begin each meeting by forming a physical circle, lighting a single central candle to symbolize God's promise. Invite each member to share one Scripture promise they are thanking God for in advance—a pattern drawn from Romans 4:17's "calls into being… the things that do not exist." After each sharing, the group responds with "Amen—Thank You, Lord!" reinforcing communal affirmation. Rotate leadership weekly so every person practices guiding the circle and praying for the next member's promise. Incorporate short silence between shares, allowing space for personal reflection and the Holy Spirit's prompting. Track shared promises in a communal notebook, revisiting them monthly to celebrate any movement or answered praise. Introduce simple "objects" like index cards with written promises placed under the candle, visually reminding the circle of ongoing expectations. Encourage group members to text or call one another mid-week with thanksgiving updates, sustaining momentum. Through consistent Gratitude Circles, small groups cultivate a shared culture of anticipatory faith, emboldened to witness God's unfolding answers together.

7.8.2 Family "Thank-You" Jars for Daily Practice

Families can nurture anticipatory thanksgiving by placing a jar in a central location—kitchen counter or living room shelf—labeled "Thank-You Jar." Each day, family members write on slips of paper what they're thanking God for in advance—answers to prayer, upcoming events, or growth in character. During family devotions or meals, choose one or two slips to read aloud, then pray a brief collective "Thank You" over those items. Parents can guide children to pick verses from a family "Promise Bowl," inscribed on stones with promises like Jeremiah 29:11 or Matthew 6:33, and then add that promise to the jar with a pre-thanksgiving note. At month's end, open the jar and review promises: have any been fulfilled, partially answered, or revealed in unexpected ways? This review becomes a celebratory family festival, perhaps accompanied by a special dessert. Record fulfilled promises in a "Praise Wall" picture frame nearby, encouraging children to connect prayer, praise, and provision. Holiday seasons provide natural expansion—letting extended family write "thank-you" notes to place in the jar during reunions. By making anticipatory gratitude tangible and routine, families train hearts to see God's hand moving even before answers arrive.

7.8.3 Digital Walls of Thanks: Virtual Testimony Platforms

In our connected age, digital walls of thanks extend worship beyond physical walls. Platforms such as church intranets, social media groups, or dedicated apps can host "Virtual Gratitude Walls" where members post GIFs, images, or text statements of thanks for future promises. Each post tags a Bible verse and the anticipated answer date, enabling others to pray and follow up. Moderators curate highlights into weekly "Thankful Thursday" newsletters, amplifying community expectancy. Live-stream prayer events can integrate chat-based "thank-you" reposts, displaying them on screen to spur online and in-person participants. Devotional apps send push notifications prompting users to add new anticipatory thanks or celebrate past entries. Virtual walls can be organized by categories—healing, provision, reconciliation—helping users navigate needs and join intercession. Regular webinars teach how to craft effective digital testimonies that combine transparency, theological grounding, and hope. Privacy settings allow sensitive needs to be kept within small groups, maintaining confidentiality while fostering trust. Through digital walls of thanks, prayer communities transcend geography, weaving anticipatory gratitude into the digital fabric of daily life.

7.9 Overcoming Obstacles to Thankful Prayer

7.9.1 Distinguishing Presumption from Faith (James 4:13–16)

James warns against boasting of tomorrow—"Come now, you who say, 'Today or tomorrow we will...'—yet you do not know what tomorrow will bring" (James 4:13–14). Anticipatory thanksgiving risks sliding into presumption if divorced from humble dependence on God's timing. True faith acknowledges uncertainty—"If the Lord wills, we will live and do this or that" (v. 15)—while still offering thankfulness for his promised work. Teaching on this balance helps prayer groups avoid rote "I'm expecting X" statements that ignore divine sovereignty. Small-group facilitators can introduce checklists distinguishing presumption ("God must...") from faith ("God can... and I trust He will"). Incorporating confession prompts— "Forgive me for presuming upon Your will"—prevents arrogance in prayer. Devotional writers can model conditional thanksgiving—"Thank You for the provision You will bring, Lord willing"—demonstrating reverent expectancy. Sermon series on wisdom literature (Proverbs 16:9) reinforce humility in planning and praising. Personal prayer journaling includes margin notes of "Lord willing" to temper certainty with submission. By distinguishing presumption from faith, believers secure their anticipatory thanks in genuine trust rather than unchecked entitlement.

7.9.2 Acknowledge Grief While Giving Thanks (Ecclesiastes 3:4)

Ecclesiastes 3:4 reminds us there is "a time to weep, and a time to laugh; a time to mourn, and a time to dance." Thankful prayer does not banish grief but holds both lament and gratitude in tension. In practice, prayer models can begin with "Let us weep together over…" before moving to "Let us thank God for…" acknowledging both present pain and future hope. Support groups for trauma survivors incorporate "lamentful thanksgiving," offering space to express sorrow then pivot to anticipation of God's healing. Worship services may include a lament psalm (Psalm 42) followed by a thanksgiving chorus (Psalm 30:11–12). Pastors can teach that laments themselves are prayers laden with expectation—"How long, O Lord? Yet I will hope in You" (Psalm 13:5). In family rhythms, parents validate children's tears before guiding them into "thank-you" prayers for comfort promised in Scripture. Counseling sessions might assign "grief letters" to God alongside "gratitude letters," then unify them in prayer. Art therapy in churches uses dual canvases: one for grief imagery, one for thanksgiving symbols. By acknowledging grief while giving thanks, the church practices holistic prayer that honors present reality and embraces future deliverance.

7.9.3 Counteracting Cultural Skepticism toward Praise

Contemporary culture often views overt praise as naïve or gimmicky. To counter skepticism, the church must demonstrate that anticipatory thanksgiving is rooted in rich tradition and sound theology. Educational workshops can present historical practices—Old Testament songs, early church eucharistic thanksgiving—as foundations rather than novelty. Testimonies of scientific studies on gratitude's benefits lend credibility to faith-based thankfulness. Public events like "Praise in the Park" show that gratitude gatherings can be culturally relevant and authentic, drawing curious onlookers. Media teams produce short videos explaining the spiritual logic of thanking God before answers, framing it as an act of trust, not delusion. Leaders must model sober, reflective praise—avoiding "happy-clappy" tropes that fuel cynicism—while maintaining joy in the Lord. Encouraging questions and open dialogue about the rationale for anticipatory gratitude builds trust. Research partnerships with local universities on the psychology of gratitude reinforce the church's practices. By addressing skepticism thoughtfully and transparently, the church fosters an environment where anticipatory praise is both respected and practiced widely.

Conclusion As we bring our journey through anticipatory thanksgiving to a close, may you carry with you the liberating truth that praise is not merely a response to what God has done but a declaration of what he will do. When you speak thanks in the face of fear, you fasten your hope to God's unchanging character and open the door for his power to break through. Let this practice become the drumbeat of your prayer life: a steady rhythm of trust that beckons resurrection where there is death, provision where there is lack, and joy where there is despair. Go forth, offering gratitude before you see, and watch as the stone rolls away—not by your strength, but by the loving hand of the One who delights to answer the prayers of a thankful heart.

Chapter 8. "Unbind Him and Let Him Go" — Ministry of Release

As Jesus commands the bystanders to "unbind him and let him go," we witness the final act in a cascade of resurrection power—an invitation not only to remove grave-clothes but to release a life into its full potential. This moment encapsulates the heart of ministry: setting captives free from whatever entangles them, whether chains of past sins, fears that shackle the soul, or systemic injustices that restrict whole communities. In this chapter, we will explore how the church is called to partner with Christ in unbinding every form of bondage, moving from compassion that sees pain to action that delivers freedom. From personal healing to societal transformation, the ministry of release reflects God's redemptive design, empowering individuals and collectives to walk unencumbered into the abundant life Christ intends.

8.1 The Command to Unbind: From Tomb to Freedom

8.1.1 Jesus' Final Instruction (John 11:44)

After commanding life from the tomb, Jesus turns to the bystanders with a precise order: "Unbind him, and let him go" (John 11:44). This instruction completes the resurrection act, moving Lazarus from passive recipient to active participant in his own freedom. The command assumes that disciples will move Lazarus's grave-clothes—strips that once signified death—so he can walk freely. It underscores that divine miracles often culminate in human responsibility: God brings life, but we must remove the bindings. In ministry, we too hear Christ's voice calling us to unbind those he has quickened— releasing them from sins, fears, or oppressive systems. This directive models spiritual authority: Jesus gives both the power (to raise) and the commission (to unbind), teaching that release ministry flows from Christ's lordship. Liturgically, this moment has inspired "unbinding" rituals, where participants symbolically remove cloths or ties representing personal shackles. Pastoral teams can replicate this pattern in counseling sessions—after a prayer of deliverance, clients physically remove items (journals, chains) that symbolize old bondage. In worship, leaders may invite congregants to come forward and lay down burdens at the altar, acting out Jesus' command. Thus, John 11:44 becomes the blueprint: God raises, we unbind, and the newly liberated step into abundant life.

8.1.2 Tomb-Bands as Symbols of Bondage

The linen cloths and burial shrouds that bound Lazarus represent more than physical restraints; they symbolize any force that holds people captive. In ancient Jewish burial, tomb-bands were long strips wrapped tightly, ensuring the dead remained sealed. Spiritually, these bands parallel guilt that constricts the conscience (Hebrews 10:22), shame that imprisons identity (Romans 8:1), and patterns of habit that ensnare the will (John 8:34). When Jesus commands "unbind him," he calls us to identify and remove the metaphorical wrappings that choke life—addiction, unforgiveness, fear of rejection. In deliverance ministry, leaders teach participants to visualize these bands as part of their testimony and to pray for Christ to loosen each knot. Art therapy workshops may use strips of cloth that participants tie around a model or silhouette, then physically cut or unwrap them in prayer, embodying unbinding. In pastoral counseling, asking clients to write their sins or fears on strips of paper and then ceremonially discard them enacts release. The imagery also extends to institutional bindings—policies and structures that restrict community flourishing—urging churches to dismantle systemic oppression. By viewing tomb-bands as universal symbols of bondage, the church gains a versatile metaphor for both personal and corporate release ministry.

8.1.3 Immediate Obedience and Its Impact

The crowds do not debate Jesus' command; they immediately roll away the stone and loosen Lazarus' grave-clothes. This swift obedience highlights the importance of prompt faith in the ministry of release. Delay or doubt after a divine directive risks prolonging bondage, whereas immediate action clears the way for full restoration. Similarly, when individuals receive a word of knowledge or inner prompting to forgive, reconcile, or break a sinful pattern, prompt obedience prevents the re-entrenchment of the very chains God wants to break. Training sessions for deliverance teams emphasize the "moment of obedience"—the split-second decision to act in faith. Congregational workshops might simulate this by giving participants symbolic directives (e.g., unwrapping a prepared "burial cloth" package) to practice responsive trust. Testimonies reflecting on lives radically changed by immediate obedience—leaving abusive relationships, entering recovery programs—underscore its transformative power. Theologically, James 1:22–25 warns against being hearers only; unbinding requires doing. When the church embraces immediate obedience, it becomes a community where freedom is consistently activated, and people learn to trust God's voice enough to act without hesitation.

8.2 Biblical Models of Release

8.2.1 The Exodus: Pharaoh's Deliverance of Israel (Exodus 12:31–42)

God's first great act of national unbinding occurs when Pharaoh finally says, "Go, serve the Lord" after the Passover judgment (Exodus 12:31). Israel had been bound for centuries in Egyptian slavery—forced labor, broken families, and oppressive taxes. The Passover lamb's blood signified deliverance, yet liberation required action: lining up at the border and marching into the wilderness. Moses served as God's agent, instructing Israel to break their domestic bondage by gathering provisions, smearing blood on doorposts, and departing immediately (Exodus 12:11). Their obedient exodus reveals ministry of release as a partnership: divine power to liberate and human responsibility to move. In modern liberation theology, Exodus serves as the paradigm for fighting systemic injustice—churches advocate for victims of human trafficking or mass incarceration, echoing Moses' intercession before Pharaoh. Bible studies on Exodus draw parallels between Israel's bondage and today's marginalized communities, teaching advocacy as unbinding. Visual drama in churches—recreating the Red Sea crossing—immerses participants in the Exodus narrative. By studying Israel's deliverance, the church learns that ministry of release can transform entire peoples, not only individuals.

8.2.2 Release from Spiritual Bondage: Paul and Silas (Acts 16:25–34)

In Philippi, Paul and Silas find themselves imprisoned—chains, stocks, and a guard maintaining order. Yet at midnight, they pray and sing hymns (v. 25), unleashing spiritual power that shakes the prison's foundations and opens every door (v. 26). Their release is both divine intervention and human participation: the jailer, awakened and witnessing the miracle, asks how to be saved (v. 30), then washes their wounds and houses them (v. 33). This narrative illustrates that unbinding ministry often results in both physical liberation and spiritual emancipation. Churches can emulate this model by combining worship with intercession in prayer gatherings focused on spiritual strongholds—addiction, demonic oppression, legalism. Freedom groups use psalms and hymns in deliverance meetings to activate the same spiritual dynamics. Urban ministries might hold "Midnight Praise" events in neighborhoods plagued by violence, praying and singing until breakthrough occurs. The jailer's conversion reminds us that release ministry often leads to evangelistic opportunities. By following Paul and Silas' example, believers learn that prayerful praise opens prisons—literal and spiritual—and brings captives into the family of God.

8.2.3 Forgiveness as Unbinding: Parable of the Unforgiving Servant (Matthew 18:21–35)

Jesus' parable tells of a servant forgiven a vast debt by his master, only to refuse releasing a fellow servant's small debt (Matthew 18:32–34). The master's subsequent judgment—binding the unforgiving servant and casting him into prison—reveals that failing to unbind others condemns oneself. Forgiveness thus functions as ministry of release: letting go of someone's offense unbinds both parties from the bonds of resentment. Counseling ministries teach "forgiveness exercises," where participants list hurts and symbolically forgive offenders—tearing up lists or releasing stones into water. Small groups might facilitate guided conversations on Matthew 18's implications, stressing that bitterness is a self-binding chain. Pastoral care resources—workbooks and online modules—guide individuals through steps of forgiveness, reconciliation, and restoration. Corporate confession services on "Forgiveness Sunday" integrate prayer and symbolic foot-washing, emphasizing mutual release. By linking forgiveness to unbinding, the church practices liberation not only from external chains but from internal prison bars of unforgiveness, embodying Christ's grace to both forgive and set free.

8.3 Identifying Modern Bindings

8.3.1 Emotional Bindings: Guilt, Shame, and Fear

Emotional bindings manifest as internal prisons where guilt, shame, or fear restrict joy and obedience. Guilt binds conscience under the weight of past sin (Romans 8:1), while shame convinces the soul it is unworthy of God's love (Isaiah 54:4). Fear—of failure, rejection, or the future—paralyzes potential (2 Timothy 1:7). Emotional unbinding ministry begins with safe spaces for lament and confession, recognizing wounds before healing. Inner-healing prayer models guide participants to dialogue with Jesus about painful memories, inviting him to loosen the grip of shame. Cognitive-behavioral Christian counseling integrates Scripture to reframe false beliefs—replacing "I am unlovable" with "I am loved with an everlasting love" (Jeremiah 31:3). Worship gatherings include testimonies of emotional breakthrough, encouraging others to trust God's love over past failures. Creative arts—journaling, painting—help externalize internal chains before ceremonially releasing them. Pastors preach messages on freedom from fear, urging congregations to walk in the liberty Christ purchased. By identifying and addressing emotional bindings, the church becomes a sanctuary where hearts are unshackled and emotions realigned to God's truth.

8.3.2 Relational Bindings: Unhealthy Attachments and Codependency

Relational bindings occur when ties to people—family, spouses, friends—become unhealthy, leading to codependency or toxic control. Scripture warns against bound partnerships: "Do not be unequally yoked" (2 Corinthians 6:14), urging believers to maintain Christ-first relationships. Codependency often masquerades as care but results in mutual bondage, enabling destructive patterns. Ministry of release includes teaching on healthy boundaries, integration of emotional maturity curricula, and support groups for adult children of dysfunctional families. Pastoral counseling offers attachment-based interventions, helping individuals unbind from controlling relationships. Divorce care ministries address the release process for those leaving unhealthy marriages. Small groups discuss relational health in light of biblical commands to love but not enslave (Matthew 18:15–17). Leadership training includes conflict mediation skills, enabling churches to intervene when relational bindings endanger spiritual health. By identifying and unbinding relational chains, the church upholds both compassion and boundary integrity, freeing members to flourish in Christ-centered connections.

8.3.3 Systemic Bindings: Oppression, Injustice, and Poverty

Beyond personal and relational chains, entire communities can be bound by systemic injustices—racism, economic exploitation, or political oppression. Biblical examples of God shattering shackles (Psalm 146:7) inspire modern advocacy. The church must diagnose and confess corporate sins— segregation, economic disparity—and commit to unbinding through justice initiatives (Isaiah 1:17). Community listening sessions uncover local "stones" of injustice, generating grassroots action plans. Partnerships with legal aid organizations and social service agencies facilitate systemic change. Educational programs teach congregants about advocacy tools—lobbying, peaceful protest, policy research— equipping them to unbind structures of poverty and discrimination. Churches can host "Justice and Mercy" summits, aligning compassion ministries with systemic interventions. Case study workshops analyze successful unbinding campaigns—abolition of slavery, civil rights movements—drawing lessons for today. By tackling systemic bindings, the church extends release ministry from individual souls to societal transformation, embodying the kingdom's larger vision of restored creation.

8.4 Principles of Ministry of Release

8.4.1 Empathy Before Action: Entering the Prison of Another's Pain

Effective release ministry begins with empathetic engagement—Jesus first wept (John 11:35) before he acted. Empathy requires willingly entering another's emotional or spiritual confinement, listening without judgment to understand the nature of their bondage. In pastoral care, this looks like creating confidential environments where individuals can share wounds—abuse, addiction, or fear—without fear of shame. Training in active listening (James 1:19) equips ministry teams to reflect back feelings and needs, validating the person's experience before moving to intervention. Empathy also demands cultural sensitivity, recognizing how social stigma or trauma histories shape each person's stones of bondage. In inner-healing prayer models, counselors first walk prayers of lament and blessing through a person's story, ensuring that theological truth meets lived reality. Community immersion—spending time in neighborhoods affected by systemic oppression—deepens understanding beyond surface charity. Empathy prevents premature action that can retraumatize; only after truly grasping the chains can one call forth release effectively. By entering the prison of another's pain, ministers mirror Christ's compassion (Matthew 9:36) and lay the groundwork for authentic unbinding.

8.4.2 Authority of the Name: "In Jesus' Name, Be Loosed" (Luke 10:17–19)

Jesus empowered his disciples, saying, "By your name...demons are subject to you" (Luke 10:17–19). In ministry of release, invoking the name of Jesus carries divine authority to break every chain—spiritual, emotional, or relational. This is not magical formula but reliance on Christ's victory over evil (Philippians 2:9–11). Training in deliverance ministry emphasizes understanding legal authority—ensuring no hidden unconfessed sin or ungodly vow gives demonic footholds, as depicted in Mark 6:7–13. Prayer sessions often include corporate declarations: "In Jesus' name, I break every chain of fear," anchoring release in Christ's finished work. Testimonies of healed addictions and transformed lives underscore the name's power when coupled with faith (Mark 16:17). Worship teams can integrate simple choruses—"Jesus, Name Above All Names"—to reinforce authority in song. Virtual prayer rooms train intercessors to lead people through naming Jesus over specific struggles. Theologically, preaching on Luke 10:19 grounds practical ministry in biblical precedent, preventing overreliance on technique. By wielding the name of Jesus with understanding and faith, the church channels God's power to unbind captives.

8.4.3 Gentleness and Respect: Paul's Advice in Galatians 6:1

Paul instructs, "Restore…in a spirit of gentleness. Keep watch on yourself, lest you too be tempted" (Galatians 6:1). Release ministry must be gentle—aware of the vulnerability of those bound—and marked by humility. Rather than domineering, ministers walk alongside covenant partners, offering encouragement without coercion. Gentle restoration recognizes the possibility of relapse and the need for ongoing support. Respect for autonomy prevents spiritual abuse; individuals are invited to participate in their own unbinding, not forced. Training includes modeling nonviolent communication techniques and trauma-informed care principles—avoiding language that shames or re-traumatizes. Ministry teams hold self-care debriefs to guard against pride or burnout, as Paul warns. Visitation and prayer sessions begin with consent, ensuring people feel safe to decline or pause. Corporate codes of conduct—confidentiality agreements, boundaries around physical touch—reinforce respect. By following Galatians 6:1, the church practices release ministry that honors God's gentle spirit and the dignity of every person.

8.5 Spiritual Disciplines for Personal Unbinding

8.5.1 Confession and Repentance: Loosening the Grip of Sin (1 John 1:9)

John assures, "If we confess our sins, he is faithful...to forgive us... and cleanse us from all unrighteousness" (1 John 1:9). Personal unbinding begins with recognizing sin as a binding force—pride, anger, lust—and bringing it into the light. Regular confession rhythms—journaling sins, corporate confession services, or sacramental reconciliation—break shame's hold. In accountability partnerships, confession catalyzes mutual release: confessing a secret struggle invites prayer and accountability without judgment. Repentance includes turning away and making restitution where possible, embodying true reversal. Counseling programs use the "Three R's"—Recognition, Repentance, Restoration—to guide people through unbinding spiritual chains. Discipleship classes teach practical steps—confession prayers, public or private, tied to specific commitments. Liturgies on Ash Wednesday or Reconciliation Sundays embed confession into church calendar, normalizing vulnerability. As sin's grip loosens, individuals experience new freedom to obey and worship. Through confession and repentance, we enact the unbinding decree, trusting Jesus' cleansing power to set us free.

8.5.2 Forgiveness Exercises: Releasing Others from Debts (Colossians 3:13)

Paul commands: "Bear with one another... forgiving each other, as the Lord has forgiven you" (Colossians 3:13). Unbinding ministry extends to forgiving others—loosing relational bindings of bitterness and resentment. Structured forgiveness exercises guide participants to list offenses, pray for offenders, and offer symbolic acts—writing names on paper and releasing them into flowing water. Small groups facilitate "forgiveness workshops," where guided prompts help members articulate hurts and then verbally forgive. Pastoral letters and counseling tools emphasize that forgiveness does not condone wrongdoing but severs emotional chains. Family ministries include forgiveness ceremonies—reconciling siblings or generational grudges through storytelling and blessing. Role-plays equip people with phrases to express forgiveness sincerely, such as "I release you from this debt." Churches can host "Healing from Hurt" retreats focused on forgiveness, integrating worship and art. Teaching on Jesus' command to forgive "seventy times seven" (Matthew 18:22) underscores forgiveness as ongoing discipline. As forgiveness exercises unfold, individuals move from bondage to freedom, embodying Christ's unbinding ministry.

8.5.3 Inner Healing Prayer: Confronting Roots of Bondage

Inner healing prayer addresses deep-seated wounds—childhood trauma, spiritual oppression, identity crises—that bind the soul. This discipline involves guided prayer steps: invitation of the Holy Spirit, remembrance of wounds, confession of lies believed, receipt of God's truth, and declaration of freedom (Ephesians 1:7). Prayer teams trained in inner healing listen sensitively, offering Scripture-based declarations into each person's memory and soul. Use of imagination prayer—visualizing Jesus ministering on the cross—facilitates emotional release. Retreats often include "quiet zones" where participants journal dialogues with Jesus, unwrapping spiritual debris layer by layer. Art and music therapy complement inner healing, allowing non-verbal expression of pain before release. Pastoral care handbooks provide protocols for referral if deeper trauma emerges, ensuring safe boundaries. Small groups can incorporate monthly inner-healing sessions, normalizing spiritual depth in community. Theologically, teaching on Christ's "binding of the strong man" (Mark 3:27) frames inner healing as reclaiming territory. Through inner healing prayer, long-hidden roots of bondage are unearthed and unbound, enabling full participation in Christ's freedom.

8.6 Counseling and Pastoral Care in Release Ministry

8.6.1 Safe Spaces for Vulnerability: Confidential Listening and Prayer

Effective pastoral care creates environments where people feel secure to share their deepest struggles. Confidentiality agreements, private settings, and clear assurances of non-judgment establish trust (Proverbs 11:13). Training in trauma-informed care emphasizes physical comfort—comfortable seating, water, tissues—and psychological safety—active listening, validating language, and consent for all prayer actions. Pastors and counselors use open-ended questions to invite storytelling, gently guiding from pain into prayer. Prayer ministries designate "safe rooms"—spaces with calming décor and prayer resources—where individuals meet for unhurried ministry. Small group facilitators receive training in confidentiality, referral protocols, and self-care to prevent burnout. Volunteer teams include debriefing sessions after intense ministry to maintain emotional health. Pastoral care handbooks outline procedures for crisis situations—suicidal ideation or abuse disclosures—ensuring proper intervention. By prioritizing safe spaces, the church honors Galatians 6:2's "bear one another's burdens" in compassionate confidentiality. These environments become grounds where the unbinding ministry can take root in trust.

8.6.2 Tools for Unbinding: Freedom Groups and Support Networks

Structured Freedom Groups offer ongoing support for those seeking release from specific bindings—addiction, grief, or trauma. Models like Celebrate Recovery adapt twelve-step principles with a Christ-centered framework, integrating teaching, confession, and accountability. Support networks pair novices with mentors—seasoned believers who model freedom and guide new members through the unbinding journey. Resource kits—including workbooks, video curricula, and prayer guides—equip group leaders to deliver consistent, biblically grounded sessions. Topics cover confession, forgiveness, boundary-setting, and identity in Christ. Online support networks extend reach to those unable to attend in person, using secure video conferencing and moderated forums. Churches collaborate with professional counselors to co-host specialized groups for PTSD or domestic violence survivors. Quarterly Freedom Conferences include testimonies, worship, and workshops, uniting multiple groups for mutual encouragement. By deploying these tools, the church institutionalizes ministry of release, ensuring no one must carry bindings alone.

8.6.3 Referral to Professional Care: When Bindings Require Expert Help

Some bindings—severe trauma, mental illness, addiction—require professional intervention alongside spiritual ministry. Pastoral counselors should maintain a vetted referral list of Christian therapists, psychiatrists, and addiction specialists. Clear referral protocols guide when and how to recommend professional care, safeguarding individuals from harm. Joint care teams—pastor plus therapist—coordinate to integrate spiritual support with clinical treatment, ensuring holistic freedom. Confidentiality and consent are paramount: ministry leaders respect boundaries of medical confidentiality and legal requirements. Continuing education for pastors includes recognizing red flags—suicidal ideation, severe dissociation—that necessitate professional engagement (2 Timothy 4:5). Community seminars on mental health destigmatize seeking help, casting therapy as an extension of Christ's healing ministry. Follow-up care plans include both spiritual counsel and clinical check-ins, tracking progress. By collaborating with experts, the church demonstrates humility and wisdom, ensuring that the ministry of release honors both God's sovereignty and the complexity of human healing.

8.7 Corporate Release: Breaking Community Chains

8.7.1 Public Confession and Corporate Repentance (2 Chronicles 7:14)

2 Chronicles 7:14 promises, "If my people who are called by my name humble themselves, pray and seek my face and turn from their wicked ways, then I will hear from heaven..." Corporate confession acknowledges that communal sin—whether racial prejudice, economic exploitation, or moral failure—binds entire communities. Churches can organize "Day of Repentance" services where congregations confess known corporate sins: neglect of the poor (Isaiah 58:6–7), complicity in injustice (Micah 6:8), or failure to love neighbors (Mark 12:31). Liturgies include responsive readings: leader names a corporate sin, congregation repeats a confession and plea for mercy. Testimonies from community leaders or activists can highlight real-world impacts of these sins, giving voice to those harmed. Following confession, the congregation engages in symbolic acts—washing feet to represent cleansing (John 13:14–15) or laying hands on a city map while praying for healing. Public confession builds shared humility, breaking the pride that sustains systemic bondage. It also fosters accountability: covenants or public commitments to specific justice initiatives emerge from these gatherings. Partnering with local civic bodies—mayors, councils, nonprofits—bridges church confession to tangible community action. Over time, regular corporate repentance cultivates a repentant culture, paving the way for sustained release from entrenched communal chains. Thus, God's promise in 2 Chronicles 7:14 unfolds as the church both humbles itself and sees revival in its neighborhoods.

8.7.2 Advocacy and Justice: Unbinding Victims of Injustice (Isaiah 1:17)

Isaiah 1:17 commands, "Learn to do good; seek justice, correct oppression; bring justice to the fatherless, plead the widow's cause." Advocacy ministries live out unbinding by confronting laws, policies, and power structures that oppress vulnerable populations. Churches can establish "Justice Teams" trained to research local issues—housing inequity, mass incarceration, wage theft—and lobby for legislative reform. Volunteer legal clinics sponsored by the church offer pro bono counsel to immigrants or low-income families, directly unbinding legal chains. Partnerships with organizations combating human trafficking allow congregants to serve survivors and advocate for stricter enforcement against perpetrators. Social action campaigns—letter-writing drives, phone-a-thons, public demonstrations—give voice to marginalized citizens. Educational forums on systemic racism help unmask unconscious bias and promote equitable practices within the congregation and beyond. Regular "Justice Sunday" sermons unpack biblical mandates for justice, inspiring congregational participation. Measuring impact—tracking reduced eviction rates or improved community services—demonstrates the fruit of advocacy. By pressing for structural change, the church extends Christ's unbinding ministry from individual hearts to social institutions, embodying kingdom justice in action. This advocacy settles living stones in society's foundation, replacing chains with covenantal compassion.

8.7.3 Community Healing Rituals: Stones of Remembrance (Joshua 4:1–7)

In Joshua 4, twelve stones memorialize Israel's crossing of the Jordan, reminding each generation of God's deliverance. Similarly, community healing rituals use symbols to mark milestones in collective unbinding. Churches might create a "Freedom Wall," where community members write personal testimonies of liberation on stones and place them in a public display—each stone commemorating an unbound life. Annual "Healing Pilgrimages" could lead participants through dozen ritual stations: confession, forgiveness, lament, proclamation of freedom, service, restitution, and celebration. At each station, individuals place a symbolic item—chain links removed, debt documents burned, forgiveness letters buried—illustrating specific bonds broken. Dramatized processions echo Joshua's crossing: the body of Christ moves through neighborhood streets, pausing at markers of historical trauma or reconciliation, praying for release. Art installations—murals composed of community-painted stones—tell collective narratives of bondage and freedom. Digital story maps capture these testimonies online, allowing wider audiences to engage with the community's journey. By embedding symbols in public spaces, these rituals both remember God's past deliverance and anticipate ongoing unbinding. Community healing rituals thus become landmarks of God's faithfulness, testifying that where stones once symbolized death, now they commemorate life—and freedom to "let him go."

8.8 Empowering Testimonies: Stories of Unbinding

8.8.1 Biblical Case Studies: Peter's Release from Prison (Acts 12:5–17)

In Acts 12, Peter languishes in Herod's prison, chained between two guards. The church prays earnestly "without ceasing" (v. 5), and an angel miraculously frees him—chains fall off, doors open (vv. 7–10). The deliverance emphasizes both divine initiative and the power of corporate prayer. Peter's unbinding becomes a testimony that galvanizes the early church, leading believers to glorify God (v. 17). Preachers can unpack this narrative in sermons, highlighting how prayer and praise coalesce to unleash God's power. Bible studies might map the sequence—prayer, praise, release—and invite groups to emulate each step. Dramatic readings or short film re-enactments help congregations engage emotionally with Peter's story. Pastors can encourage congregants to journal their "Acts 12 experiences," noting instances where prayer preceded deliverance. By rooting release ministry in Peter's example, the church draws from Scripture's own testimonies to fuel present faith in unbinding. This case study reminds modern believers that the same God who freed Peter still hears and releases today.

8.8.2 Modern Testimonies: Freedom from Addiction and Abuse

Countless lives bear witness to Christ's unbinding power over modern chains—addiction to substances, patterns of abuse, or self-destructive behaviors. Recovery ministries often host "Testimony Nights" where individuals share journeys from bondage to freedom, crediting spiritual breakthroughs. A man might recount how surrendering his addiction to Christ led him to a twelve-step group and ultimately restoration in family relationships. A survivor of domestic abuse might testify that inner-healing prayer freed her from fear and enabled reconciliation or safe separation. These testimonies often emphasize a pivotal "unbind moment"—an act of faith such as forgiving an abuser, entering rehab, or repenting before God. Churches can curate multimedia presentations—video interviews, audio clips, written narratives—to compile a "Modern Unbinding Gallery." Recovery coaches or pastoral counselors participate in panels, tying personal stories to biblical truths like "where the Spirit of the Lord is, there is freedom" (2 Corinthians 3:17). Hosting support groups adjacent to testimony events offers immediate pathways for others seeking release. Celebrating answered prayers publicly reinforces the church's commitment to unbinding contemporary chains. Modern testimonies thus become beacons of hope, illustrating that the ministry Jesus began at Lazarus' tomb continues powerfully today.

8.8.3 Congregational Spotlights: Celebrating Released Lives

Every congregation has stories of individuals whom God has unbound from various chains—health crises, broken marriages, financial ruin. Periodic "Freedom Spotlights" during services honor these journeys, allowing released members to share concise testimonies and receive affirmation. Spotlight moments can include before-and-after photos, short video montages, or displayed token objects—crutches discarded, debt statements torn—to symbolize released burdens. Church newsletters and websites publish "Freedom Spotlights" as written features, broadening reach beyond Sunday gatherings. Recognition events—luncheons or receptions—

give released individuals platforms to network, mentor, and inspire others. Administrative teams maintain a "freedom archive," cataloging testimonies by category (e.g., healing, relational, financial) for resource–sharing and historical memory. Spiritual gift assessments can connect those recently freed to ministry roles, harnessing newly regained strengths. Congregational spotlights reinforce corporate identity as a community of unbinding, encouraging new faith steps among attendees. By regularly celebrating released lives, the church embeds release ministry into its narrative, reminding all that unbinding is both possible and promised.

8.9 Equipping the Church for Release Ministry

8.9.1 Training Workshops: Developing Release Ministry Teams

To steward unbinding effectively, churches must equip teams through structured workshops. Training covers biblical foundations (John 11:44; Isaiah 61:1), spiritual authority in Christ's name (Luke 10:19), and practical skills like active listening and trauma-informed care. Workshops blend didactic teaching, role-plays, and supervised practice, ensuring participants experience both theological depth and hands-on application. Trainers from deliverance ministries, clinical counseling, and social justice organizations co-teach modules—addressing spiritual, emotional, and systemic chains. Certification pathways validate team readiness, requiring ongoing mentorship and continued education. Retreat-style intensives model safe spaces for vulnerability, giving trainees personal unbinding opportunities. Post-training support includes monthly peer supervision and case study reviews, preventing isolation. Leaders integrate ethical guidelines—confidentiality, consent, referral thresholds—to safeguard all involved. By investing in training, the church builds a robust release ministry that is theologically sound, emotionally wise, and practically effective.

8.9.2 Resource Libraries: Books, Videos, and Curriculum on Freedom

A centralized resource library empowers church members to learn and engage release ministry at their own pace. Collections include classic texts—C.S. Lewis on penitence, Neil Anderson on freedom in Christ—and up-to-date deliverance curricula like Freedom in Christ materials. Video libraries offer recorded interviews with freedom ministers, case-study documentaries, and instructional webinars. Curricula from reputable organizations—Celebrate Recovery, Inner Healing USA—provide ready-made small-group lessons. Digital access via church intranet or mobile app ensures resources are available anytime. Curated reading lists and recommended viewing guides help newcomers navigate entry points. Resource librarians host "Freedom Open Houses," demonstrating tools like prayer guides, worksheets, and symbolic artifacts. Partnering with theological seminaries ensures academic rigor and access to research on trauma and deliverance. By maintaining and promoting resource libraries, the church democratizes access to knowledge, equipping anyone to engage in ministry of release thoughtfully and confidently.

8.9.3 Ongoing Support: Mentorship and Accountability Circles

Sustainable release ministry depends on ongoing support structures. Mentorship pairs new deliverance ministers with seasoned practitioners, fostering skill transfer and personal growth. Accountability circles—small cohorts meeting monthly—provide spaces for case debriefing, prayer, and mutual encouragement. These circles follow a structured agenda: personal check-in, review of ministry actions, prayer for specific challenges, and setting action steps. Retention of ministry volunteers improves when they experience companionship and shared vision. Leadership teams conduct quarterly retreats to refresh team identity, worship together, and process emotional burdens. Online forums—moderated by care coordinators—offer asynchronous support, enabling peer advice and resource sharing. Supervisors track metrics—number of people ministered to, referral outcomes, team wellbeing indicators—to guide resourcing and training needs. Celebrating milestones—one year free from a particular bondage, first successful deliverance case—boosts morale. Through mentorship and accountability, the church ensures that its ministry of release remains vibrant, healthy, and deeply rooted in Christ's command to "unbind and let go."

Conclusion When the grave-cloths fall away and the freed person steps into the open air, we glimpse the breadth of God's liberating love—a love that refuses to leave anyone imprisoned by guilt, fear, or oppression. Our calling is to carry that same unbinding ministry into every sphere of life: to pray deliverance over hidden wounds, to champion justice for the marginalized, and to foster communities where chains are broken and dignity restored. May we go forth with courageous hearts, equipped by Scripture and guided by the Spirit, ready to declare Christ's victory over every bondage and to usher in the freedom he so generously offers.

Chapter 9. From Death to Life — Personal Transformation

Every person carries within a story of brokenness—a history of choices, wounds, and fears that leave the soul feeling lifeless and bound. Yet in the resurrection of Lazarus we see the same power at work in our own hearts: the God who calls the dead to life invites us into a personal metamorphosis. In this chapter, we'll journey through the stages of awakening from spiritual slumber, experiencing the new birth that pulses with divine life, and embracing an identity anchored in Christ's victory over death. Along the way, we'll explore how daily rhythms, inner healing, and community support shape our transformation, equipping us to bear the fruit of the Spirit and step confidently into the mission for which we were made.

9.1 Awakening to Spiritual Death

9.1.1 Recognizing the Signs: Apathy, Shame, and Despair

Spiritual death often begins with a creeping sense of apathy toward God—prayers become perfunctory, Scripture reading feels hollow, and worship rings empty. Shame steals into our hearts, convincing us that our failures disqualify us from God's love, even though the gospel insists "there is now no condemnation for those who are in Christ Jesus" (Romans 8:1). Despair follows, whispering that change is impossible and that we are irredeemably broken. This trio of symptoms—apathy, shame, despair—parallels the physical signs of death: coldness, pallor, and stillness. Just as a physician diagnoses physical death by external markers, spiritual mentors learn to discern these signs in others' lives through prayerful conversation and pastoral sensitivity (Galatians 6:1). In small-group settings, leaders can gently ask, "When was the last time you felt alive in worship?" or "What lies about yourself do you still struggle to reject?" Honest dialogue helps individuals name their spiritual numbness. Personal inventories—journaling questions like "What excites me most about following Jesus?"—reveal hidden apathy. Shame can be unmasked by sharing testimonies in safe spaces, bringing medical light into spiritual wounds (James 5:16). Recognizing despair as a lie from the enemy (1□Peter 5:8) empowers us to confront it with prophetic truth.

9.1.2 The Biblical Diagnosis: "Dead in Trespasses and Sins" (Ephesians 2:1)

Paul's stark assessment—"You were dead in the trespasses and sins in which you once walked" (Ephesians 2:1)—frames spiritual death as universal before Christ's intervention. The phrase "dead in trespasses" indicates an inability to respond to God's commands, just as a corpse cannot move toward health. Scripture repeatedly portrays sin as the power that enslaves and cuts us off from the Source of life (Isaiah 59:2). The prophet Ezekiel envisioned dry bones—an image of Israel's spiritual paralysis—before God breathed resurrection life into them (Ezekiel 37:1–10). Recognizing our condition is the first step of healing: without admission of death, one cannot seek life. In preaching, pastors highlight that spiritual death is not moral "mistakes" but a fundamental severing from God. Theologians teach that original sin renders every person naturally dead, underscoring the necessity of divine grace (Romans 5:12). Counseling frameworks incorporate

Ephesians 2:1 as a diagnostic tool, moving clients from self-help to spiritual dependence. By naming our deadness in Christ-less living, we become poised to receive the new birth only he can impart.

9.1.3 Testimonies of Awakening: Coming Face-to-Face with Inner Death

Personal stories of awakening illustrate the moment when individuals recognize their spiritual deadness and cry out for life. One woman describes her "road to Emmaus" moment—walking through daily routines until Scripture suddenly sprang to life, revealing her heart's barrenness (Luke 24:32). A man recounts crashing in addiction and hitting a "rock-bottom realization" that nothing earthly could revive his soul. In inner-healing retreats, participants share breakthroughs: an image of Christ's nail-scarred hands reaching into their emptiness catalyzed a profound "yes" to new life. Each testimony underscores that awakening often begins with grace-illumined awareness of death, not spiritual commitment. Small-group "Awakening Nights" provide forums for sharing these turning points, reinforcing communal empathy. Video interviews—edited into short clips—serve as powerful catalysts when shared in services or social media. Counselees hearing others' awakening feel permission to face their own deadness without shame. By encountering real stories, individuals sense that God's revival fire can ignite even the most arid hearts.

9.2 The New Birth: Experiencing Spiritual Resurrection

9.2.1 Jesus' Invitation: "You Must Be Born Again" (John 3:3–7)

In his nocturnal conversation with Nicodemus, Jesus declares, "Truly, truly, I say to you, unless one is born again he cannot see the kingdom of God" (John 3:3). This radical statement underscores that spiritual life begins not with deeds but with divine rebirth. Birth imagery emphasizes powerlessness and dependency: just as infants cannot initiate their own birth, we cannot regenerate ourselves (James 1:18). The encounter highlights the necessity of both water and Spirit—physical cleansing and supernatural renewal—demonstrating the holistic nature of new birth. In evangelistic settings, sharing John 3:3–7 challenges seekers to consider whether their faith rests on mere moral improvement or on Spirit-wrought transformation. Baptism classes often unpack this text, preparing candidates to receive the sacrament as an outward sign of inward rebirth. Churches hold "Born Again" testimonies during services, inviting recent converts to articulate the moment they encountered spiritual awakening. Discipleship curricula guide new believers through steps of growth, affirming that the new birth initiates a lifelong journey. By centering on Jesus' invitation, the church clarifies that personal transformation begins with the miracle of rebirth alone he can accomplish.

9.2.2 Water and Spirit: Sacramental and Spiritual Life (Titus 3:5)

Titus 3:5 describes our salvation as "not because of works done by us in righteousness, but according to his own mercy, by the washing of regeneration and renewal of the Holy Spirit." The "washing" metaphor recalls baptism's sacramental role, symbolizing cleansing and new birth. Meanwhile, "renewal of the Holy Spirit" emphasizes ongoing spiritual vitality beyond the initial rite. The dual imagery of water and Spirit invites believers to both remember their rebirth baptism and depend daily on Spirit empowerment. Liturgical practices reinforce this: baptismal fonts remain visible in sanctuaries, and periodic "renewal services" invite worshippers to be anointed or prayed over for fresh filling of the Spirit. Small-group devotions might include water symbolism—sprinkling bowls— paired with brief times of silent Spirit-inviting prayer. Pastoral teaching on Titus 3:5 cautions against sacramentalism or Spiritless moralism, affirming the necessity of both elements. Confirmation classes or new member orientations explore this text, ensuring that reception of sacraments aligns with personal repentance and Spirit-filled living. Through the interplay of water and Spirit, believers experience both the authority of visible symbols and the reality of invisible renewal.

9.2.3 Stories of New Birth: From Skepticism to Spiritual Life

Accounts of skepticism turned to faith powerfully illustrate the new birth's reality. A former atheist recalls attending a church service as a dare, expecting empty ritual, only to feel an overwhelming presence of love—prompting an emotional surrender and dramatic life change. Another describes growing up in a nominally Christian home, never truly believing until a friend's authentic testimony triggered a spiritual breakthrough. In multiple contexts, seekers describe a moment when eternal realities became tangible, akin to Lazarus stepping out of the tomb into sunlight. Churches capture these stories in "Born Again Testimony" videos, interweaving candid interviews with Scripture and worship footage. Pastoral teams host "Alpha" or "Christianity Explored" courses, inviting skeptics to explore the gospel, then featuring testimonies of those who crossed from doubt into new life. Baptism services become celebratory points where testimonies precede immersion, underscoring the new birth's personal impact. Youth group retreats often include "Skeptic's Night," where young people voice doubts before witnessing peers' conversion stories. These narratives affirm that the new birth is not theoretical but vibrantly real, turning spiritual corpses into living witnesses of resurrection power.

9.3 Union with Christ: Identity Transformed

9.3.1 Crucified, Buried, and Raised with Him (Romans 6:4)

Paul teaches that in baptism, believers "are buried with [Christ] by baptism into death, in order that…we too might walk in newness of life" (Romans 6:4). This union with Christ's death and resurrection reframes our identity: the old self is considered crucified, and the new self is empowered to live under grace, not law. Symbolic immersion illustrates burial; emerging from the water signifies resurrection. Discipleship groups study Romans 6:1–14 to grasp implications: no longer slaves to sin, we now offer ourselves to God. Counseling integrates this truth into identity work—clients replace self-condemning narratives with affirmations of being "dead to sin" and "alive to God" (v. 11). Graphic teaching—diagrams of self-crucifixion and resurrection—helps visual learners. Churches may celebrate symbolic "dying Sunday" and "rising Sunday," deepening grasp of spiritual union. Baptism anniversaries become opportunities to revisit Romans 6, reminding believers of initial transformation and ongoing union. By embracing our participation in Christ's death and resurrection, we adopt an identity fully realigned from bondage to freedom.

9.3.2 Adoption and Sonship: "In Christ You Are a New Creation" (2 Corinthians 5:17; Galatians 4:5–7)

Paul declares, "If anyone is in Christ, he is a new creation" (2 Corinthians 5:17), and later describes believers as adopted sons—"God sent the Spirit of his Son into our hearts" (Galatians 4:6). Adoption language underscores relational transformation: we move from orphan status—alienated and powerless—to heirs with Christ. New creation imagery signals that old patterns of death are replaced with fresh life forms, like a butterfly emerging from a cocoon. Identity formation curricula teach new believers to claim "child of God" as their primary identity, displacing fear and insecurity. Worship songs echo this: refrains such as "No longer slaves, but children of God" reinforce adoption truth. Pastors preach on inheritance—the promises and privileges that come with sonship, including access to God's throne (Ephesians 3:12). Counseling sessions use family-tree metaphors to help individuals see spiritual lineage, fostering belonging. Small groups conduct "Identity Workshops," where participants write "I am" sentences—"I am God's beloved child"—and share in affirming circle. By internalizing adoption and new creation, believers experience deep-rooted transformation that reshapes self-image and relational dynamics.

9.3.3 Living Out New Identity: Practical Implications for Self-Image

Embracing our union with Christ demands practical shifts in self-perception and behavior. Knowing we are a new creation prompts us to discard old self-talk ("I'm a failure") and replace it with gospel-based affirmations ("I am forgiven and empowered to change"). Spiritual disciplines—daily confession of identity statements, Scripture memorization of identity verses (e.g., 1□Peter 2:9)—reinforce new self-image. Small groups practice "identity declarations" at the start of meetings, speaking aloud truths such as "I am chosen" and "I am empowered by the Spirit." Christian counseling integrates identity-focused Cognitive Behavioral Therapy, challenging core beliefs and rooting new cognitive patterns in spiritual reality. In workplace and school ministry, believers learn to respond to criticism with "Identity Reframing"—replying with "I am God's workmanship" (Ephesians 2:10) rather than defensiveness. Visual reminders—post-it notes on mirrors with identity phrases—help rescript self-image throughout the day. Leadership development includes coaching on embodying Christian identity in ethical decisions, reflecting Christ's character in professional contexts. Through these practices, union with Christ moves from theological concept to lived reality, allowing transformed identity to drive transformed living.

9.4 Walking in Newness of Life

9.4.1 Daily Disciplines: Prayer, Scripture, and Sacrament as Rhythms of Life (Colossians 2:6–7)

Walking in newness of life begins with intentional rhythms that root us in Christ's presence day by day. Colossians 2:6–7 urges believers "to walk in him, rooted and built up in him and established in the faith, just as you were taught." First, daily prayer—both listening and speaking—cultivates ongoing communion rather than a once-a-day transaction. A structured morning and evening prayer time, even for ten minutes, anchors our identity in Christ before the world's demands engulf us. Second, regular Scripture reading—whether through a chronological plan, thematic study, or lectio divina—feeds the mind with life-shaping truth (Psalm 119:105). Practically, many find reading one chapter each morning and journaling a verse that speaks to them cements God's word in their hearts. Third, participation in the sacraments—baptism remembered and Eucharist celebrated—externalizes our union with Christ's death and resurrection (1 Corinthians 11:26), transforming routine worship into personal encounter. Home altars or simple communion kits enable believers to partake in the Lord's Supper outside formal services, reinforcing new-life rhythms. Accountability apps or prayer partners ensure consistency, gently reminding us when we skip disciplines. Over time, these three anchors—prayer, Scripture, and sacrament—form a resilient foundation, so that even amid trials, our steps remain in the trajectory of resurrection life.

9.4.2 Overcoming Old Patterns: Putting to Death the Flesh (Romans 8:13)

Transformation requires more than positive habits; it demands decisive rupture with former patterns that enslave us. Romans 8:13 teaches, "If by the Spirit you put to death the deeds of the body, you will live." This "putting to death" involves identifying specific flesh-driven tendencies—anger outbursts, envy, compulsive behaviors—and bringing them into God's light through confession and accountability (John 3:20–21). Practical steps include maintaining a "sin log," where each day one records moments of temptation and action taken to resist. Coupling that with immediate confession to a trusted friend or mentor prevents secret sins from regaining power. Spiritual victory groups meet weekly to share struggles and prayers, embodying Proverbs 27:17's principle: "Iron sharpens iron." Fasting targeted at a particular stronghold—social media, unhealthy food, gossip—breaks habitual patterns by demonstrating control of the Spirit over the flesh (Matthew 17:21). Replacing old patterns with new ones—journaling instead of scrolling, prayer instead of complaining—rewires our desires. Pastoral counseling integrates cognitive reframing: transforming the thought "I must have this to feel happy" into "My satisfaction comes from Christ alone." Over time, putting the flesh to death leads not to legalistic striving but to liberated living, marked by increasing fruitfulness of the Spirit.

9.4.3 Community Accountability: Iron Sharpens Iron (Proverbs 27:17)

We cannot walk in newness of life in isolation; transformation thrives in community. Proverbs 27:17 declares, "Iron sharpens iron, and one man sharpens another." Small groups designed for mutual growth provide structured times for confession, encouragement, and prayer, creating safe spaces for vulnerability. Weekly check-ins—sharing victories and struggles—build trust and prompt timely intervention when someone drifts. Mentorship relationships pair mature believers with younger ones, modeling new-life habits and providing personalized guidance. Accountability partners agree to daily or weekly reporting on specific commitments, such as devotional time or resisting particular temptations. Churches can host quarterly "Accountability Summits," bringing multiple small groups together for teaching, worship, and recommitment. Online platforms—secure group chats or apps—enable rapid encouragement and prayer when real-time challenges arise. Annual retreats focus on renewal, allowing groups to step away from routine and refocus on Christ. By sharpening one another in truth and love, the community sustains transformation, ensuring that new-life rhythms are not just individual disciplines but shared journeys toward Christlikeness.

9.5 Fruit of Transformation: Character and Conduct

9.5.1 The Fruit of the Spirit as Evidence (Galatians 5:22–23)

The hallmark of personal transformation is the visible fruit that springs from Christ's life within us. Galatians 5:22–23 lists love, joy, peace, patience, kindness, goodness, faithfulness, gentleness, and self-control—qualities that contrast sharply with the "works of the flesh." Monitoring these virtues becomes part of discipleship: individuals keep a "fruit journal," noting daily instances when they exhibited or lacked a fruit quality. Small groups can use "fruit-assessment tools"—self-scoring surveys that track growth areas and prayer needs. Preaching on one fruit at a time—e.g., a sermon series on "The Joy Revolution"—equips congregations to cultivate specific character traits. Worship songs that focus on the Spirit's work in producing these virtues reinforce their centrality. Parenting ministries integrate fruit talks, helping children recognize and practice kindness or patience in family dynamics. Mentors model faithfulness by their consistent presence and gentle guidance. When congregants share fruit testimonies—"I responded in gentleness instead of anger"—they encourage one another in transformation. Over time, the community becomes a living orchard, testifying that where death once reigned, new life bursts forth through the Spirit's work.

9.5.2 Holiness and Love: The Twin Marks of New Life (1□Peter 1:15–16; 1□John 4:7–8)

Holiness—being set apart for God—and love—self-giving concern for others—are inseparable signposts of transformation. Peter commands, "As he who called you is holy, you also be holy…for it is written, 'You shall be holy, for I am holy'" (1□Peter 1:15–16). John emphasizes, "God is love, and whoever abides in love abides in God" (1□John 4:16). Holiness shapes our internal motivations—seeking purity of thought and intention—while love animates our external actions toward neighbor. Practical holiness disciplines include regular confession, boundary setting around media consumption, and cultivating modesty in speech and lifestyle. Love is practiced through service ministries—visiting the sick, feeding the hungry, advocating for the marginalized. Churches can hold "Holy Love Workshops" combining biblical teaching on holiness with hands-on service projects. Marriage enrichment programs teach couples how holiness—in fidelity—and love—in sacrificial care—go hand in hand. Youth groups engage in "love challenges," performing anonymous acts of kindness around campus. By pursuing holiness and love together, believers display the visible evidence of internal new-life transformation, fulfilling Christ's command to be "perfect as your heavenly Father is perfect" (Matthew 5:48).

9.5.3 Testimonies of Changed Lives: From Anger to Patience, Fear to Courage

Personal stories of marked character shifts inspire listeners toward transformation. A man who once exploded in rage recounts how regular confession, anger management courses, and accountability led to patient restraint (James 1:19). A woman plagued by social anxiety tells how stepping out in faith—volunteering to lead prayer—grew her courage (2 Timothy 1:7). During worship services, scheduled "Transformation Testimony" segments allow brief, powerful narratives that highlight before-and-after contrasts. Video testimonies—edited with Scripture overlays—can be shown during midweek gatherings, reinforcing the gospel's power to change. Small groups dedicate meeting time to "Character Stories," analyzing real-life growth against fruit-of-the-Spirit benchmarks. Leadership development programs invite emerging leaders to share how practicing self-control or kindness has reshaped their influence. Annual "Freedom Festivals" celebrate testimonies across all ages, from teen overcoming envy to elder growing in gentleness. These stories do more than inspire—they provide roadmaps, showing concrete steps others took to move from old vices to new virtues. By spotlighting changed lives, the church testifies that resurrection life yields transformative conduct in every domain.

9.6 Healing the Inner Self: Mind, Emotions, and Will

9.6.1 Renewing the Mind: Taking Every Thought Captive (Romans 12:2)

The first battleground for transformation is the mind, where thoughts shape beliefs and actions. Romans 12:2 urges, "Do not be conformed to this world, but be transformed by the renewal of your mind." Renewing the mind involves identifying thought patterns—negative self-talk, cynical assumptions—and replacing them with God's truth. Cognitive disciplines include Scripture meditation: journaling verses like Philippians 4:8 and memorizing them for recitation when toxic thoughts arise. Thought-monitoring exercises—recording recurring negative thoughts and then disputing them with biblical promises—adapt cognitive behavioral therapy into spiritual practice. Prayer of the mind, such as "Jesus, guard my thoughts," invites divine oversight. Seminars on "Mind-Body-Spirit Integration" teach how physical practices—exercise, proper sleep—support mental renewal. Small groups can host "Truth Nights," debating cultural narratives vs. gospel truths to sharpen discernment. Pastors preach series on the mind's renewal—"Head Change, Heart Change"—linking theology to psychology. Over time, as thought patterns realign, emotional responses and willful choices follow suit, evidencing metamorphosis from death to life.

9.6.2 Emotional Restoration: Washing Wounds with Scripture (Psalm 147:3)

God "heals the brokenhearted and binds up their wounds" (Psalm 147:3), promising emotional restoration. Inner healing prayer addresses emotional wounds—grief, betrayal, anxiety—by bringing them to Christ's compassionate care. Guided imagery exercises invite individuals to picture Jesus ministering to each wound point, applying Scripture balm like Isaiah 43:1. Journaling prompts such as "Lord, where do I still feel pain?" followed by "What truth counters this wound?" help process emotions. Creative outlets—art therapy, music therapy—allow expression of grief and hope beyond words. Support groups for trauma survivors integrate Bible studies on God's comfort (2 Corinthians 1:3–4). Pastoral counselors use "emotion mapping" tools to trace triggers and scriptural responses. Worship evenings titled "Healing Waters" incorporate gentle music, darkened rooms, and candlelit prayer stations for reflection. Couples' counseling includes emotional check-ins framed by gratitude—"Name one joy even in this season." As wounds are washed by Scripture and Spirit, emotional life is restored, enabling freedom in relationships and ministry.

9.6.3 Strengthening the Will: Choosing Obedience Daily (Philippians 2:12–13)

Transformation requires not only renewed mind and healed emotions but a strengthened will that chooses obedience daily. Paul writes, "Work out your own salvation… for it is God who works in you, both to will and to work for his good pleasure" (Philippians 2:12–13). Will-strengthening practices include setting concrete obedience goals—praying each morning, serving weekly—and reviewing progress each evening. Accountability partners help sustain motivation, gently reminding each other of commitments. Spiritual disciplines like fasting test and strengthen the will (Matthew 4:1–4), demonstrating reliance on divine provision. Decision-making frameworks, anchored in Scripture (Psalm 119:105), guide choices: "Does this align with God's word?" In small groups, "Will-Workout" sessions include challenges like a 24-hour digital fast or daily generosity acts, followed by shared reflections. Retreats focused on "Willful Surrender" immerse participants in extended silence and guided prompts, clarifying desires. Leaders model willful obedience by sharing their own daily disciplines with transparency and humility. As believers learn to choose obedience moment by moment, the new life birthed in them gains strength and momentum, reflecting the continual work of the Spirit within.

9.7 Integrating the Shadow: Grace for the Wounded Self

9.7.1 Facing Brokenness: Acknowledging Hidden Sins (Psalm 32:3–5)

David describes the agony of unconfessed sin—"When I kept silent, my bones wasted away through my groaning all day long" (Psalm 32:3). Confronting our "shadow" means naming the sins and wounds we prefer to hide: envy, pride, bitterness, or past traumas. Spiritual transformation stalls when we refuse to bring these into the light (John 3:20–21). In personal reflection, journaling questions like "What recurring guilt do I suppress?" surface hidden patterns. Small groups can facilitate "shadow sessions," where carefully guided confession prompts and active listening create safe space to share. Pastoral counselors employ Scripture reading—Psalm 32:5: "I acknowledged my sin to you... and you forgave"—to underscore God's invitation to honesty. Art therapy exercises ask participants to depict their "dark side" on paper before praying over the image. Corporate worship might include a responsive reading of Psalm 32, moving from lament to thanksgiving. Over time, acknowledging hidden sins dismantles their covert power, freeing the conscience for genuine new-life fruit. By facing brokenness head-on, we clear the way for God's grace to penetrate every recess of our wounded self.

9.7.2 Receiving Grace: Healing Through God's Unconditional Love (Ephesians 1:7)

Ephesians 1:7 proclaims that "in [Christ] we have redemption through his blood, the forgiveness of our trespasses, according to the riches of his grace." While acknowledgment of sin is crucial, it must immediately lead to receiving grace. Inner healing prayer guides individuals to silence self-accusation and hear God's words of pardon—"There is therefore now no condemnation" (Romans 8:1). Worship songs focused on grace—"Amazing Grace," "Who Am I?"—create emotional entry points to grasp unconditional love. Small groups practice "grace circles," where each person receives an affirming statement from others rooted in biblical truth. Pastors teach sermons on the parable of the prodigal son (Luke 15:11–32), emphasizing the father's unabated love despite the son's rebellion. Counselors supplement Scripture with empirically supported practices like positive affirmations, helping clients internalize grace. Families can adopt "grace statements" at meals—each member approvingly names one truth they thank God for about another. Quarterly "Grace Retreats" allow deeper immersion into themes of mercy, identity, and acceptance. As grace washes over hidden wounds, individuals begin to embody their new identity as forgiven and beloved children of God.

9.7.3 Reconciliation with Self and Others: The Ministry of Inner Forgiveness

Forgiveness of self and others is the bridge from receiving grace to living freely. Jesus teaches that we forgive "as the Lord has forgiven you" (Colossians 3:13), linking self-forgiveness to divine pardon. Inner work often involves forgiving our own past—poor choices, personal failures—before we can extend grace outward. Guided exercises ask participants to write letters of forgiveness to themselves, sealed and later symbolically buried or burned. Small groups facilitate "reconciliation dialogues," where each person practices forgiving a specific offender under prayerful supervision. Pastors preach on Matthew 5:23–24, urging believers to reconcile before worship, emphasizing relational wholeness. Counseling integrates boundary work: forgiving an offender does not always mean restoring unsafe relationships, but freeing oneself from resentment. Role-plays teach assertive communication that both forgives and protects healthy identity. Communities may hold "Healing of Memories" services, combining testimony, prayer, and symbolized laying down of burdens. Over time, practicing inner forgiveness dismantles the chains of bitterness that block new-life transformation, enabling both self-acceptance and authentic love for others.

9.8 Mission as Transformation: Becoming Agents of New Life

9.8.1 Witnessing by Example: "You Will Know Them by Their Love" (John 13:35)

Jesus declared, "By this all people will know that you are my disciples, if you have love for one another" (John 13:35). Personal transformation naturally overflows into visible love that serves as gospel witness. When neighbors see Christians forgiving, serving, and blessing others, they encounter tangible signs of resurrection life. Communities can launch "Love in Action" initiatives—meal trains for new parents, neighborhood clean-ups, or hospital visits—demonstrating self-giving compassion. Testimonies during services highlight how transformed character leads to outreach—e.g., a recovering addict mentoring others. Small groups practice "Love Walks," walking through local streets praying for houses and looking for practical ways to help. Training in cultural sensitivity ensures that love bridges divides, respecting diverse backgrounds. Workplace ministries encourage employees to exhibit patience and kindness under stress, influencing corporate culture. By witnessing through love, transformed individuals embody John 13:35's mandate, attracting seekers to the source of the change.

9.8.2 Empowered for Service: Gifts of the Spirit in Action (1 Corinthians 12:4–7)

Transformation is not only about character but also about empowerment for ministry. Paul describes spiritual gifts—wisdom, healing, prophecy—as distributions of the Spirit "for the common good" (1 Corinthians 12:7). Identifying and deploying these gifts allows transformed believers to contribute uniquely to God's mission. Churches can offer gift-assessment workshops, helping members discover their gifting profiles. Service pathways—children's ministry, hospitality teams, intercession—provide contexts for gifts to flourish. Training cohorts equip gift bearers: prophecy teams learn ethical protocols; healing prayer teams study pastoral care; serving volunteers develop hospitality skills. Mentorship connects established ministry leaders with new volunteers, modeling gift use in real ministry. Celebrating gifts in worship—testimonies and commissioning prayers—inspires others to step into service. When individuals operate in their Spirit-empowered roles, the body of Christ functions healthily, and communities see the reality of the Spirit's transformative power.

9.8.3 Stories of Multiplied Life: Disciple-Making as Ongoing Resurrection

The ultimate mark of transformation is multiplication—disciples making disciples, communities birthing new communities. Jesus modeled this as he mentored the Twelve, who in turn mentored others (2 Timothy 2:2). Personal transformation thus seeds further new life. Churches can highlight stories of discipleship "snowballs"—a believer sharing faith with a friend who then leads a small group. Mentoring programs formalize this: trained disciplers commit to investing in one or two newer believers over time. Long-term discipleship structures include curricula like "The Navigators" or "Discipleship Path," tracking growth from new birth to mature witness. Retreats focus on "Reproduce Retreat" themes, encouraging participants to identify whom they will invest in next. Digital platforms support virtual discipleship pairs when geography separates mentors and mentees. Celebrating milestones—first baptism through a disciple's witness, first small group led by a new believer—spotlights multiplication. Through these stories, the church sees that personal transformation is not an end but the beginning of a ripple effect that carries resurrection life across generations.

9.9 Perseverance and Growth: Sanctification as a Journey

9.9.1 Trials as Promoters of Growth: Refining Fire (James 1:2–4)

James exhorts believers to "count it all joy…when you meet trials of various kinds," because testing produces steadfastness (James 1:2–3). Trials expose remaining weaknesses—pride, impatience, insecurity—then refine character much like fire purifies gold. Personal transformation thus advances not in ease but under pressure. Faith communities can reframe suffering—loss of job, relationship breakdown, health crisis—as opportunities for sanctification. Testimony services featuring "trial to triumph" stories illustrate how believers emerge stronger in faith and character. Counseling integrates resilience training: teaching clients to identify lessons in hardship and to pray through refined perspectives. Small groups practice "trial sharing," supporting members through current struggles with prayer anchored in James' promise. Retreats include "wilderness weekends," simulating solitude and challenge to foster dependence on God. Pastors preach on biblical examples—Joseph's slavery to leadership, Paul's imprisonments to evangelistic impact—modeling trial-driven growth. As trials refine us, we learn perseverance, producing maturity and completeness so that our transformation reflects Christ's own tested faith.

9.9.2 The Role of Suffering in Conforming to Christ (Romans 8:17–18)

Paul reminds us that "if we suffer with him, we will also be glorified with him" (Romans 8:17) and that present sufferings are not worth comparing with future glory (v. 18). Suffering unites us with Christ's own path—his passion and resurrection life—and shapes us into his image. The "school of suffering" curricula teach that discipleship includes both comfort and cost, inviting believers to view hardships as participation in Christ's work. Support groups for bereavement or chronic illness draw on Romans 8:18, offering hope that pain has redemptive value. Worship services during Holy Week focus on the cross as the ultimate pathway to glory. Retreats labeled "Crossroads" incorporate activities that symbolize bearing a cross—literally carrying a wooden beam—paired with meditation on Christ's suffering. Pastors model vulnerability by sharing personal trials and their role in shaping their faith. Bible studies on Philippians 3:10—knowing Christ and the power of his resurrection, sharing his sufferings—link suffering directly to transformation. By embracing suffering's role, believers move from passive victims to active participants in Christ's sanctifying journey.

9.9.3 Celebrating Milestones: Remembering God's Faithfulness

Transformation is a marathon marked by milestones of growth and divine intervention. Celebrating these milestones—first month of sobriety, first time teaching a Bible study, confession of a sin pattern—reinforces perseverance. Churches can host "Milestone Sundays," inviting members to share recent breakthroughs and commemorating anniversaries of significant spiritual decisions. Visual displays—"Faithfulness

Boards"—highlight milestones with photos and testimonies throughout the building. Families practice "Memory Nights" around the table, recalling answered prayers, times of provision, and spiritual victories. Digital archives—blogs, podcasts, social media—record stories of faithfulness for personal and communal encouragement. Pastoral letters or certificates acknowledge individual growth, affirming the Holy Spirit's work. Annual "Faithfulness Festivals" combine worship, testimonies, and commissioning for the next season's journey. By regularly remembering God's past faithfulness, believers strengthen hope and stickability for the road ahead. These celebrations weave past, present, and future into a tapestry of transformation that honors the God who moves us from death to life.

Conclusion From the moment when God's light breaks through our darkness to each step of growth that follows, personal transformation testifies to the reality of resurrection power living within us. As we shed old patterns and learn to think, feel, and act in the freedom Christ secured, we reflect his life to a world longing for hope. May the truths and practices you've encountered here guide you in your ongoing journey—lifting you in times of trial, grounding you in grace, and sending you forth as a living demonstration that where death once reigned, life now triumphs.

Chapter 10. Many Believed Because of Him — Witness & Evangelism

When Lazarus emerged from the tomb, bound no longer in burial linens, his very presence spoke louder than any sermon ever could. This cascade of belief among witnesses reveals the power of authentic encounter: when people see the living Christ transform death into life, they cannot help but trust and proclaim his name. In this chapter, we will explore how that ancient breakthrough informs our own efforts at witness and outreach—showing how clear testimony, relational connection, and Spirit-empowered deeds converge to draw people into the circle of faith. Whether through a personal story shared over coffee or a digital video capturing a moment of breakthrough, the principles that sent ripples through Judea still guide us today in bringing others face-to-face with the one who gives life.

10.1 The Impact of Lazarus' Resurrection on Belief

10.1.1 Immediate Belief among the Jews (John 11:45)

When Lazarus walked out of the tomb, John records that "many of the Jews therefore, who had come with Mary and had seen what he did, believed in him" (John 11:45). Their belief was not abstract assent but rooted in eyewitness evidence—they saw a man confirmed dead restored to life. This immediate conversion demonstrates that miracles serve as divine credentials, inviting onlookers to place their trust in the Messiah's authority over death. In first-century Judaism, resurrection was associated only with the end-times (Daniel 12:2); Lazarus's return to life gave them a foretaste of the coming age. Yet their belief was fragile, contingent upon the sign itself rather than deep discipleship—many would later waver when the cross loomed. Contemporary evangelism learns from this: powerful testimonies can spark faith, but must be followed by teaching to anchor belief beyond the initial experience (Ephesians 4:14). Churches often begin outreach by sharing recent "Lazarus stories"—testimonies of radical change—to kindle interest. Small groups then disciple new believers through study of the teachings behind the sign, ensuring they mature in faith. This two-stage pattern—sign that provokes belief, followed by grounding in truth—echoes the Gospel's own method (John 20:31). Thus, the Jews' immediate belief exemplifies the catalytic power of resurrection testimony, while reminding us of the need for ongoing discipleship.

10.1.2 Pharisaical Fear and Plotting (John 11:46–53)

Not all who witnessed Lazarus's resurrection responded with faith; John notes that "some of them went to the Pharisees and told them what Jesus had done" (11:46). The ruling religious leaders reacted with fear, recognizing that Jesus' growing influence threatened both their authority and the fragile peace with Roman occupiers. Caiaphas, the high priest, presciently—if cynically—asserts that it is better for one man to die than for the whole nation to perish (11:50), inadvertently prophesying Jesus' sacrificial death for many (Matthew 26:24). Their plot to kill Jesus (11:53) showcases how opposition to genuine witness often springs from self-preservation rather than theological debate. In modern contexts, effective evangelism may provoke institutional resistance—church-planting efforts can unsettle established denominational hierarchies or political interests. Recognizing this pattern, missionaries prepare for both warm reception and backlash, trusting that opposition can amplify rather than silence the gospel (Philippians 1:12). Pastors warn congregations that proclaiming life-giving truth may trigger social or familial conflict, but remind them that God's purposes cannot be thwarted (Acts 5:29–32). Training in gospel resilience—based on Jesus' own obedience unto death—equips believers to endure persecution without losing heart (Romans 8:35–39). Thus, the Pharisees' plotting in response to Lazarus's resurrection teaches that genuine witness may be met with both transforming faith and fearful resistance.

10.1.3 The Ripple Effect into Jerusalem and Beyond (John 12:17–18)

John describes how "the people…went and told the crowds that Lazarus was raised from the dead, and…a great many of the Jews went to meet him for they heard that he had done this sign" (12:17–18). This illustrates the ripple effect: one sign, shared enthusiastically, can mobilize crowds and redirect public attention. In Jerusalem, this mass movement contributed to Jesus' triumphal entry, fulfilling Zechariah 9:9's prophecy and intensifying the city's expectations. For contemporary witness, the ripple principle encourages believers to share personal testimonies not only within small circles but to wider networks—social media, community events, and public gatherings. Strategic use of digital platforms—short video clips of transformation stories—can ignite viral interest in Christ's work today. Church-wide "Testimony Campaigns" invite members to share one life-change story each month, multiplying impact. Local mission teams leverage small-group testimonies to launch larger outreach events, trusting that one changed life fuels many conversions (Matthew 13:31–33). Evangelistic training emphasizes creating "ripple plans": identifying key influencers, timing public stories, and coordinating prayer cover. Thus, the movement from a handful of witnesses in Bethany to multitudes in Jerusalem models how personal encounter with resurrection power can cascade through communities, inviting widespread belief.

10.2 The Nature of Biblical Witness

10.2.1 Eyewitness Credibility: "We Have Seen" (1□John 1:1–3)

The apostle John anchors his Gospel in eyewitness testimony: "What we have seen with our eyes…we proclaim also to you" (1□John 1:1–3). Emphasizing "we have seen" establishes the Gospel's historical reliability and invites listeners to trust reports based on firsthand experience. In a court-like presentation, John stakes his apostolic authority on tangible encounters with the incarnate Word. For modern witness, this underscores the importance of personal credibility: sharing what one has directly experienced of Christ's saving power, rather than merely quoting second-hand stories. Training in personal narrative includes tips on clarity: specifying when and where events occurred, what changed, and how new life persists. Churches can host "Apostolic Night" events where veteran missionaries recount their original experiences, imparting a sense of firsthand authenticity. Video interviews with long-time believers—captured in documentary style—offer visual proof of lived faith. Incorporating archaeological and historical research into teaching buttresses confidence in scriptural accounts. By anchoring witness in "we have seen," the church follows the biblical pattern of credible, firsthand proclamation that calls others to faith.

10.2.2 Transformation as Proof: Changed Lives Testify (Acts 4:20)

Peter and John, rebuked for proclaiming Jesus' name, responded, "For we cannot but speak of what we have seen and heard" (Acts 4:20), pointing to the transformed lives of believers as living testimonies. When people observe real change—from addiction to sobriety, alienation to community—they encounter compelling evidence of the gospel's power. Contemporary ministries highlight "before & after" testimonies: photographs, video testimonies, or written narratives that illustrate tangible transformation. In discipleship classes, members are encouraged to reflect on specific areas where Christ has changed their attitudes, behaviors, or circumstances, compiling personal transformation portfolios. Healing ministries track progress through measurable indicators—emotional health assessments, restored relationships—to underscore credibility. Churches often integrate testimonies into worship: mid-service "Story Moments" allow individuals to briefly share life-change, reinforcing the sermon's theme. Small groups practice "Transformation Interviews," where one member asks another guided questions about their journey, deepening understanding. By showcasing changed lives, the church demonstrates that the gospel is more than ideology—it is a living force that reshapes hearts and communities, validating witness through visible proof.

10.2.3 Narrative Power: Storytelling in the Early Church (Luke 1:1–4)

Luke's prologue declares his intent "to write an orderly account...so that you may have certainty concerning the things you have been taught" (Luke 1:1–4). His narrative approach weaves eyewitness testimonies into a coherent story, making complex theology accessible through compelling accounts. Storytelling in the early church served to teach, persuade, and anchor communal identity around shared events. In modern evangelism, narrative workshops train believers to craft their faith stories with attention to structure—setting the scene, detailing conflict, describing the turning point, and illustrating new reality. Faith communities can host "Story Camps," teaching participants how to use narrative elements—character, tension, resolution—to engage listeners. Digital storytelling through podcasts and short films replicates Luke's model, delivering ordered accounts to global audiences. Sermon series structured as "First-Century Stories" connect contemporary believers with the narrative texture of scripture. By leveraging narrative power, the church bridges ancient testimony and modern communication, ensuring the gospel story resonates deeply in every context.

10.3 The Great Commission in Light of Lazarus

10.3.1 Jesus' Final Charge: "Go and Make Disciples" (Matthew 28:18–20)

After demonstrating authority over death, Jesus commissions his followers: "Go therefore and make disciples of all nations" (Matthew 28:19). The impulse behind witnesses drawn by Lazarus's sign is transcended by this mandate—to not merely invite belief but to cultivate lifelong followers. "Go" implies movement beyond comfort zones: returning to Jerusalem, Judea, Samaria, and the ends of the earth (Acts 1:8). Effective discipleship requires contextual sensitivity—adapting methods to diverse cultures without diluting gospel truths (1□Corinthians 9:19–23). Churches translate this into local outreach plans: blessing neighborhoods, cross-cultural partnerships, and short-term mission trips. Discipleship pathways—bible courses, mentorship, service opportunities—equip new believers to reproduce faith in others. Leadership training emphasizes theological grounding alongside practical skills for evangelism and mentoring. Regular commissioning services send out workers with prayer and laying on of hands, echoing the early church's practice (Acts 13:3). By linking Lazarus's sign to the Great Commission, the church embodies both the catalyst of belief and the ongoing call to spiritual multiplication.

10.3.2 Witnessing by Word and Sacrament (Acts 2:38–42)

Peter's post-Pentecost sermon pairs proclamation—"Repent and be baptized" (Acts 2:38)—with sacramental action, leading to three thousand conversions. Word and sacrament function together: preaching harvests hearts, baptism publicly unites new believers to Christ's death and resurrection (Romans 6:4), and the Lord's Supper sustains communal memory of his life-giving work. Contemporary churches integrate evangelistic invitations with immediate baptism classes and accessible communion services. Outreach events conclude with an altar call that offers both prayer for salvation and an invitation to baptism preparation. Careful teaching ensures newcomers understand the sacramental significance rather than viewing it as mere ritual. Small groups studying Acts 2 learn how word and sacrament formed the early Christian identity. Worship planners sequence services so that testimonies and sermons lead naturally into sacrament participation. By combining clear gospel proclamation with tangible signs, the church embodies the biblical pattern that nurtures faith from initial belief into sustained life in Christ.

10.3.3 Baptism as First Testimony of Resurrection Life (Romans 6:3–5)

Baptism proclaims publicly that believers have died and risen with Christ (Romans 6:3–5), signaling to the world that resurrection life is now operative in them. As the first public act of obedience, it serves as a powerful testimony—new believers step into water bound by sin and emerge bound instead to Christ's new life. Churches can craft baptism liturgies that include personal testimonies shared just before immersion, linking individual stories to the symbolic act. Video highlight reels of baptisms, shown in services or online, leverage the visual impact to encourage others toward faith. Follow-up support groups for the newly baptized help them integrate into community and continue growth. Pastors remind congregations that every baptism is both a celebration and a commission—each baptized person is sent into the world as living evidence of Jesus' victory over death. By centering baptism as the first testimony, the church anchors evangelistic strategy in the tangible demonstration of resurrection life, inviting observers to consider the transformative power that baptism represents.

10.4 Personal Testimony: Sharing Your Story

10.4.1 The Three-Act Structure: Before, Encounter, After

Crafting an effective testimony often follows a three-act arc: life before Christ ("Before"), the moment of encounter ("Encounter"), and life after transformation ("After"). In the "Before" phase, describe your context—what longings, failures, or emptiness characterized your life. For example, Paul describes his former zeal that led him to persecute the church (Philippians 3:6). The "Encounter" phase pinpoints how you met Christ—through reading Scripture, a friend's invitation, or a moment of crisis. Nicodemus, coming by night, encountered Jesus' radical offer of new birth (John 3:3–7). In "After," illustrate tangible changes—new freedoms, healed relationships, or fresh purpose. Lydia's household believed after hearing Paul, then acted immediately by being baptized and hosting the church (Acts 16:14–15). Keeping each section concise—one to two minutes when spoken—maintains listener attention. Writing your story in bullet points under these headings ensures clarity when nerves set in. Practice with a friend who can offer feedback on pacing and emotional impact. By structuring testimony this way, listeners easily follow your journey and feel invited into each phase of transformation.

10.4.2 Vulnerability and Authenticity: Inviting Identification (2□Corinthians 1:3–7)

Paul models vulnerability when he shares his sufferings—flogged, shipwrecked, faced death—so others might know comfort (2□Corinthians 1:3–7). Authentic testimony acknowledges hardship without glossing over pain, demonstrating God's presence in real brokenness. Sharing specific emotions—fear, shame, anger—allows listeners to connect emotionally rather than perceive a polished, impersonal account. For instance, Peter's denial of Jesus (Luke 22:54–62) becomes powerful when he later recounts his shame and Christ's restoration. Including moments of doubt or struggle gives credibility: "I wrestled with believing God could forgive me" invites empathy. Maintaining boundaries—avoiding graphic or overly private details—respects the dignity of others involved. Always point back to Christ's work, preventing the story from becoming self-glorifying. Use "I" statements ("I felt," "I experienced") to own your narrative and avoid making universal claims. Invite listeners to ask questions, fostering two-way engagement rather than a monologue. When vulnerability is rooted in gospel truth, it becomes a bridge to others' hearts, opening them to the resurrection life you testify to.

10.4.3 Undergirding Testimony with Scripture (Psalm 107:2)

Psalm 107:2 declares, "Let the redeemed of the Lord say so...," linking testimony with corporate declaration of God's deeds. Every personal story gains theological depth when anchored to Scripture: referencing God's promises and fulfilled prophecy frames your experience within God's larger redemptive work. For instance, aligning your "Before" shame with Isaiah 54:4 ("...you will not be put to shame") shows God's word speaking into your life. When recounting deliverance from fear, Psalm 34:4 ("I sought the Lord, and he answered me; he delivered me from all my fears") gives listeners a biblical lens. Integrating brief Scripture citations prevents your testimony from floating as mere anecdote. Memorizing a handful of key verses equips you to weave them naturally into your story. Visual aids—PowerPoint slides or handouts—can display your reference verses, reinforcing their authority. Small-group leaders can host "Scripture & Story" nights, pairing testimonies with group reading of related passages. This fusion of narrative and text echoes early evangelists who preached Christ's death and resurrection "according to the Scriptures" (1 Corinthians 15:3–4). By undergirding testimony with Scripture, you show that your story is not anecdotal curiosity but evidence of God's consistent, trustworthy character.

10.5 Relational Evangelism: Hearing and Speaking

10.5.1 Listening as Ministry: "Murmur No More" (1☐Peter 3:15)

Peter instructs believers always to be "ready to give a defense…yet do it with gentleness and respect" (1☐Peter 3:15). More than having an answer, relational evangelism begins with active listening—hearing another's story without rushing to speak. Techniques such as reflective listening ("So you're saying…") validate concerns and build trust. In a coffee-shop conversation, pausing to let the other finish shows respect and invites openness. Jesus modeled this in his encounter with the Samaritan woman, engaging her need before revealing his identity (John 4:1–26). Asking open-ended questions—"What has shaped your view of God?"—uncovers spiritual longings. Listening without judgment creates a safe space where the gospel can be introduced gently. Training workshops in spiritual conversation include role-plays where one person practices listening for "spiritual cues." Churches can host "Listening Labs," gathering laypeople to refine listening skills in pairs. When we murmur no more—ceasing inner evaluation and offering full attention—we embody Christ's compassionate presence and lay the foundation for credible witness.

10.5.2 Asking Life-Story Questions of Seekers

Turning generic quiz-style questions into heartfelt life-story inquiries invites deeper sharing. Instead of "Do you believe in God?" ask "What experiences have shaped your spiritual journey?" Questions like "What gives you hope on hard days?" or "Where have you felt most alive?" open windows into a person's soul. In Acts 8, Philip begins with the Ethiopian eunuch's reading of Isaiah 53 and asks, "Do you understand what you are reading?" (Acts 8:30), guiding the seeker to see Christ as the fulfillment. Relational evangelists prepare a mental list of such "story questions" to adapt to any context. Professionals in counseling and coaching back this approach, noting that deeper questions yield more meaningful dialogue. Small groups can practice interviewing one another using these prompts, then debrief on insights gained. Journaling personal responses to these questions equips believers to relate when roles reverse. By asking life-story questions, we demonstrate genuine interest and invite seekers into a conversational space where the gospel feels less like salesmanship and more like shared discovery.

10.5.3 Inviting to Community: Hospitality as Evangelism (Romans 12:13)

Paul urges believers "to contribute to the needs of the saints and seek to show hospitality" (Romans 12:13), highlighting that relational evangelism often unfolds over time within community contexts. Inviting a seeker to your home dinner or small-group gathering extends the gospel by demonstrating love in action. Shared meals break down social barriers and model the kingdom table (Luke 14:12–14). Hosting "Alpha" or "Explore Christianity" courses in a living-room setting combines hospitality with structured teaching. Churches can train hospitality volunteers to greet newcomers by name, offer guided tours, and follow up with invitations to home-based events. Neighborhood block parties sponsored by the church create informal contexts where seekers and believers mingle naturally. Care packages—meals, prayer cards, devotion booklets—serve as tangible expressions of welcome and concern. In multiethnic contexts, hosting cultural-theme potlucks honors backgrounds and invites curiosity about faith's relevance. Through intentional hospitality, we incarnate the gospel's love, making community itself a powerful evangelistic tool.

10.6 Signs and Wonders: The Role of Miracles Today

10.6.1 Beyond Lazarus—Biblical Patterns of Sign-Driven Belief (John 20:30–31)

John concludes his Gospel: "these are written so that you may believe that Jesus is the Christ...and by believing you may have life in his name" (John 20:30–31). He frames signs as written records to evoke belief. Throughout Scripture, signs— water to wine (John 2), healing the blind (John 9), the leper cleansed (Luke 5)—function to validate Jesus' identity. Contemporary ministry recognizes that modern miracles— healings, deliverances, miraculous provisions—continue this pattern, directing attention to Christ rather than sensationalism. Careful documentation of signs, with testimonies and medical verifications, parallels early Gospel writers' "orderly accounts." Healing rooms network believers skilled in prayer for physical restoration, partnering with Scripture like James 5:14–15. Teams trained in discernment ensure that claims align with biblical criteria (Deuteronomy 13:1–3). Regularly sharing verified signs in preaching and small groups reinforces faith in the same Jesus who performed the original signs. By situating modern wonders within the biblical pattern, the church invites both seekers and skeptics to consider Jesus' ongoing authority over creation.

10.6.2 Discernment: Testing the Spirits (1 John 4:1–3)

John warns, "Beloved, do not believe every spirit, but test the spirits to see whether they are from God" (1 John 4:1). While valuing signs, we guard against counterfeit miracles that distract or deceive. Discernment involves checking whether the results—conviction of sin, transformation in Christlikeness—align with the Spirit's fruit (Galatians 5:22– 23). Evaluating a claimed healing includes both prayer for the individual's ongoing care and medical follow-up. In cases of prophetic utterance, church elders verify content against Scripture's authority (Isaiah 8:20). Training in spiritual warfare and deliverance equips leaders to distinguish genuine freedom from manipulation. Accountability structures—peer review groups, oversight councils—assess sign-ministry integrity. Workshops on "Healthy Charismata" teach theological and practical criteria, preventing sensationalism. By rigorously testing every spirit, the church preserves its witness, ensuring signs point to God's glory rather than human vanity.

10.6.3 Balancing Word and Deed in Contemporary Ministry (James 2:14–18)

James insists, "What good is it…if someone says he has faith but does not have works?… faith by itself, if it does not have works, is dead" (James 2:14, 17). Effective witness integrates the preaching of the Word with compassionate deeds—feeding the hungry, visiting the sick—reflecting the holistic gospel. The Good Samaritan (Luke 10:30–37) illustrates that neighborly action and spiritual witness co-occur. Community outreach programs—food banks, free medical clinics—serve as platforms for sharing the resurrection message. Training curricula for evangelists include modules on social justice and mercy, preventing narrow definitions of ministry. Churches partner with nonprofits, leveraging combined resources to address both spiritual and material needs. Volunteer teams receive spiritual formation alongside practical training in aid distribution. Evaluating outreach impact includes measuring both tangible outcomes (meals served) and spiritual fruit (decisions for Christ). By balancing word and deed, the church embodies James' vision of vibrant faith and authentic witness, mirroring Christ's holistic ministry that proclaimed good news and healed every disease (Matthew 4:23).

10.7 Contextualization: Speaking in Cultural Code

10.7.1 Paul at Athens: Finding Common Ground (Acts 17:22–23)

When Paul preached on Mars Hill, he began by observing Athenian worship of an "unknown god" (Acts 17:23), using their altar as an entry point for the gospel. He affirmed their religiosity before introducing the true Creator, thus building rapport. Contextualization requires learning the cultural "altar" of your audience—its values, symbols, and unspoken beliefs—and speaking into that space. In multiethnic or secular settings, this might mean referencing popular art, local sayings, or communal struggles. Ethnographic listening—spending time in community events, cafés, or online forums—reveals these contextual touchpoints. Mission teams equip themselves with cultural guides—local historians, anthropologists, or long-time residents—to avoid missteps. When sharing the resurrection story, they translate theological terms into everyday language—"new start" for regeneration, "life restored" for resurrection. Paul's approach also included quoting local poets (Aratus) to demonstrate respect for their heritage (v.28). In our day, quoting song lyrics or film quotes can serve a similar function, provided the source aligns with biblical truth. By finding common ground like Paul did, evangelists open ears and hearts to deeper gospel conversations.

10.7.2 Bridging Worldviews without Compromise (1 Corinthians 9:19–23)

Paul's ministry philosophy—becoming "all things to all people" (1 Corinthians 9:22)—demonstrates flexibility in methods while remaining unwavering on core truths. Bridging worldviews requires understanding contrasting belief systems—materialism, pluralism, scientism—and translating the gospel in terms they can grasp. For example, addressing secular audiences might involve framing Christ as the fulfillment of existential longings, not merely a religious figure. Apologetic training helps believers articulate why Christian theism best accounts for objective morality, human dignity, and the origin of the universe. Yet this must be done gently, avoiding intellectual arrogance or cultural imperialism. Contextual evangelism also adapts worship styles, liturgies, and community practices to local customs—using indigenous music, culturally relevant illustrations, and community rhythms. Churches in diaspora communities often blend traditional liturgy with host-culture elements, modeling unity in diversity. Theological workshops emphasize preserving the gospel's substance—Christ's deity, atoning death, bodily resurrection—while adjusting its form for cultural intelligibility. Field teams produce contextualized discipleship materials—scripts, films, study guides—designed by and for local believers. In this way, the church fulfills Paul's mandate: entering each worldview respectfully, yet never compromising the gospel's unchanging message.

10.7.3 Using Local Languages, Metaphors, and Symbols

Language shapes thought, so sharing the gospel in a person's heart language enhances clarity and resonance (Acts 2:6–8). Translating Scripture and testimony into local dialects, idioms, and proverbs makes the message accessible. Metaphors drawn from common experiences—fishing nets for evangelism in coastal towns, harvest imagery in farming communities—connect biblical truth to daily life. Symbols—such as water jars in regions with water scarcity—communicate spiritual realities in tangible form. Ethnolinguistic engagement involves collaborating with local translators and cultural insiders to avoid literal but misleading renderings. Visual arts—murals, comics, digital graphics—incorporate indigenous aesthetics, affirming cultural dignity. Storytelling events leverage folk tales that echo gospel themes—lost sheep, prodigal journeys—before unveiling their fulfillment in Christ. Music ministries compose worship songs in local musical modes, carrying theological depth through familiar rhythms. Training programs teach believers to craft their own cultural metaphors, ensuring the gospel becomes a living narrative within each community. By using local languages, metaphors, and symbols, the church incarnates the message of resurrection life in ways that speak directly to every person's context.

10.8 Digital Evangelism: Opportunities and Pitfalls

10.8.1 Social-Media Testimonies: Short-Form Storytelling

Platforms like Instagram, TikTok, and YouTube allow believers to share bite-sized testimonies—60-second videos capturing before/after snapshots of God's work. Short-form storytelling emphasizes emotional hooks: identifying a pain point, declaring the gospel pivot, and showcasing life's transformation. Utilizing captions and hashtags (#ResurrectionLife, #TestimonyTuesday) increases discoverability and encourages community engagement. Teams produce professionally edited clips—mixing personal footage, text overlays, and Scripture citations—to maintain credibility and visual appeal. Viewer comments become avenues for follow-up, with moderated responses guiding seekers to deeper conversations. Churches can coordinate "Digital Testimony Campaigns," asking members to submit short videos on a theme (healing, forgiveness, purpose). Analytics track reach, watch time, and engagement rates, informing content refinement. Caution: digital testimonies must avoid sensationalism or privacy violations; consent and theological vetting are essential. By leveraging social media's reach responsibly, the church brings resurrection stories into millions of timelines, inviting virtual witnesses to real faith encounters.

10.8.2 Online Apologetics: Equipping for Digital Dialogue

In a world inundated with competing worldviews, online apologetics addresses intellectual objections in comment threads, forums, and live streams. Churches and ministries host webinars on topics like "Does the Resurrection Stand Up to Historical Scrutiny?" or "Is Christianity Intolerant?" Participants learn how to articulate evidence for the empty tomb, the reliability of the Gospels, and the coherence of the Christian worldview. Resources—e-books, podcasts, and FAQ pages—provide quick reference for digital conversations. Volunteers trained in civility and digital etiquette engage skeptics without hostility, following 1☐Peter 3:15's admonition to give answers with "gentleness and respect." Online "Ask Me Anything" sessions feature pastors, scholars, and lay apologists addressing real-time questions. Multimedia presentations use infographics and short animations to explain complex arguments accessibly. Churches monitor comment moderation to ensure safe spaces for seekers. By combining solid biblical grounding with digital savvy, online apologetics transforms comment sections into front-porches for the gospel.

10.8.3 Building Virtual Communities and Discipleship Pathways

Beyond initial contact, digital evangelism must offer pathways for sustained growth—virtual small groups, online courses, and mentoring. Video conferencing platforms host Bible studies, prayer meetings, and alpha courses, enabling geographical barriers to fall. Learning management systems deliver tiered discipleship content—foundational courses, spiritual-formation modules, leadership training—to online members. Mentorship pairs can meet via video calls, using chat apps for daily encouragement and accountability. Community platforms integrate forums, resource libraries, and event calendars, creating a sense of belonging. Annual online conferences and virtual "Faith Festivals" bring tens of thousands together for worship, teaching, and fellowship. Effective digital discipleship tracks participant progress— course completion, group attendance, mentoring sessions— and prompts follow-up. Privacy settings ensure that vulnerable discussions remain secure. By intentionally building virtual communities and discipleship pathways, the church extends the promise of "abundant life" into the digital realm, making the message of resurrection accessible and sustaining it through relational engagement.

10.9 Discipleship: From First Belief to Maturity

10.9.1 Initial Follow-Up: Grounding New Believers in Truth (Colossians 2:6–7)

After someone trusts in Christ, immediate follow-up prevents shallow faith from fading. Colossians 2:6–7 calls believers to "walk in him, rooted and built up in him." Churches implement a "Welcome Path" where new believers receive a personalized welcome package—New Believers' Bible, discipleship book (e.g., "The" Christianity Explored Handbook), and a welcome card. Assigned "discipleship buddies" contact them within 24 hours, sharing their own faith journey and inviting them into a New Believers' class. A structured first-month plan outlines weekly steps: memorizing a foundational verse (John 3:16), learning a simple prayer model, attending a basic doctrine session, and practicing sharing their testimony. Digital tools—apps sending daily devotionals—reinforce initial teachings. Accountability check-ins at weeks 2 and 4 address challenges and celebrate milestones, helping newcomers feel seen and valued. Pastors preach a "First Steps" series, ensuring that congregational teaching aligns with follow-up content. By swiftly grounding new believers in core truths and habits, the church fosters roots strong enough to withstand life's storms.

10.9.2 Incorporation into Local Church Life (Hebrews 10:24–25)

Believers grow best when woven into the fabric of a faith community. Hebrews 10:24–25 exhorts us to "consider how to stir up one another to love and good works, not neglecting to meet together." After initial follow-up, new members are invited to join a small group aligned with their life stage—young adults, families, singles, or interest-based groups (arts, sports, service). Integration events—new members' luncheons, "Coffee with the Elder"—introduce them to leadership and fellow believers. Service-opportunity fairs match newcomers with ministry roles, affirming their gifts and building ownership. Church applications map member interests, spiritual gifts, and availability, facilitating meaningful connections. A "Member Mentor" program pairs new believers with established families, accelerating assimilation. Celebrations of new member baptisms and testimonies in worship reinforce communal support. By embedding believers into church life early, the body functions as intended—a living organism where every part contributes and grows.

10.9.3 Multiplication through Mentoring and Leadership Development (2☐Timothy 2:2)

Per Paul's directive—"what you have heard from me… entrust to faithful men who will be able to teach others also" (2☐Timothy 2:2)—discipleship multiplies when leaders intentionally invest in emerging believers. Churches establish tiered mentoring cohorts: one-on-one mentorship for spiritual formation, group mentorship in theology or ministry skills, and peer mentoring for mutual encouragement. Leadership development tracks guide participants from basic volunteer roles to team leader, small-group facilitator, and eventually trainer or missionary. Regular "mentor summits" equip mentors in communication, theology, and coaching, ensuring high-quality replication. Apprenticeship models—shadowing pastors, worship leaders, and missions coordinators—provide hands-on experience. Assessment tools measure readiness for leadership, focusing on character, competence, and calling. Upon readiness, emerging leaders are commissioned in worship services, publicly affirming their new role and encouraging the congregation to support them. This deliberate multiplication ensures that personal transformation catalyzes the next generation of Christ's witnesses, fulfilling the Great Commission through exponential discipleship.

Conclusion As we step into the world bearing our own Lazarus-stories, may we do so with humility, boldness, and reliance on the Spirit's power to validate our words. True evangelism is never about clever techniques or rote presentations, but about inviting people into real encounters where Christ's resurrection life becomes undeniable. When we weave together the courage to testify, the grace to listen, and the compassion to serve, many more will believe—not because of our eloquence, but because they glimpse the resurrected Lord in us and through us. May each step of witness you take echo the life-changing moment at Bethany, opening hearts to the eternal hope that only he can offer.

Chapter 11. Rising Opposition — Counting the Cost of Miraculous Ministry

When the power of God breaks into our world through signs and wonders, it often triggers a fierce reaction from forces determined to maintain the status quo. From the whisperings in the council chambers to the shifting allegiances of the crowds, the aftermath of miraculous ministry exposes the hidden fears and agendas that rise to oppose God's work. In this chapter, we will examine how heavenly interventions provoke earthly resistance—revealing both the spiritual realities at play and the very real costs borne by those who dare to stand with the resurrected Lord.

11.1 The Sanhedrin's Backlash

11.1.1 Caiaphas and the High Council's Decree (John 11:47–48)

As news of Lazarus' resurrection reached the Sanhedrin, "the chief priests and the Pharisees gathered the council and said, 'What are we to do? For this man performs many signs'" (John 11:47). Their immediate reaction was political panic rather than theological reflection: they feared that Jesus' growing following would provoke Roman reprisals. Caiaphas, the high priest that year, bluntly asserted, "You know nothing at all. Nor do you understand that it is better for you that one man should die for the people" (John 11:49–50). Though Caiaphas spoke cynically to protect the nation, John remarks that he spoke prophetically, foreshadowing Jesus' atoning death. The council's decree to eliminate Jesus illustrates how religious leadership can prioritize institutional survival over fidelity to God's redemptive purposes. Their decision-making process— closed, fear-driven, self-serving—stands in stark contrast to Jesus' openness and sacrificial love. Modern ministry leaders face similar temptations: protecting budgets, reputations, or denominations can lead to watered-down gospel witness. Churches must guard against fear-based governance by maintaining accountability and inviting prophetic critique. Training in spiritual discernment equips elders to recognize when ministry decisions stem from faith or from institutional self-interest. By studying Caiaphas' decree, contemporary leaders learn the high cost of choosing preservation over partnership with God's transformative work.

11.1.2 Fear of Rome and Preservation of Power (John 11:49–53)

Within the council, the overriding concern was Roman reaction: loss of privileges, high taxes, and potential destruction of the Temple. Under the terms of Pax Romana, any disturbance could draw punitive measures (Josephus, *Antiq.*). Caiaphas' logic—"that the Romans may come and destroy both our holy place and our nation"—reflects realpolitik more than covenantal trust (John 11:48). Their fear-driven alliance with Rome exemplifies how spiritual authority can become entangled with secular power, leading to moral compromise. The council's plot to kill Jesus (John 11:53) thus becomes an act of misguided patriotism, sacrificing truth for stability. In today's context, churches navigating relationships with governments—regarding tax exemptions, zoning laws, or education policy—must avoid compromises that undermine gospel integrity. Advocacy training helps Christians engage civil authorities without losing prophetic voice (Proverbs 29:2). Historical examples—churches cooperating with apartheid regimes or totalitarian states—warn of the dangers of such alliances. Cultivating a theology of the kingdom that transcends earthly powers protects congregations from fear-driven capitulation. By examining the Sanhedrin's fear of Rome, ministers can learn to place ultimate trust in God rather than in human empires.

11.1.3 Formal Charges and Attempts at Discrediting

Following their decree, the Sanhedrin set about gathering evidence to justify Jesus' arrest: they scrutinized his teachings, sought false witnesses, and manipulated public perception (Mark 14:55–59). The formal charges—blasphemy, claiming to be the Messiah, threatening Temple authority—were crafted to appear religiously legitimate. Yet the courts employed illicit methods: bribing witnesses, twisting Jesus' words, and ignoring contradictory testimony. The Temple trial's illegality—held at night, in Caiaphas' house, without defense counsel—reveals a judiciary more concerned with outcome than justice (John 18:12–14). This pattern of discrediting through manipulated evidence echoes in modern contexts: religious whistleblowers or minority ministers can face defamation and institutional pushback. Educating congregations on ethical leadership and transparency prevents similar miscarriages of justice. Legal ministries within the church teach members to uphold due process and resist character assassination. Pastors model integrity by providing open forums for critique and inviting external oversight. By dissecting the Sanhedrin's formal charges, believers learn to anticipate opposition's tactics and maintain righteousness under scrutiny.

11.2 Hostile Crowds and Popular Shifts

11.2.1 From Hosannas to Hisses: The Volatility of Public Opinion

Jesus' triumphal entry into Jerusalem was met with cries of "Hosanna!" (Mark 11:9), yet days later the same crowds chanted "Crucify him!" (Matthew 27:22). This rapid reversal underscores how public sentiment, once swayed by spectacle, can be redirected by fear-mongering and demagoguery. Crowd psychology studies reveal that large groups often latch onto the loudest voices and can be manipulated through emotional appeals (Le Bon, *The Crowd*). In Jerusalem, the chief priests stoked anger by depicting Jesus as a political threat (John 19:12). Modern ministries must recognize that viral campaigns and social-media outrage can fuel similar volatility. Training in crisis communication equips church leaders to respond calmly when public opinion shifts due to rumor or sensational headlines. Engaging in honest dialogue with community influencers and providing transparent information helps stabilize perceptions. Pastors can preempt backlash by maintaining consistent messaging rooted in character rather than chasing popularity. Churches that memorize Jesus' counsel—"Blessed are you when men revile you… rejoice and be glad" (Matthew 5:11–12)—stand firm amid shifting crowds. Understanding the fickle nature of mass sentiment prepares believers to persevere when the applause turns to jeers.

11.2.2 Propaganda and Rumor: Shaping the Narrative

Following Lazarus' resurrection, the Pharisees and chief priests commissioned false witnesses and spread rumors that Jesus performed miracles by demonic power (Matthew 12:24). This propaganda campaign aimed to sow doubt and discredit genuine signs. Political movements throughout history have used similar tactics—spreading fear-inducing misinformation to undermine opponents. In our age of "fake news," churches must proactively guard against rumor by establishing official channels for communication. Equipping members to fact-check viral claims and encouraging responsible social-media sharing combats misleading narratives. Media-training programs teach pastors and lay leaders how to craft clear, concise statements and rapidly correct falsehoods. Partnering with reputable journalists and using press-release protocols helps control the story's framing. Small groups practice critical media literacy, learning to distinguish credible sources from manipulative propaganda. By countering rumor with truth and transparency, the church preserves its witness and protects the vulnerable from defamation.

11.2.3 Lessons for Managing Public Perception

Jesus never abandoned the crowds but engaged them with parables, healing, and teaching, demonstrating authenticity rather than spin control. He modeled that consistent character over time builds trust beyond any single event (John 7:46). For modern ministries, long-term visibility through genuine service—feeding the poor, advocating for justice—establishes credibility that outlasts fleeting controversies. Implementing feedback loops—listening sessions, surveys—helps leaders gauge community perception and address concerns before they escalate. Pastors should appoint "public perception teams" responsible for outreach, community relations, and proactive storytelling. Hosting open-house events invites neighbors into church life, humanizing its mission. Regular transparency reports—on finances, decision-making, and community impact—build sustained public trust. In crisis, swift acknowledgment of mistakes and clear corrective action, modeled on Jesus' confession of wrongdoing (if any), limits reputational damage. By learning from the volatile Jerusalem crowds, the church adopts strategic, character-driven approaches to public perception, ensuring that its miracles point back to God rather than to institutional agendas.

11.3 Political Entanglements

11.3.1 Pilate's Dilemma: Balancing Justice and Order (Luke 23:4–12)

Pilate faced a classic colonial dilemma: uphold justice or appease local elites to maintain order. He interrogated Jesus personally, finding no guilt warranting death (Luke 23:4), yet ultimately capitulated to the crowd's demands to avoid a riot. His compromise—symbolic hand-washing of responsibility (Matthew 27:24)—revealed the emptiness of political gestures unanchored in truth. Modern church–state interactions mirror this tension: when religious freedoms intersect with public policy, political leaders may feign neutrality while enforcing popular opinion. Churches must navigate these waters by advocating for justice (Micah 6:8) while respecting legitimate governmental roles (Romans 13:1–7). Engaging in civic education helps congregants understand their rights and responsibilities as both citizens and believers. Partnerships with faith-based advocacy groups ensure that church voices are heard in the legislative process on matters of morality and social welfare. Ethical lobbying training equips church leaders to represent their communities without coercion or partisanship. By examining Pilate's dilemma, believers learn to resist expedient compromises and uphold God's justice even under political pressure.

11.3.2 Collusion of Religious and Secular Authorities

The trial of Jesus showcases how religious authorities manipulated secular power: they leveraged Pilate's fear of unrest to achieve their own ends (John 19:12–16). This collusion between temple leaders and the Roman governor exemplifies how unchecked alliances between church and state can pervert both Gospel witness and civil administration. Today, religious institutions that align too closely with political parties risk losing prophetic independence and becoming mere extensions of government policy. Historical examples—state churches in medieval Europe, modern theocracies—demonstrate the dangers of such alliances. Churches maintain integrity by affirming their dual citizenship: in Christ's kingdom and in earthly nations (Philippians 3:20). Developing clear policies on political engagement—encouraging voter registration and issue-based advocacy but discouraging partisan endorsements—protects congregations from undue influence. Pastors and staff receive training in ecclesial ethics, understanding boundaries set by law and denomination. Interfaith coalitions on social issues allow churches to partner without compromising core convictions. Learning from the collusion against Jesus, believers commit to speaking truth to power rather than using power to enforce religious conformity.

11.3.3 Navigating Church–State Boundaries Today

Balancing respect for government with prophetic critique requires wisdom and courage. Churches operate under legal frameworks—nonprofit status, zoning regulations, employment law—that set boundaries for political activity. Educating leadership teams on the juridical limits of advocacy ensures compliance and preserves tax-exempt status. Teaching congregations about the distinction between issue advocacy and candidate endorsements empowers informed participation. Advocacy toolkits provide templates for letter-writing campaigns on policy matters—immigration reform, poverty alleviation—while avoiding prohibited electioneering. Regular forums—"Civic Sundays"—offer neutral presentations on current affairs from multiple perspectives, fostering critical engagement rather than noise. Establishing "Justice Commissions" within the church coordinates long-term policy work with theological grounding (Isaiah 1:17). Partnerships with legal aid societies extend the church's reach in defending religious freedom while upholding the rule of law. By thoughtfully navigating church–state boundaries, congregations honor both their heavenly mandate and their civic responsibilities, modeling integrity in every sphere of influence.

11.4 Spiritual Warfare behind the Scenes

11.4.1 Satan's Counter-Miracle: Fear and Intimidation (Ephesians 6:12)

While Jesus wrought life from death, Satan marshaled his resources to sow fear and intimidation among witnesses. Ephesians 6:12 reminds us that our struggle is "against the spiritual forces of evil in the heavenly places," indicating a reality beyond mere human antagonism. The disciples, fresh from Lazarus's resurrection, soon faced dread-induced paralysis—a spiritual tactic designed to neutralize their testimony. Demonic intimidation often manifests as sudden, unexplainable dread, nightmares, or relational conflict that distracts believers from gospel proclamation. In Bethany, the plot to kill Jesus and Lazarus (John 12:10) likely involved fear-mongering intended to terrify followers into silence. Today, ministry leaders report burnout, anxiety, and conflict inexplicable by human factors alone, suggesting spiritual assault. Recognizing such counter-miracles demands prayerful discernment (1 John 4:1) and reliance on God's armor (Ephesians 6:13–17). Corporate fasting and prayer vigils—modeled on Jesus' own 40-day fast (Matthew 4:1–11)—break the fear's grip. Pastors equip congregations to "take every thought captive" (2 Corinthians 10:5) when panic threatens. By naming Satan's intimidation tactics, the church stands ready to resist the enemy's counter-miracles and uphold Christ's victory.

11.4.2 Demonic Activity versus Divine Intervention

In the same hour that the evil one rallied forces against God's purposes, the Spirit of God moved freely to empower Jesus' followers. Demonic activity—possession, oppression, and temptation—often masquerades as unassailable strongholds, yet Scripture shows that every power of darkness is inferior to Christ's authority (Luke 10:17–19). While demons instilled terror in the Sanhedrin, the resurrection miracle dismantled their claims over death. Distinguishing demonic interference from God's intervention requires grounding in biblical truth: if an event leads away from Christ's character, it is not from God (1□John 4:1–3). For instance, physical ailments used in deliverance sessions may have spiritual roots requiring prayer, but genuine healings align with Scripture's patterns (Acts 3:1–10). God's interventions bring peace, clarity, and faith, whereas demonic incursions breed confusion and despair (John 10:10). Deliverance ministers learn to declare divine authority—"In Jesus' name, depart!"—while also practicing humility and pastoral care (Galatians 6:1). Teaching on spiritual warfare integrates both offensive and defensive prayer stances, mirroring Jesus' commissioning of the Seventy (Luke 10:1–12). Through consistent reliance on Scripture and Spirit, the church navigates the tension between dark scheming and divine power.

11.4.3 Equipping for Overseer Warfare in Ministry

Ministry leaders are called not only to preach but to intercede in spiritual battles that afflict their congregations. Paul's charge to "put on the whole armor of God" (Ephesians 6:11) applies first to elders who must model and teach spiritual warfare. Training programs for overseers include theological foundations—understanding the nature of angels and demons (Hebrews 1:14)—and practical exercises in prophetic prayer, binding, and loosing. Mentorship cohorts pair new leaders with seasoned intercessors, transferring insights on discerning spiritual strongholds. Workshops simulate conflict scenarios— internal strife, community opposition—equipping teams to pray scripturally for breakthrough. Regular "War Room" gatherings create dedicated times for focused spiritual warfare on behalf of church and community. Accountability structures ensure that spiritual leaders remain grounded in personal holiness, preventing pride or error (James 4:6). Pastors incorporate teaching on spiritual authority into discipleship classes, normalizing warfare as part of everyday faith. By intentionally equipping overseers, churches sustain miraculous ministry despite rising opposition.

11.5 Personal Persecution of Witnesses

11.5.1 Disciples' Fears and Fainting Hearts (Luke 9:51–56)

Even as Jesus set his face to Jerusalem, his disciples struggled with fear and misunderstanding. When Samaritans refused him lodging, James and John asked to call down fire (Luke 9:54), revealing their zeal but also their impatience and warlike hearts. Their reaction underscores how persecution can distort even well-intended followers, leading them to respond in anger rather than grace. As the pathway down from Bethany to Jerusalem narrowed, each step carried the threat of arrest, beatings, or worse, causing hearts to faint (Isaiah 29:8). Modern evangelists often confess similar tremors before hostile crowds—public ridicule, legal threats, or physical danger. Churches can hold "Courage Clinics" where testimonies of fear overcome through faith (Matthew 14:30–31) encourage boldness. Small-group rehearsals of gospel presentations in safe spaces build confidence. Mentoring relationships help individuals process fear before it paralyzes witness. Prayer partners commit to interceding for one another in moments of fainting faith. By addressing disciples' fears head-on, the church cultivates resilient witness rather than fragile bravado.

11.5.2 Imprisonment, Whipping, and Exile (Acts 5:40–41)

After preaching Christ's resurrection, Peter and the apostles were flogged by the Sanhedrin, yet "rejoiced that they were counted worthy to suffer dishonor for the name" (Acts 5:41). Paul endured imprisonments, beatings, and shipwrecks (2 Corinthians 11:23–27), each wound marking his faithfulness. The early church's embrace of suffering as "joyful endurance" contrasts sharply with modern aversion to discomfort. Today, in many regions, believers face arrest for preaching, eviction for faith-based schools, or exile for refusing to recant. Solidarity networks—legal aid for imprisoned Christians, resettlement assistance for refugees—reflect the body's commitment to those suffering. Training in nonviolent resistance prepares ministries to maintain witness under coercive pressure. Pastoral care teams provide trauma counseling for survivors of persecution. Advocacy ministries leverage international law and human-rights frameworks to secure religious freedom. Celebrating the stories of martyrs and modern victims fosters a theology that values truth over personal comfort. By honoring the cost of persecution, the church undergirds witness with communal support and global solidarity.

11.5.3 Costly Discipleship: When Following Costs Everything

Jesus warned, "Whoever does not bear his own cross and come after me cannot be my disciple" (Luke 14:27). True discipleship demands willingness to lose reputation, economic security, and even family ties (Matthew 10:37–39). In contexts hostile to Christianity, choosing to follow Christ can mean forfeiting professional licenses, facing social ostracism, or risking a death sentence. Missionary biographies from China, North Korea, and parts of the Middle East recount believers who choose prison over apostasy. Churches in safe contexts cultivate cross-cultural awareness by sponsoring short-term mission trips to sensitive regions, training participants in cost assumptions. Seminary courses in missiology emphasize "theology of martyrdom," preparing future leaders for potential ultimate sacrifices. Discipleship groups engage in "Cost-Count" exercises—journaling what one would risk for Jesus—fostering perspective on material comforts. Corporate worship includes hymns of surrender—"I Surrender All"—to remind congregations of Christ's call. By reckoning the cost of discipleship honestly, the church ensures that its witness is authentic and its faith robust enough to endure opposition.

11.6 Theological Reflections on Suffering

11.6.1 Christ's Suffering as Paradigm (Philippians 3:10)

Paul earnestly desired to "know Christ and the power of his resurrection, and may share his sufferings, becoming like him in his death" (Philippians 3:10). Christ's passion—betrayal, mocking, scourging, crucifixion—serves as the paradigm for believers' suffering. His willingness to endure the cross reveals that redemptive pain transforms sin's curse into covenant blessing (Galatians 3:13). Theologically, participation in Christ's suffering links us to his resurrection power in a profound union (Romans 6:5). Preachers unpack this paradigm in passion-week sermons, showing how Jesus' voluntary suffering shapes understanding of our own trials. Spiritual retreats focus on "Cross Imagination," meditating on the actual events of Good Friday to cultivate empathy and solidarity with Christ. Artistic expressions—stations of the cross, liturgical dramas—help congregants internalize the depth of Jesus' suffering. Pastoral resources—sermon guides, devotional booklets—explore Pauline reflections on suffering's role in sanctification. By orienting our theology of trials around Christ's example, believers find both meaning and motivation to endure cost of fruitful ministry.

11.6.2 Redemptive Suffering: Joining in Christ's Passion (Romans 8:17)

Romans 8:17 states, "if children, then heirs—heirs of God and fellow heirs with Christ—provided we suffer with him in order that we may also be glorified with him." Suffering becomes redemptive when understood as participation in Christ's own passion, forging solidarity with his mission and confidence in future glory. The early church viewed martyrdom as "baptism in blood" that guaranteed union with Christ (Tertullian, *Apologeticus*). Current theological frameworks highlight how personal trials, when offered to God, join the cosmic story of redemption (Colossians 1:24). Support groups for chronic illness counsel members to view ongoing pain as offering to God, transforming suffering into spiritual fruit (2 Corinthians 1:3–7). Worship songs that affirm "my tears are gifts, my pain refines" help communities articulate redemptive suffering. Teaching series—"The Gospel and the Grind"—explore biblical case studies where adversity yielded deeper dependence on God (Hebrews 12:3–11). Retreats incorporate symbolic rituals—writing sufferings on paper and placing them at the cross—signifying release and consecration. By reframing suffering as redemptive participation in Christ's passion, the church sustains hope and purpose even amid opposition.

11.6.3 Hope amid Persecution: The Promise of Resurrection (1□Peter 4:12–14)

Peter encourages believers not to be surprised at trials but to rejoice "so that you may share in his sufferings" and in the revelation of his glory (1□Peter 4:12–13). Suffering for the name associates us with Christ's resurrection, offering a hope that transcends present pain. Early Christians often sang hymns in prison, anticipating the life-beyond (Acts 16:25). Stories of modern persecuted church members who "count it joy" amid hardship demonstrate this hope in action. Churches cultivate this perspective through teaching on eschatology—reminding congregations that present troubles are transient compared to eternal glory (2□Corinthians 4:17). Visual arts—stained-glass windows depicting the empty tomb—serve as constant reminders of victory over suffering. Prayer gatherings include readings of Revelation 7:9–17, painting a picture of the great multitude adorned in white robes. Personal reflection exercises—journaling promises of resurrection against current trials—anchor hearts in future hope. By living out the promise of resurrection amid persecution, believers testify that death's final word has been spoken—and it is not death, but life.

11.7 Pastoral Care for Wounded Ministers

11.7.1 Recognizing Burnout and Trauma in Deliverers

Those on the front lines of miraculous ministry often carry emotional and spiritual scars. Chronic exposure to intense prayer environments and spiritual warfare can lead to compassion fatigue, a form of burnout where ministers feel numb to pain rather than empathetic (Galatians 6:9). Trauma from personal attacks—defamation, threats, or physical danger—may result in PTSD-like symptoms: nightmares, hypervigilance, and emotional withdrawal (Psalm 34:18). Pastoral caregivers must learn to recognize warning signs: irritability, unexplained physical ailments, or a pervasive sense of spiritual dryness. Peer support teams provide confidential spaces for ministers to share their burdens without fear of judgment (Romans 15:1). Regular "debriefing retreats" allow deliverance workers to process encounters, receive encouragement, and reboot spiritually. Training in trauma-informed care helps pastors differentiate between normal stress and deeper wounds requiring professional referral (Proverbs 11:14). Integrating Sabbath rhythms— intentional rest in God's presence—guards against the culture of nonstop ministry (Exodus 20:8–10). Accountability partners check in weekly, asking direct questions about ministers' well-being. By proactively identifying burnout and trauma, the church honors those who bear the cost of miraculous work, ensuring they receive the care they need to continue faithfully.

11.7.2 Providing Safe Spaces for Lament and Healing

Scripture models lament as a legitimate response to suffering—David pours out his soul in the Psalms (Psalm 42:3), and early Christians wept at Stephen's martyrdom (Acts 8:2). Creating designated "lament services" offers corporate permission to grieve losses: failed ministries, persecuted colleagues, or suppressed testimonies. These gatherings incorporate lament psalms, silent prayer stations, and symbolic acts—placing stones on a "grief altar" to represent unspoken sorrows. Trained pastoral teams guide participants through structured lament liturgies, ensuring emotional expression remains tethered to hope (Lamentations 3:22–23). Small groups called "Healing Circles" meet regularly, using journal prompts to surface hidden pain and then praying for God's restorative touch (Isaiah 61:1). Incorporating creative arts—spoken word, painting, or movement—allows non-verbal expression of deep wounds. Confidentiality agreements within these spaces foster trust and freedom to share without fear of gossip. Following lament, worship leaders transition to songs of assurance—"Though I walk through the valley, you are with me" (Psalm 23)—reminding participants of God's presence. Over time, these safe spaces become battlegrounds where sorrow is transformed into strength for service. By normalizing lament, the church provides wounded ministers both validation and pathways to healing.

11.7.3 Rebuilding Vision after Crushing Opposition

After the storm of backlash, ministers may question God's calling or lose enthusiasm for service. Nehemiah faced such moments: opposition threatened to halt the wall's rebuilding, yet he refocused on God's purpose (Nehemiah 4:14). Vision-renewal gatherings bring leaders together to revisit original callings, share renewed testimonies, and pray corporately for fresh direction (Habakkuk 2:2). Pastoral retreats incorporate silence and solitude to discern God's voice apart from the clamor of criticism. Mentorship conversations revisit early leadership victories, reinforcing identity in Christ rather than in performance (2 Corinthians 1:21–22). Strategic planning sessions, grounded in prayer, help recalibrate ministry goals in light of lessons learned from opposition. Story-sharing panels featuring leaders who overcame similar setbacks inspire perseverance. Workshops on "Resilient Leadership" teach emotional agility and adaptive strategies. Encouraging ministers to set new micro-goals—small, achievable steps—rekindles momentum. By systematically rebuilding vision, the church ensures that those who have weathered crushing opposition emerge with renewed purpose and strengthened resolve.

11.8 Strategic Responses to Opposition

11.8.1 Pray, Persevere, and Proclaim (Acts 4:23–31)

When Peter and John were released after being flogged, the early church "lifted their voices together to God" (Acts 4:24), praying for boldness. Their prayer acknowledges God's sovereignty, perseveres in unity, and ends with renewed proclamation. Contemporary ministries facing opposition can adopt this model: convening urgent prayer gatherings, repenting for any sin that hinders, and asking for courage to continue witnessing. Intercession maps identify specific threats—legal actions, defamation campaigns, spiritual attacks—assigning prayer teams to each. Perseverance is cultivated through testimony rotations, where leaders share how past prayers were answered, building collective faith

(Hebrews 12:1). Prayer-and-proclamation nights integrate worship with evangelistic outreach—singing praises followed by preaching in public spaces. Recording and sharing stories of God's intervention stokes congregation-wide expectancy. Leadership communicates transparently about challenges and invites communal prayer, preventing isolation of those under fire. By combining prayer, perseverance, and proclamation, ministries resist intimidation and maintain momentum under fire.

11.8.2 Legal and Advocacy Channels for Religious Freedom

In contexts where opposition turns to legal enforcement—church closures, fines, or arrests—understanding human-rights mechanisms is essential. Churches partner with religious-liberty organizations (e.g., ADF, Open Doors) to monitor violations and file amicus briefs if needed. Training seminars equip pastors to document incidents, prepare affidavits, and engage pro bono legal counsel. Lobbying efforts—letter-writing campaigns to legislators, public petitions—raise awareness of religious-freedom infringements. Churches host "Know Your Rights" workshops for congregants, clarifying limits of permissible expression under local law. Strategic litigation can set precedents protecting worship and evangelism (e.g., Supreme Court rulings in the U.S. that defend free exercise). Public-interest lawyers within the congregation serve as ongoing advisors. Collaboration with interfaith coalitions broadens support and underscores universal value of freedom of conscience. Maintaining diplomatic relationships with government officials through respectful dialogue prevents misunderstandings and fosters goodwill. Through legal and advocacy channels, the church transforms opposition into opportunities to advance religious freedom for all.

11.8.3 Adaptive Ministry Models in Hostile Contexts

When direct public ministry is prohibited, adaptive models sustain gospel witness. Underground house churches—small groups meeting in homes—mirror the early church's practices (Acts 2:46). Digital platforms host encrypted worship services and discipleship courses, reaching believers without physical gatherings. Distribution of "Bible on a Chip" micro-SD cards allows discreet access to Scripture. Bi-vocational ministry—leaders holding secular jobs—provides cover for community engagement and ethical witness in workplaces. Training in "Contextual Evangelism" helps believers use culturally acceptable venues: tutoring, service projects, or business networks, to share faith. Mobile mission teams rotate meeting locations to avoid detection. Education-based ministry—teaching English, vocational skills, or health education—builds trust and opens doors for gospel conversations. Regular evaluation ensures safety protocols are effective: anonymized reporting of incidents, emergency extraction plans, and covert communication channels. By innovating ministry forms, the church continues its mission where overt opposition seeks to silence it.

11.9 Perseverance and Victory

11.9.1 Scriptural Examples of Endurance (Hebrews 12:1–3)

Hebrews exhorts believers to "run with endurance the race that is set before us, looking to Jesus...the founder and perfecter of our faith" (Hebrews 12:1–2). This marathon metaphor emphasizes long-term perseverance, shedding every weight and sin that entangles. Biblical heroes like Abraham, who waited decades for Isaac (Romans 4:18–21), and Job, who maintained integrity amid loss (Job 1:21–22), exemplify steadfast faith. Studying these lives in sermon series or small-group curricula provides role models for modern trials. Facilitated "Endurance Workshops" use interactive timelines, mapping key moments where faith triumphed over adversity. Churches commemorate "Faithful Service Awards" for members who minister under duress, encouraging others to persist. Personal devotion resources—journals with daily encouragements from Hebrews 12—equip believers for the long haul. Periodic "Perseverance Retreats" allow deep reflection on one's race, realignment of goals, and rekindling of hope. By anchoring present struggles in scriptural examples of endurance, the church nurtures resilient faith that outlasts every opposition.

11.9.2 Celebrating Small Triumphs under Pressure

Victory in persecution is often incremental—answers to prayer, salvations, moments of peace amid chaos. Recognizing these small triumphs provides emotional fuel to continue. Weekly "Victory Boards" in church halls display post-its celebrating any breakthroughs—legal reprieves, healed relationships, new courage. Testimony segments in services spotlight these small wins, reminding congregations that God is at work even when large-scale change is slow. Prayer group leaders maintain "Answered Prayer Logs," periodically reviewing and sharing progress. Celebratory gatherings—potlucks or informal "victory lunches"—honor those who have stood firm. Digital newsletters highlight these milestones, encouraging remote supporters. By consistently marking small triumphs, the church reinforces that every act of faith, no matter how modest, contributes to the larger victory in Christ.

11.9.3 The Ultimate Triumph of Resurrection over Resistance

The final chapter of opposition is eclipsed by the certainty of resurrection victory—"Death is swallowed up in victory" (1 Corinthians 15:54). Jesus' rising from the dead guarantees that no scheme of darkness can prevail (Revelation 1:18). Early martyrs rejoiced knowing they shared in his triumph, singing hymns as they faced execution (Revelation 7:13–14). This eschatological perspective sustains believers: present sufferings are temporary compared to the glory to be revealed (Romans 8:18). Churches incorporate this promise into baptism services, linking new life in water with eternal resurrection life. Easter celebrations emphasize victory themes, not only commemorating Christ's rising but anticipating ours. Artistic expressions—resurrection iconography, music, drama—proclaim the final overthrow of resistance. Discipleship classes on eschatology teach that every cost paid for the gospel contributes to the culmination of God's redemptive plan. By focusing on resurrection's ultimate triumph, the church marches through opposition with unshakeable hope, confident that every cost is redeemed in the risen Christ.

Conclusion As we confront the backlash that follows in the wake of divine power, may we be neither naïve about the opposition nor shaken in our resolve to press on. To count the cost is not to surrender but to prepare—to ground our courage in Christ's suffering, to stand firm in prayer and proclamation, and to care tenderly for one another when trials come. For every scheme devised against the gospel, the same resurrection life that raised Lazarus equips us to endure, persevere, and ultimately witness the triumph of God's kingdom over every form of resistance.

Chapter 12. Foreshadowing Calvary — The Sign That Points to the Empty Tomb

The astonishing sight of Lazarus stepping forth from the tomb, still wrapped in burial cloths, carries a prophetic weight far beyond Bethany's hillside. In that moment, Jesus offers a living parable of his own journey through death to new life— previewing the cross and the empty tomb. As we unpack this "seventh sign," we will trace the shadows it casts forward onto Calvary and beyond, revealing how every detail—from stones to spices—anticipates the ultimate victory over death. This chapter invites us to see Lazarus's resurrection not as an isolated wonder but as an early chapter in the larger story of Christ's passion, death, and triumphant rising.

12.1 The Irony of Resurrection before Crucifixion

12.1.1 Lazarus Raised to Die Again (John 11:44)

When Jesus orders, "Unbind him, and let him go" (John 11:44), Lazarus emerges alive only to later face mortality once more. His resurrection serves as a temporary victory over death, yet he inevitably returns to dust—underscoring that this divine act, powerful though it is, does not break death's final barrier. In this sense, Lazarus's return foreshadows Christ's own passage: a preliminary sign that points to the ultimate defeat of death on Calvary and resurrection morning. The disciples who witnessed Lazarus live out this irony had to learn that true life would come only through Jesus' own death and rising (Romans 6:5). This paradox calls the church to discern between provisional miracles and the consummating miracle of the empty tomb. In pastoral teaching, Lazarus's second mortality can illustrate that temporal healings and deliverances, while glorious, leave us longing for the eternal life Christ secures (John 3:16). Theologically, Lazarus's fate reminds us that Christ's resurrection alone offers unbroken, everlasting life. Liturgically, raising Lazarus becomes a pre-Easter motif, inviting congregations to anticipate both sorrow and joy. Artistic depictions often show Lazarus stepping forward while shadows of Calvary loom in the background, capturing this layered meaning. Thus, the irony of Lazarus's temporary life sets the stage for the gospel's climactic turning point.

12.1.2 The Temporary Triumph: Life That Precedes Ultimate Sacrifice

In Bethany, the crowd exults at Lazarus's resurrection, but within days, the same crowd will demand Jesus' crucifixion (John 12:18–19; 19:15). This fleeting celebration highlights how human praise can be as transient as the raised man's second death. Jesus allows this temporary triumph precisely to teach that genuine transformation requires the giving of his own life. His death would not only raise the dead but abolish death itself, rendering all previous resuscitations mere foreshadows. Church history has recognized Lazarus's miracle as the "dress rehearsal" for Calvary—showing power, yet pointing beyond itself (John 20:30–31). Preaching on this theme invites congregations to move beyond craving sensational signs to embracing the costly path of cruciform discipleship (Philippians 2:8). It also cautions against conflating temporary spiritual awakenings with the permanent renewal achieved in Christ's atoning work. Sacramental theology ties this temporary triumph to Eucharistic anticipation: we celebrate Christ's body given and blood shed in each communion as the once-for-all sacrifice that overcomes death forever (Hebrews 10:10). Thus, the brevity of Lazarus's victory deepens our appreciation for the permanence of Christ's.

12.1.3 How Pre-Calvary Miracles Set the Stage for Good Friday

The raising of Lazarus catalyzes the plot to kill Jesus (John 11:53), driving the narrative toward Good Friday. Each sign Jesus performed—turning water to wine, healing the blind—prepared hearts and provoked opposition, intensifying God's redemptive drama. In Bethany, Lazarus's resurrection escalates tensions to a breaking point, making Jesus' sacrifice imminent. This pattern of sign leading to slander and climax in the cross is repeated throughout the Gospel of John (John 2:23–25; 6:26–27). For preachers, mapping this progression offers a powerful sermon series: each miracle builds anticipation for the cross. Devotional guides might structure Holy Week reflections around the "seven signs," ending with the definitive sign of the empty tomb. In pastoral care, understanding this trajectory helps believers see that opposition often intensifies just before breakthrough. Small-group studies on the "schedule of signs" reveal how God's timeline seamlessly weaves wonder with suffering. By tracing pre-Calvary miracles' role in shaping the Passion narrative, the church gains insight into God's sovereign orchestration of redemption.

12.2 Prophetic Echoes in the Passion Narrative

12.2.1 "Take Away the Stone" and "Take Up Your Cross" (John 11:39; Matthew 16:24)

Jesus' command to roll away the stone (John 11:39) and later his summons to "take up your cross" (Matthew 16:24) carry parallel symbolism. Both involve moving a heavy burden: the stone seals in death; the cross signals submission to death's means. Lazarus's unbinding prefigures Jesus' own unbinding from the grave clothes at his resurrection (John 20:6–7). Simultaneously, disciples are called not only to witness resurrection but also to bear sacrificial suffering. The juxtaposition warns that one cannot bypass the cross to reach the empty tomb; glory follows obedience to the call of self-sacrifice. Thirteen-week Easter series often contrast these passages, inviting believers into both reflection on daily cross-bearing and anticipation of resurrection victory. Artistic meditations pair images of the stone's removal and the cross's lifting, illustrating inward transformation. In discipleship curricula, participants practice "stone-mapping" and "cross-mapping" exercises—identifying personal barriers and counting costs. Theologically, these echoes underscore the unified trajectory of Jesus' ministry: resurrection power is inseparable from redemptive suffering (Philippians 2:8–9). By exploring these prophetic parallels, the church embraces the full scope of gospel message.

12.2.2 "Unbind Him" and "Forgive Them" (John 11:44; Luke 23:34)

At Lazarus's tomb, Jesus commands, "Unbind him" (John 11:44); on the cross he prays, "Father, forgive them" (Luke 23:34). Both acts demonstrate Jesus' power to reverse bondage—physical and spiritual—and highlight his compassionate authority. Unbinding Lazarus frees him to walk; forgiving executioners frees them to receive grace. These paired commands reveal the two-fold scope of Christ's liberation: deliverance from death and from sin's penalty.

Pastoral sermons tracing these commands emphasize that resurrection power brings holistic freedom. Inner-healing workshops link unbinding prayers with forgiveness exercises, teaching participants to release both self and others from bondage. In liturgical practice, the church binds symbolic grave clothes and then washes feet, enacting both unbinding and forgiveness. Theological reflections note that Christ's forgiveness—declared in the midst of suffering—serves as the definitive unbinding of sinners (Colossians 2:13–14). By connecting "unbind" and "forgive," the church proclaims comprehensive redemption that extends beyond physical restoration to the heart's deepest needs.

12.2.3 Linen Wrappings: Burial Cloths of Lazarus and Shroud of Christ (John 11:44; John 20:6–7)

John carefully notes that Lazarus emerged "bound hand and foot with linen strips" (11:44), and that Peter saw "the linen cloths lying there" and the face cloth folded separately (20:6–7). These parallel details draw a typological line between Lazarus's temporary unbinding and Christ's permanent victory over death. The burial cloths represent death's claim on the body, while their presence in the empty tomb signals that death has been vanquished. Archaeological finds of first-century Jewish burial practices corroborate the Gospel's precise descriptions (Gezer 7:1–4). In meditation, participants are invited to visualize unwrapping personal grave clothes— habits, fears, sins—while meditating on John 20:6–7. Liturgical installations may display linen strips and folded cloths as Easter symbols. Sermons unpack how the orderly placement of Christ's face cloth indicates intentionality, contrasting with Lazarus's hasty unbinding. By focusing on linen wrappings, the church engages all the senses—visual, tactile—in Easter remembrance. Typological preaching on cloths helps congregations grasp the continuity between Lazarus's sign and Christ's climactic work. These woven threads of narrative bind together the two resurrections into one redemptive tapestry.

12.3 Judicial Injustice: From Bethany's Council to Pilate's Bench

12.3.1 Sanhedrin's Plot against Lazarus and Jesus (John 11:47–53)

After Lazarus's resurrection, the Sanhedrin convened a council and decided, "If we let him go on like this, everyone will believe in him" (John 11:48). Their response reveals judicial corruption: rather than weigh evidence, they plotted to silence God's sign because it threatened their power. Caiaphas's fatalistic solution—"that one man should die for the people"—exposes the misuse of legal authority for political ends. Jewish legal traditions required due process and witness corroboration, yet these were abandoned to secure a predetermined verdict (Deuteronomy 19:15). This miscarriage of justice foreshadows the illegal trial of Jesus, showing systemic bias from the outset. Modern parallels emerge when religious authorities manipulate courts to suppress honest ministry or activist witnesses. Churches must teach biblical justice principles—fair hearing, impartial judges, and the defense of the vulnerable (Proverbs 31:9). Legal-ethics seminars for ministry leaders underscore the importance of integrity in any judicial interaction. By studying the Sanhedrin's plot, believers learn that true justice aligns with God's heart for equity and truth (Isaiah 1:17). This awareness equips the church to challenge unjust systems in faithful obedience.

12.3.2 Legal Farce: Trials without Evidence (Mark 14:55–59)

During Jesus' trial before the council, "many bore false witness" but their testimonies "did not agree" (Mark 14:56). Desperate for a charge, the authorities ignored contradictory evidence, highlighting that their aim was condemnation, not truth. These proceedings flouted Deuteronomy's safeguards against false testimony (Deuteronomy 19:16–21), transforming the trial into a theatrical farce. Similarly, Pilate's trial—an afternoon session devoid of proper legal formality—served political expedience over justice (John 19:13). Contemporary church-state relations sometimes suffer similar abuses: religious dissidents face show trials designed to intimidate rather than ascertain truth. Training in legal ministry emphasizes documentation of abuses, advocacy for fair hearing rights, and international legal recourse (e.g., UN special rapporteurs). Pastors can equip congregations with "Know Your Rights" resources and partner with NGOs to monitor trials of religious prisoners. By exposing legal farces for what they are, the church stands in solidarity with the oppressed and upholds biblical justice standards.

12.3.3 Prophetic Parallels: Innocent Suffering Foretold

Scripture foretold the Messiah's unjust suffering—Isaiah 53 describes one "despised and rejected" who "had done no violence, nor was any deceit in his mouth" (Isaiah 53:3–9). The judicial injustices at Bethany and Jerusalem fulfill these prophecies, confirming Jesus as the Suffering Servant. Peter's sermon in Acts 3 ties Jesus' trial and resurrection to Psalm 2's prediction of the Anointed One (Acts 4:25–27). Recognizing these parallels deepens theological understanding that opposition is integral to the messianic mission. Preachers can craft sermon series tracing Old Testament oracles to New Testament fulfillment in the Passion. Bible studies on Isaiah 53 prepare groups to hear the Gospel with fresh insight into justice and redemption. Dramatic readings of the Suffering Servant's song alongside trial narratives accentuate continuity. Artistic installations—combining courtroom imagery with prophetic texts—engage hearts in the prophetic dimension. By highlighting these prophetic parallels, the church sees that what appears as injustice is woven into God's redemptive blueprint, ensuring that suffering leads to glory rather than defeat.

12.4 The Crowd's Crescendo: Hosannas to "Crucify Him!"

12.4.1 Palm Sunday's Praise Echoed in Lazarus' Shout (John 12:12–13 vs. 11:43–44)

When Jesus entered Jerusalem, the crowd waved palm branches, crying "Hosanna!" (John 12:13), echoing the earlier moment when witnesses to Lazarus' resurrection shouted in awe (John 11:43–44). In both cases, the people recognized God's power breaking into history, yet their understanding remained shallow—praise for a sign rather than for the Sign-Bearer himself. Palm Sunday's hosannas drew directly from Psalm 118:25–26, linking messianic expectation to visible deliverance. Similarly, the raising of Lazarus invoked Old Testament hope of life triumphant over death. Yet within days, the same voices demanded Jesus' crucifixion (John 19:15), revealing public devotion built on spectacle rather than sustained discipleship. This pattern warns modern ministries against relying solely on emotional highs; authentic faith must be rooted in Christ's person and work, not just in miracles. Preachers can juxtapose these two shout-moments in sermons to illustrate fickle popular opinion and call congregations to deeper allegiance. Worship teams might incorporate both hosanna choruses and laments within Holy Week, guiding hearts from celebration to sober reflection. Small groups can discuss personal experiences of fleeting enthusiasm versus enduring faith, learning to guard against "Palm Sunday syndrome." Recognizing this crescendo cycle equips believers to remain steadfast even when the crowd turns.

12.4.2 The Swing of Public Opinion: From Belief to Blasphemy

Public opinion in Jerusalem swung dramatically—from belief in Jesus' power (John 12:18) to charges of blasphemy and calls for his death (John 19:7). Such volatility often reflects underlying fears: fear of losing social status, of provoking authorities, or of theological dissonance. Crowd psychology teaches that groupthink and mob mentality can override personal convictions, leading to sudden reversals. In Bethany, spontaneous belief at Lazarus' tomb gave way to orchestrated outrage when religious leaders stoked anxiety about Rome (John 11:48). Modern parallels include viral outrage campaigns that can vilify previously celebrated figures. Churches must teach discernment: evaluating gospel witnesses by biblical criteria rather than by majority sentiment (Acts 17:11). Training in apologetics and critical thinking helps believers resist emotional manipulation. Community forums that encourage respectful debate protect against herd impulses. By understanding how easily public opinion can pivot, ministries prepare to stand firm on truth, regardless of popularity.

12.4.3 Lessons for Modern Witness in Volatile Climates

Believers laboring in culturally volatile contexts learn from Jerusalem's crowds: prepare for both acclaim and accusation. Strategic witness plans anticipate backlash—identifying likely criticisms and rehearsing gracious responses (1 Peter 3:15). Developing core messaging—unshakable gospel truths— prevents mission drift under pressure. Building alliances with community leaders and interfaith partners fosters credibility when accusations arise. Training in crisis communication ensures timely, transparent responses to rumors or attacks. Spiritual formation that emphasizes identity in Christ rather than in public approval grounds believers in internal assurance. Regular "resilience retreats" reinforce faith under trial, drawing on stories of early martyrs. Digital platforms can host moderated dialogues to counteract misinformation swiftly. By modeling integrity in volatile climates, the church demonstrates the constancy of resurrection hope amidst shifting social tides.

12.5 Symbolic Actions: Spices, Stones, and Sacrifice

12.5.1 Mary's Anointing with Costly Perfume (John 12:3; cf. John 11:2)

Mary of Bethany breaks open an alabaster jar of expensive perfume to anoint Jesus' feet, a gesture of lavish devotion (John 12:3). The perfume's cost—worth nearly a year's wages in her society—underscores the extravagance of worship that anticipates Jesus' burial (Matthew 26:12). This act parallels Lazarus' foreshadowing: anointing both signifies preparation for death even amid life-restoring wonders. The fragrance's potency symbolizes Christ's impending sacrifice, filling the air as death approaches. Cultural studies show that anointing with oil or perfume communicated honor, hospitality, and prophetic insight in first-century Jewish practice. In homiletics, Mary's action models worship that transcends ceremony—offering one's best in anticipation of Christ's supreme act. Liturgists incorporate anointing rites during Holy Week, reenacting Mary's devotion. Small groups might practice symbolic anointing with fragrant oils while praying through the Passion narrative. By linking spices with sacrifice, the church remembers that true worship flows from recognition of both Jesus' life-giving power and his sacrificial love.

12.5.2 The Stone Rolled Away and the Open Tomb of Jesus (John 11:39–41; John 20:1)

In both Lazarus's and Jesus' resurrections, a stone seals the tomb—then is rolled away. At Bethany, it requires human effort prompted by Divine command (John 11:39–41); at the empty tomb, angels and risen Lord set it aside (Matthew 28:2–4). The stone symbolizes death's barrier; its removal signifies divine conquest. Liturgical reenactments during Easter Vigil often include symbolic rolling of a stone and unveiling of a lighted cross. Artistic depictions—from icons to modern installations—contrast the sealed tomb and the glorious emptiness that follows. The difference in agency—human in Lazarus's case, divine in Jesus'—teaches that only Christ's power fully overcomes death. Preachers connect these events to Romans 6:9, affirming Christ's permanent triumph. Small-group devotions might guide members to roll away "stones" of personal doubt and stand before the risen Christ. By meditating on stones and tombs, believers internalize the gospel's transformative message of barriers removed.

12.5.3 From Incense to Blood: Worship Gestures Foreshadowed

Jewish worship in the Temple used incense, a visual and olfactory offering symbolizing prayers ascending to God (Psalm 141:2). Lazarus's burial spices (John 11:2) and Mary's perfume link Old Covenant incense with New Covenant sacrifice—Christ's blood as the ultimate fragrant offering (Revelation 5:8). The transformation from plant-based aroma to sacrificial blood marks the shift from symbol to substance. Liturgically, Eastern Orthodox churches burn incense in Good Friday services, then shift to the Eucharistic elements on Easter, embodying this transition. The Mass's prayers likening Christ's sacrifice to "a fragrant offering" marry Temple imagery with Calvary's reality (Ephesians 5:2). Hymns such as "Let All Mortal Flesh Keep Silence" evoke incense-laden worship pointing toward the cross. Teaching on sacramental theology highlights how every true act of worship in Christ's body becomes a sweet aroma to God (2 Corinthians 2:15). By tracing worship gestures from spices to blood, the church perceives the continuity of divine worship across covenants.

12.6 Theological Significance of the "Seventh Sign"

12.6.1 Lazarus as the Seventh Sign in John's Gospel (John 20:30–31)

John's Gospel organizes seven public signs culminating in the resurrection of Jesus himself. The raising of Lazarus is the seventh and climactic sign before the Passion, intended to move readers to faith in Jesus as the Messiah (John 20:30–31). This structure—six signs pointing forward, the seventh pointing to the cross—frames Lazarus as both pinnacle and prelude. Scholars note that each sign addresses a facet of Jesus' identity—water into wine reveals his glory, healing the blind reveals spiritual sight, and raising Lazarus reveals his authority over death. The seventh sign, therefore, carries dual meaning: it displays life-giving power and foreshadows the death that would break death's power once and for all. In preaching series on the "seven signs," Lazarus's resurrection serves as the hinge between Jesus's ministry and his sacrificial mission. Small groups exploring John's narrative structure gain insight into the gospel writer's theological artistry. By recognizing Lazarus as the seventh sign, believers appreciate its strategic placement in guiding faith toward the empty tomb.

12.6.2 Incomplete Resurrection versus Complete Victory

Lazarus's resurrection is incomplete—he remains mortal and will die again—whereas Christ's resurrection is final, inaugurating a new creation (1□Corinthians 15:22–23). This contrast underscores that only Christ's rising fulfills God's promise of eternal life. The provisional nature of Lazarus's deliverance warns against equating any human miracle with the comprehensive salvation Jesus accomplishes. Theologians term Lazarus's case a "type," a temporary pattern pointing ahead to the "antitype" in Christ (Hebrews 10:1). Pastoral teaching clarifies that while healings and signs testify to God's compassion, they do not secure ultimate redemption. Sacramental reflection on baptism highlights that our union with Christ in death and resurrection brings a permanent new life (Romans 6:4). Hymns linking "new birth" to Christ's triumph over the grave reinforce this distinction. By contrasting incomplete and complete resurrections, the church maintains Christ's centrality as the sole foundation of eternal hope.

12.6.3 Christ's Death and Rising as the Definitive Sign

While signs in John's Gospel authenticate Jesus's ministry, his own death and resurrection constitute the definitive sign— the ultimate revelation of God's love and power (1□Corinthians 1:23–24). Paul calls the cross "the power of

God and the wisdom of God," affirming its supremacy over all other signs (1□Corinthians 1:18). The empty tomb, witnessed by women, disciples, and over five hundred at once (1□Corinthians 15:6), offers irrefutable proof that death has been defeated. Easter longings in Jewish prophecy—"Your dead shall live; their bodies shall rise" (Isaiah 26:19)—find fulfilment in Christ alone. Christian worship centers on this event: the proclamation "Christ is risen!" defines liturgy, hymnody, and preaching. Doctrinal formulations—Nicene Creed's affirmation of resurrection—anchor the church's faith in this definitive sign. Mission statements echo the resurrection mandate: "Declare his glory among the nations" (Psalm 96:3). By homing in on Christ's death and rising as the ultimate sign, the church proclaims a gospel that transforms every other miracle into pointers toward the empty tomb.

12.7 Sacramental Dimensions: Baptism, Communion, and the Empty Tomb

12.7.1 Baptism into Death and Resurrection (Romans 6:3–5)

Paul teaches that in baptism we "are buried with him by baptism into death, in order that...we too might walk in newness of life" (Romans 6:4). The imagery of descending into water and rising again visually echoes both Lazarus's emergence and Christ's resurrection. In foreshadowing Calvary, Lazarus's unbinding reminds us that baptism points backward to Christ's death and forward to new life. Early church fathers linked Lazarus's rite-like raising with the baptismal font as a tomb from which believers emerge cleansed (Tertullian, *De Baptismo*). Liturgically, many traditions baptize catechumens during the Easter Vigil to underscore solidarity with the resurrected Christ. Catechumenate programs teach postulants the typology of Lazarus—raised temporarily—to highlight their need for the definitive life Christ gives. Pastors preach on Romans 6:3–5 in baptism services, inviting the congregation to remember their own "Lazarus moments" before eternal rebirth. Small groups use water-symbol meditations, recalling Lazarus and personal spiritual awakenings. By rooting baptism in the

Lazarus-to-Christ typology, the church affirms that every baptism participates in the once-for-all resurrection that calms death's claim forever.

12.7.2 Eucharist as Participation in Calvary and Empty Tomb (1 Corinthians 11:23–26)

When Jesus instituted the Lord's Supper, he linked the bread to his body "given for you" and the cup to "the new covenant in my blood" (1 Corinthians 11:24–25). This meal both memorializes Calvary and proclaims the empty tomb until he comes. Just as Lazarus's raising was remembered with spices and fellowship (John 12:1–3), the early church shared communal meals to celebrate Christ's saving work (Acts 2:42). The Eucharist reverses death's sting: we eat of the crucified yet living Lord, tasting resurrection life in our midst. Liturgical prayers often reference Lazarus-type imagery—"We partake of life that death could not hold"—linking the seventh sign to the sacrament. Musical settings of the Agnus Dei ("Lamb of God…grant us peace") weave themes of sacrifice and risen victory. Communion classes teach that each element embodies both Christ's sacrifice (Calvary) and triumph (empty tomb). Home communion kits for the suffering enable isolated believers to join in this sacramental typology. By celebrating Eucharist in this dual light, the church lives between the cross and the empty tomb, anticipating Christ's return.

12.7.3 Lazarus-Christ Typology in Sacramental Theology

Lazarus's raising serves as a "type" of Christ's greater resurrection ("antitype") in biblical hermeneutics (Hebrews 10:1). Sacramental theology employs this typology to show how Old Covenant events and signs prefigure New Covenant realities. Baptism and Eucharist thus become the church's ongoing re-presentation of the Lazarus-to-Calvary-to-empty-tomb narrative. The typology underscores continuity: just as Lazarus's life was extended, our baptism extends eternal life through Christ's death and rising. Pastoral curricula incorporate typology charts, mapping Lazarus's miracle to sacramental practice. Theologians lecture on how typological events lend sacramental efficacy—

water and wine symbolize deeper realities uncovered in Christ. Visual art in sanctuaries may depict Lazarus emerging alongside baptismal and communion symbols, unifying the narrative. Seminary courses in sacramental theology assign papers tracing typological links from Lazarus through Christ's Passion to sacrament. By embedding Lazarus-Christ typology into sacramental life, the church roots every ritual in the narrative arc of redemption—from death to the empty tomb.

12.8 Christological Centerpiece: "I Am the Resurrection and the Life"

12.8.1 Asserting Divine Authority over Death (John 11:25)

Jesus declares to Martha, "I am the resurrection and the life. Whoever believes in me, though he die, yet shall he live" (John 11:25). This "I Am" statement echoes divine self-identification in Exodus 3:14, affirming Jesus' deity and authority over death. Placed in the context of Lazarus's resurrection, it reveals that raising Lazarus was not an isolated deed but an extension of Christ's own life-giving nature. Theologically, this bold assertion anchors soteriology: union with Christ secures victory over death's sting (1 Corinthians 15:55). Worship liturgies often center this verse in Easter proclamation, uniting congregations in confession of faith. Artistic installations— imprinted "I Am" in sanctuary windows—remind believers daily of Christ's authority. Small-group studies on John's "I Am" sayings devote sessions to unpacking the theological depth of "resurrection and life." Pastors preach Christ's high Christology from Ephesians 1:20–23 in conjunction with John 11:25, connecting resurrection power to cosmic Lordship. By focusing on this centerpiece, the church proclaims a Christ who is not merely messenger but the very source of life itself.

12.8.2 Foreshadowing the Ultimate Demonstration on Calvary

When Jesus calls himself "the resurrection and the life," he points beyond Lazarus's return to his own sacrificial death and rising. The foreshadowing is clear: Lazarus's temporary life and Jesus' final triumph are two acts in the same divine drama. Preachers often structure sermon series around this "I Am" saying, culminating in Good Friday and Easter messages. Dramatic presentations pair Martha's confession (John 11:27) with a portrayal of the cross, highlighting the movement from belief to vicarious atonement. The Passion narrative intertwines John 11 and 19, showing that resurrection life requires death's shedding. Worship art media—projecting images of a rising Lazarus superimposed on a crucifix—drive home the connection. Discipleship classes include exegetical assignments: comparing Lazarus's miracle account with Passion predictions (Mark 8:31). By tracing this foreshadowing, the church helps believers see that every miracle Jesus performs serves as signpost to Calvary's climactic revelation of divine love.

12.8.3 Implications for High Christology in Worship and Preaching

John's Gospel exalts Christ's divine identity through "I Am" statements, of which "resurrection and life" is central. This high Christology shapes worship language—hymns, prayers, doxologies—that affirm Jesus as God incarnate. Preaching that fails to underscore Jesus' divinity risks reducing miracles to mere moral lessons. Seminars on Christology integrate Lazarus's sign with Johannine theology, urging pastors to preach "I Am" statements systematically. Worship teams craft musical arrangements that incorporate these affirmations, immersing congregations in high-doxology. Theology courses in seminaries stress the necessity of embracing full Christology to preserve the gospel's power (Colossians 2:9). Lay training sessions on "Confessing Christ" equip members to articulate Jesus' divine identity in personal witness. By embedding the high Christology of "the resurrection and the life" into every facet of church life, believers ground their faith in the person and work of Jesus—not merely in what he does, but in who he is.

12.9 Pastoral Implications: Shepherding Between Signs and Sacrifice

12.9.1 Balancing Expectancy of Miracle with Call to Discipleship

Lazarus's raising generates fervent expectation for miraculous intervention, yet Jesus warns that belief based solely on signs falls short of genuine discipleship (John 6:26–27). Pastors must cultivate both faith in God's power and commitment to the cross-shaped life Jesus demands (Luke 9:23–24). Sermon series can alternate Miracle Sundays—celebrating God's supernatural provision—with Cross Sundays—exploring themes of surrender and cost. Small groups practice "Expectation & Obedience" sessions: sharing answered prayers alongside personal commitments to obedience. Church small-group curricula emphasize that miracles serve discipleship, not replace it (Hebrews 12:2). Pastoral counseling integrates sign-seeking tendencies with deeper exploration of the believer's call to follow Jesus. Worship planning balances celebratory praise songs with reflective hymns on sacrifice. Youth ministries teach that faith in God's power must lead to loving service and holy living. By shepherding congregations between signs and sacrifice, pastors foster maturity that rests on Christ's presence, not just on occasional wonders.

12.9.2 Preparing Congregations for Suffering in Light of Resurrection

Just as Lazarus's return presaged suffering for Jesus, congregations must understand that following Christ entails both joy and hardship. Preaching on John 11's aftermath—plotting and plague—prepares believers for trials that may arise after blessing. Pastoral letters and teaching series on suffering theology (Romans 8:17; 2 Corinthians 4:17) help congregations frame hardships within God's redemptive purposes. Support groups for those experiencing persecution or loss integrate resurrection hope into counseling practice. Prayer nights include Scripture readings on resurrection victory—1□Peter 1:3—and lament psalms—Psalm 42—to hold both realities together. Leadership training in pastoral care equips elders to accompany suffering families with both empathy and hope. Incorporating testimonies of believers who endured hardship with unwavering faith strengthens communal resolve. By preparing congregations for suffering in light of the resurrection, pastors ensure that trials refine rather than derail spiritual growth.

12.9.3 Cultivating Hope through Symbolic Remembrance

Symbols—empty tomb replicas, folded grave clothes, lit Easter candles—anchor hope in tangible reminders of Christ's victory. Teaching congregations the meaning behind each symbol ensures they carry these images into daily life. Homes can set up "Easter corners" with stones and linen strips as prompts to pray. Small groups practice "Symbolic Remembrance" exercises: lighting a candle for each personal crisis God has brought them through. Children's ministries craft devotional crafts—paper tombs that open—to tell the resurrection story visually. Worship services feature processionals with symbols—carrying a cross-cloth that later becomes an empty cloth—to narrate the Gospel physically. Pastoral newsletters include weekly reflections on symbols: stones, linens, incense, and their theological import. By embedding symbolic remembrance in church and home, the community sustains resurrection hope beyond the Easter season, living as people who have stepped forth from the tomb into abundant life.

Conclusion Standing between two tombs—one temporary, one eternal—Lazarus's deliverance summons us to embrace both the glory of present miracles and the mystery of future sacrifice. The echoes of stones rolled away, grave-clothes unbound, and heartfelt declarations of faith converge at the foot of the cross, pointing us toward the empty tomb. May this exploration deepen your appreciation for how every life-giving act of Jesus foreshadows his own passage through death into resurrection. And as you reflect on these patterns, may your heart be prepared to carry both the cost of discipleship and the promise of life that endures forever.